Domesticity, the Social Scene and Leisure

The Imperial Archives

FROM DISCOVERY TO THE CIVILISATIONAL MISSION: ENGLISH WRITINGS ON INDIA

Volume 3

Domesticity, the Social Scene and Leisure

Editor

Pramod K. Nayar

B L O O M S B U R Y

NEW DELHI • LONDON • OXFORD • NEW YORK • SYDNEY

BLOOMSBURY INDIA
Bloomsbury Publishing India Pvt. Ltd
Second Floor, LSC Building No. 4, DDA Complex, Pocket C – 6 & 7,
Vasant Kunj, New Delhi, 110070

BLOOMSBURY, BLOOMSBURY ACADEMIC INDIA and the Diana logo are trademarks of Bloomsbury Publishing Plc

First published in India 2022
This edition published 2022

Bloomsbury Academic
An imprint of Bloomsbury Publishing Plc

ISBN: HB: 978-93-54358-23-4; ePDF: 978-93-54358-70-8
2 4 6 8 10 9 7 5 3 1

Printed & bound in India by Replika Press Pvt. Ltd.

CONTENTS

Prefatory Note vii

General Introduction: Archive and Empire ix

Introduction xxiii

Acknowledgements xxv

1. Thomas Williamson. *Oriental Field Sports*. London: W. Bulmer, 1808. 2 vols. 1
2. John Malcolm. 'Notes of Instructions to Assistants and Officers Acting under the Orders of Major-General Sir John Malcolm, GCB'. In *A Memoir of Central India*, edited by John Malcolm. London: Kingsbury, Parbury and Allen, 1823. Vol. 2. 48
3. J. Frederick Pogson. *Indian Gardening*. Calcutta: Wyman, 1872. 92
4. Flora Annie Steel and Grace Gardiner. *The Complete Indian Housekeeper and Cook*. London: William Heineman, 1909. 101
5. G.F. Atkinson. *Curry and Rice, on forty plates; or the ingredients of social life at "our station" in India*. London: W. Thacker, 1911. 159
6. Maud Diver. *The Englishwoman in India*. London: William Blackwood, 1909. 174
7. E.P. Stebbing. *The Diary of a Sportsman Naturalist in India*. London: John Lane and the Bodley Head, 1920. 218
8. Edward John Buck. *Simla Past and Present*. Bombay: Times Press, 1925. 264

About the Editor 303

PREFATORY NOTE

The archival texts have been retained in their original font, style and content in order to clearly show the environment of the time when these documents were produced. It is important to show in a book such as this the views held at that time and the profound effect they had on society. We acknowledge that several of the texts are derogatory about Indians, women and communities of different religious faiths like many hundreds of other colonial-era-based works. While these are clearly unacceptable to us today, we have not attempted to change any wording or redact the texts so that the contemporary reader may experience the rhetoric, attitude and ideologies that so clearly marked the Raj. In places, where the text had been smudged and rendered impossible to read, that specific segment has been deleted.

We would like to make clear that these are not the views held by the editor or Bloomsbury India and do not reflect our mission and values which are clearly stated on our website (https://www.bloomsbury.com/in/connect/about-us/missions-and-values/)

GENERAL INTRODUCTION: ARCHIVE AND EMPIRE

That the British writings on India occupy over several miles of shelf space in the British Library, London, is an apocryphal tale, but one which *may* have substance, given that there was no aspect of the subcontinent that did not pique the curiosity of the British or generate some document or the other.

In his *The Imperial Archive: Knowledge and the Fantasy of Empire* (1993), Thomas Richards demonstrated how the documentation (the subject of considerable work, notably in Bernard Cohn and others) and archivisation not only produced knowledge about the colonies but were also instrumental in generating the fantasy of absolute control. And yet, it is never easy to read these records produced by a diverse set of English, Irish and Scottish missionaries, administrators, men of leisure, nurses, teachers, wives and/or sisters of the men who occupied official posts in the colony, soldiers, mercenaries and others—many of whom, for many reasons, had their own dynamics and tensions with the *English*.

Several approaches to the imperial record exist, and this introductory chapter sets out some of them.[1] In the process, it also flags what the archive does in terms of the imperial structure and processes.[2]

The Power of the Archive

The archive is not a mere compilation of what John Malcolm (1823) advised his officers on the right approach to the native officers, or what Thomas Williamson (1808) described as the potential for the hunt in India. The archive is not a passive reflection of imperial power—it constitutes and constructs it. As diverse commentators—such as Cohn's work on the 'survey modality' (1997) and C.A. Bayly's *Empire and Information* (1999)—have pointed out, the Empire ran on information,

---

[1] I use the term 'imperial archive' throughout to refer to the corpus of published material across genres, as diverse as maps, geographical accounts, census reports, travelogues, administrative reports, ecclesiastical documents.

[2] These volumes work only with the print archive of British India, although a vast archive of visual material also exists, and has been the subject of significant studies. See, for example, Guégan (2011), Chaudhury (2012), Pinney (2014), Dohman (2017) on colonial photography, and Tobin (1999), De Silva (2011), Eaton (2013), among others, on colonial/imperial art and paintings.

and information-gathering constituted not just an act of power but was a *constituent* of the power structure. It classified, organised and legislated on the subject peoples, through the census, the geographies and anthropological studies. In the process, it defined who is counted as a subject/citizen. For instance, writing about the Todas or the Gonds, and then examining the numbers of Muslim students in schools, both the educationist and the statesman were constructing model imperial citizens who would benefit, resist or accept from 'modern' education. In other words, the imperial archive on education was not merely advocating 'modern' education: it was constructing *educate-able* citizens from among their colonial subjects while abandoning the others. Thus, archivisation and informatisation were ultimately about the power wielded over the identity-making and rights of the subjects.[3]

Relatedly, the archive and the documentation also made the subjects *visible to themselves*. With 'modern' education, for instance, the Indian colonial subject in school or college came to identify themselves in particular ways. They learnt what it means to be a good citizen, to be modern, to develop and demand certain skills, etc. They recognised their location on the civilisational scale in the books they read and assimilated (*primitive* and *non-modern* as opposed to the modern European). In an argument that resonates with my claims above, Antoinette Burton and Isabel Hofmeyr write about the power of the English book:

> The embodiment of English manly authority, the book was not simply 'a surrogate Englishman in his highest and most perfect state,' it was the very emblem of imperial sovereignty—with the rigorous spine a testimony to its singularity, its probity, its titular power … books impressed themselves in the everyday lives of imperial subjects, manifesting the formal values of an elite or bourgeois self and modeling in their material form the coherence and commanding presence of British imperial power itself. (2014: 1–2)

The colonial subjects were told, through these English books, what kind of spiritual and moral training was required for them to 'improve'.

---

[3] It must be noted that it was not only the human subjects in the colony that became objects and subjects of the imperial archive. Fauna and flora, climate, landscape and topography—indeed the natural world in its entirety—were also archived. For studies, see Edney (1997) and Damodaran et al. (2015), among others.

As A.H. Benton of the Indian Civil Service wrote in *Indian Moral Instruction and Caste Problems*:

> [The Indian] People are on the whole kindly, docile, alert, keen-spirited, high and low, one of the best-mannered peoples in the world, and they would appear to offer a very promising field for right spiritual treatment. (1917: 92)

The education archive, and especially its insistence on moral training and moral apprenticeship of the subjects as a *preliminary* to training for political citizenship, was built on the

> founding assumption … that the native readership of English texts, and the recipients of English education, were amenable to their teachings, which led them to abandon their traditional manners and disciplines. This necessitated a solid moral training to make them good citizens. (Nayar 2020: 142)

The archive also, frequently, captures the rift and fracture within the colonial subject's responses to, say, Western/English education. See, for instance, Syed Mahmood's anguish about the Indian Muslim's refusal to accept this education:

> Such feelings of aversion towards English education entertained by the Mahomedans … stand in sharp contrast to the attitude of the Hindu community.… This difference in the sentiments of the two communities towards English education, is the real key to the reasons of the vast disparity of progress of English education which the two nationalities have respectively made. The effects of this disparity have been most baneful to the interests of British India in general, and to the Mahomedan community in particular. (1895: 23)

In time, the colonial subject, convinced of the 'truth' in the power of the Englishman's word or photographic record, not only accepted the arguments about their inferiority but also welcomed the interventions in the form of the civilisational mission of the Empire. The archive had, therefore, produced the *willing* colonial subject.

In particular cases, such as Thuggee, the archive enabled the colonial structures of law enforcement and the judiciary to enact legislation and, in the process, demonise specific cultural practices. Examining the Thuggee archive, Alexander Macfie writes:

> [W]hereas Sleeman and his colleagues tended to define the activities of the thugs in terms of wickedness, murder, deceit, cowardice and criminality, the thugs themselves tended to evaluate them in terms of courage, enterprise, bravery, daring, cunning, adventure and martial

> skill … in terms usually associated by both the British and the Indians with the heroic values of war. (2008: 396)

The Archive, the Coloniser, the Colonised and Cultural Exchanges

Shifting focus, Antoinette Burton has demonstrated how the imperial archive also fed into the coloniser's psyche, imagination and political imagination. A pithy summary of how the imperial corpus fuelled, inspired and controlled the social imaginary, policies, attitudes and responses of the Britons in the nineteenth century is available in Burton's *Empire in Question*. Victorian culture, writes Burton,

> as a racialized landscape shaped by decades, if not centuries, of colonial peoples, goods, and ideas coursing through its highways and byways … as always already imperial not just implicitly but as part of a pedagogical meta-narrative about the relationship of modernity to the world-historical phenomenon of colonialism in world history…. (2011: 2–3)

Burton proposes that English 'sensibility' was shaped by Britain's imperial role and character, and its concomitant racialised hierarchies—thus makes the production and consumption of texts (and commodities) about and from the colonised peripheries central to the making of Britain itself (also see Hall 2002).

The archive also instantiates, other than the racialised power binaries (white/black, coloniser/colonised), cross-cultural *influences* and *exchanges*. Contacts across races, ethnic groups and the coloniser–colonised divide were frequent through the colonial period.

The English language took into itself words from their colonial subjects. They also sought to document the grammars of the languages of the subcontinent for their own officers and staff. As a consequence, a vibrant field of cultural exchanges opened up in the languages, with Indian pandits and English philologists and grammarians collaborating. The imperial archive in this domain shows mutual influences of English on Indian languages and vice versa (including Sanskrit [Naregal 2001]) but also the *organisation* of knowledge around the latter (Lelyveld 1993; Rao 2004; Mir 2010; Auer 2014).[4] Scholars—the famous 'Orientalists'—translated texts from, say, Sanskrit into English. Organisations and societies, such as the Asiatic Society, the

[4] A detailed annotated bibliography on these and other aspects of English colonial discourse on India can be found in Nayar 2021.

Zoological Survey of India, the Archaeological Survey of India, were spaces through which the English statesman, *memsahib* and trader encountered Indian temples, art, food practices, superstitions, systems of healing, among others.

English literary texts, as numerous commentators have shown (Leask 1993; Teltscher 1997), began to introduce Indian 'themes' and motifs, whether the *sati* or the wealth of the country's landscape. This field of literary studies was one of contestation and adaptation (Vishwanathan 1990). Be that as it may, the circulation of the English novel in nineteenth-century India catered to the Indian audience attuned to the melodramatic and informed their own creative work (Joshi 2003). Other commentators like Harish Trivedi (1993) have noted how English literature was received in India and the transactional nature of this reception.

Local experts, *writers* and translators were an integral component of the East India Company and the British government. Even account and trade books were produced through a collaborative project (Ogborn 2007). In other domains, such as translations, Indian scholars like Kasinatha Bhattacharya enabled the work of Charles Wilkins (Davis 2015).

Manners, protocols of civic interaction and norms of social, interracial interaction were also sites where cultural exchange and mutual influence were visible. Even the idea of 'civility', as Anindyo Roy has argued, was treated by the native—and projected as such by *English* textbooks and teachers—as markers of 'modern progress and mobility' (Roy 2005: 11). Therefore, both English and Indian commentators (Webb 1915; El Edroos 1922) produced advice and courtesy books for Indians and Englishmen in India (Nayar 2016, 'Civil Modernity'). These contained suggestions like:

> Members of each class, without entering into political or official discussions and avoiding personal remarks, may have much pleasant intercourse by asking about and describing the manners and customs peculiar to each other's nationality, or about their art, music, poetry and literature.... Talk about sport is most suitable at club. (El Edroos: 89)

The Archive and the Global

Another approach to the imperial archive chooses to see the archive as instantiating not just the sensibilities, attitudes and modes of the British coloniser and the subcontinent's colonised, but as enabling *global and globalising imperial networks*. That is, the archive is seen as embodying not just the binary of an imperial 'centre' and 'periphery' (the colony), but a vast network of global connections. We see this interpretation in the work of John Darwin.

In *The Empire Project: The Rise and Fall of the British World-System, 1830–1970* (2009), Darwin shows how the 'interdependence' of various regions and colonies shaped the British Empire in four specific domains. First, there is the military interdependence of various geopolitical regions:

> the most obvious forms of such inter-dependence were naval and military.... British ability to provide naval protection or to send reinforcements to the scene of a conflict would have been very limited without the resources the imperial system supplied. It was strategic control of the Cape Colony (whose economic value was derisory before 1870) that secured the naval gateway to Asia from European waters. The prime function of Egypt, occupied by the British in 1882, was to preserve British use of the Suez Canal and protect the 'Clapham Junction' of imperial communications. Malta, Aden, Ceylon, Singapore, Hong Kong, Esquimalt (on Vancouver Island), the Falklands and Halifax, Nova Scotia, formed the network of bases from which the Royal Navy patrolled the world's sea-lanes. India played several roles in the British world-system, but perhaps its critical function was to be the main base from which British interests in Asia could be advanced and defended. Indian soldiers and a British garrison paid for by Indian revenues were the 'strategic reserve' of the British system in Asia. Because India played this role, other British possessions and spheres east and south of Suez were largely exempted from the costs of defence—a fact of crucial importance to their economic viability. (3–4)

Then there is the commercial interdependence and linkages:

> Both colonial territories and 'informal' colonies had to compete for investment and credits from London to expand their economies ... with the grand exception of the United States (which had received one-fifth of British foreign investment by 1913), British capital was shuttled by the City of London between the various sectors of its commercial empire (a vast global realm among whose key provinces were Canada, Argentina, India, Australia, Southern Africa, China and the Middle East), employing a calculus of prospective return and speculative gain. (4)

The third domain of such connections would be the demographic interdependence:

> Although two-thirds of British migrants went to the United States up until 1900, almost all the rest were distributed between the four main settlement zones of Canada, Australia, New Zealand and South Africa. Indeed, their economic development was usually seen as being closely dependent upon drawing labour and skills from the British supply.... Between 1834 and 1937, India exported some 30 million people to other British possessions as indentured labour, and perhaps one-fifth remained as permanent settlers. In the tropical empire (which British migrants avoided) they supplied much of the labour and business expertise to promote commercial expansion. (4–5)

Finally,

> the spheres of British expansion were progressively linked by a complex system of communication. From the 1840s onwards, this was provided by subsidised mail services, telegraph wires, undersea cables, an expanding rail network, fast passenger steamers and (in the twentieth century) imperial air routes. (5)

In consonance with the work of Darwin, other commentators have mapped these global connections and interdependencies of the British Empire. Thus, Tony Ballantyne, Jonathan Hyslop, among others, in their contributions to the *New Imperial Histories Reader*, map racial imaginings and knowledge formations, working-class presences across the Empire, from India to Australia and Southern Africa. The migration of people and goods in the 1850–1914 period, argue Gary Magee and Andrew Thompson in *Empire and Globalisation: Networks of People, Goods and Capital in the British World, c. 1850–1914* (2010), was instrumental in the making of an international economy. This, of course, put tremendous pressure on the colonised peoples but also made '"transnationalism"—living in and identifying with more than one country or place—a normal way of life for many British people in the half-century before 1914' (5); an argument that resonates with that of Antoinette Burton about Victorian England cited earlier.

Alan Lester's work in the field of imperial humanitarianism and the 'civilisational mission' has made similar connections to argue for a trans-imperial history. Through the late eighteenth and the nineteenth centuries, notes Alan Lester, we can discern the rise of a 'moral geography of the globe', where the Europeans felt responsible for 'distant strangers' (2000: 278). Thus, imperialism intersected with, fed into and drew from humanitarian ideologies and thought in *different* parts of the world/Empire. Subsequently, Lester et al.'s work focused on not 'national boundaries' (Britain's) but on 'transnational and trans-imperial connections' (2020: 2). They argue that 'the principles of freedom, civilisation and liberalism that motivated them were dissolved in a solution of violent racism through which British power was applied' in *various* colonies and geographical locations (2). Through a reading of three years—1838, 1857 and 1879—and the archive of Victorian imperialist statesmen and legal luminaries like James Stephen, Lester et al. demonstrate the linkage and common foundations (ideological, racism, etc.):

> [T]he ending of slavery and the rise of free trade doctrine, repeated Indian famines and the Uprising of 1857, the First and Second Afghan Wars, the First and Second Opium Wars, the Great Xhosa Cattle Killing and the Anglo-Zulu War, mass emigration from the British Isles, the self-governance of settler colonies in North America, Australasia and southern Africa and the devastation of Indigenous societies. (11)[5]

The Archive in 'New Imperial Histories'

The modes through which the archive has been read and employed have come in for criticism in the *new imperial history* turn. Nicholas Dirks summarises the problem with the slide between the production of the imperial archive and the production of the historical events within imperialism. Dirks writes:

> Begins the histories behind and beneath the production of the kinds of primary sources that have represented colonial knowledge even as they have been used to determine and justify colonial policy. The archive has enshrined, in [Michel] Foucault's sense, this raw material

[5] Philippa Levine and John Marriott in their Introduction to the massive *The Ashgate Research Companion to Modern Imperial Histories* (2012) argue that for many commentators, such as C.A. Bayly, 'modernity' in Europe itself is a consequence of its imperial actions—'The putative simultaneity of Europe's imperial ascent, globalisation and the birth of the modern world has led many to see an intimate interconnectedness.' (2)

However the trouble with this reading is, they note, 'that not only did Europe (or the west if we include the Americas) continue to display significant characteristics that might be regarded as pre-modern, but many of the features identified as modern were to be found equally in societies beyond and often unconnected to Europe.' (2)

> for subsequent historical representation. In the Indian case, the archive is both the precipitate of the history of conquest and rule and the basis on which that history has been written by colonial administrators. (2010: 95)

This 'colonial history' most notably in the 'Cambridge School' of historians, argues Dirks reading the archive of John Seeley and others, was in fact 'colonial fiction', which forwarded the idea that 'Indian politics emerged as a direct reflex of administrative initiatives set in motion by colonial rule' (95). Dirks continues:

> [such colonial histories argued] that local elites, the very groups that had been the collaborators for British rule, turned nationalist—in the context of participation in the progressively enlarged electoral arenas of provincial and municipal politics—when they realized that more of the pie could be obtained through autonomous political institutions than through colonial ones.... (95)

This meant

> [The Cambridge School] proved its arguments by using colonial sources—frequently police records and confidential files—that documented the spurious activities of nationalist figures in what was a large-scale colonial effort to track, contain, and debunk the very politics that sought to overthrow colonial rule. (96)

More recent readings have shown how colonial and imperial legacies and their discursive remains, even in the postcolonial era, turn to and retain its ideologies and representational modes. Nadine Attewell writes in *Better Britons*:

> [in] the afterlife of empire insofar as the projects of nation building with which it is concerned ... sexual reproduction [is the] key to, and a potent figure for, the (re)constitution of the national body after the 'end' of empire. (2014: 6)

This implies that the archive and the historical record—even as we debate what counts as the historical record—is very much an active constituent of the present postcolonial thought and actions as well.

*

The volumes here are only a small sample of the imperial archive. The range and depth of the archive are impossible to encapsulate in a few volumes. While I have made attempts elsewhere to capture some of this variety (Nayar 2007; 2009; 2013; 2016 [*Siege and Prison Writings*]; 2017; 2019), much more is required and possible. For example, the visual archive of the Empire, with its modalities and aesthetic grammars of 'composing' the subcontinent, whether in photography or painting (some of which may be found in Archer 1972), requires much more presence in the form of collections.

The present volumes focus on select aspects of the imperial archive: the accounts of 'discovery' and exploration—flora and fauna, geography, climate—the people of the subcontinent, English domesticity and social life in the subcontinent, the wars and skirmishes—including the *Mutiny* of 1857–1858—and the *civilisational mission.* It excludes legal documents and the many Acts and laws enacted by the British government.

Volume I consists of documents that deal with England's *discovery* of India, its exploration and mapping of the Indian land. This volume includes material as diverse as the letter from India of Thomas Stephens, often called 'the first Englishman in India', chorographic and cartographic accounts from geographical, meteorological, archaeological surveys that the various organisations and societies established for the purpose produced.

Volume II includes English studies of Indian languages and the social order. Ethnographic surveys of the subcontinent's people and cultural practices were published from the late eighteenth century. Practices like female infanticide, sati and thugee, seen as emblematic of the 'barbarous' Oriental, received special attention in the documentation. The characteristics of various tribes and ethnic group were also mapped in considerable detail.

Volume III shifts the focus entirely to the English home and social life. The documents include advice on gardening—an integral part of the English home—and on housekeeping. In the latter, the English were given instructions on how to monitor the domestic economy and manage the servants. Advice manuals on hunting and field sports were also published. Given the interracial dynamics at work, officers were issued manuals on etiquette and behaviour. Accounts of hill-stations and camps, and the social life in the Presidencies make up the rest of the volume.

Volume IV is a collection of accounts of a very different British life in India: as prisoners, under siege and in conditions of war. Starting with the notorious *Black Hole* of Calcutta to the 1857 *Mutiny*, the English wrote about being assailed, besieged and tormented in their war journals and prison accounts. These documented physical and emotional suffering, the losses of families and lives, even as they strove to depict British grit and determination.

Volume V documents England's *civilisational mission*. These documents offer a glimpse into British opinions and strategies on diverse subjects. It includes Macaulay's (in)famous Minute of 1835, accounts of medical missionary activities, views on establishing missionary activities and the British views on women's education.

Works Cited

Archer, Mildred. *Company Drawings in the India Office Library*. London: HMSO, 1972.

Attewell, Nadine. *Better Britons: Reproduction, National Identity, and the Afterlife of Empire*. Toronto: University of Toronto Press, 2014.

Auer, Blain. 'Early Modern Persian, Urdu, and English Historiography and the Imagination of Islamic India under British Rule', *Études de Lettres* 2–3 (2014): 199–206.

Bayly, C.A. *Empire and Information: Intelligence-Gathering and Social Communication in India*. Cambridge: Cambridge University Press, 1999.

Benton, A.H. *Indian Moral Instruction and Caste Problems: Solutions*. London: Longmans, Green and Co., 1917.

Burton, Antoinette and Isabel Hofmeyr. 'Introduction. The Spine of Empire? Books and the Making of an Imperial Commons'. In *Ten Books that Shaped the British Empire: Creating an Imperial Commons*, edited by Antoinette Burton and Isabel Hofmeyr. Durham and London: Duke University Press, 2014.

Burton, Antoinette. *Empire in Question: Reading, Writing, and Teaching British Imperialism*. Durham and London: Duke University Press, 2011.

Chaudhury, Zahid R. *Afterimage of Empire: Photography in Nineteenth-Century India*. Minneapolis: University of Minnesota Press, 2012.

Cohn, Bernard S. *Colonialism and Its Forms of Knowledge: The British in India*. New Delhi: Oxford University Press, 1997.

Damodaran, Vinita, Anna Winterbottom and Alan Lester, eds. *The East India Company and the Natural World*. London: Palgrave Macmillan, 2015.

Darwin, John. *The Empire Project: The Rise and Fall of the British World-System, 1830–1970*. Cambridge: Cambridge University Press, 2009.

Davis, Richard. 'Wilkins, Kasinatha, Hastings, and the First English *Bhagavad Gītā*', *International Journal of Hindu Studies* 19, no. 1–2 (2015): 39–57.

De Silva, Prasannajit. 'Representing Home Life Abroad: British Domestic Life in Early Nineteenth-Century India', *Visual Culture in Britain* 12, no. 3 (2011): 313–331.

Dirks, Nicholas B. 'Coda: The Burden of the Past.' In *The New Imperial Histories Reader*, edited by Stephen Howe, 92–105. Oxford: Routledge, 2010.

Dohman, Renata, ed. *Empire and Art: British India*. Manchester, UK: Manchester University Press, 2017.

Eaton, Natasha. *Colour, Art and Empire: Visual Culture and the Nomadism of Representation*. London: I.B. Tauris, 2013.

Edney, Matthew. *Mapping an Empire: The Geographical Construction of British India, 1753–1843*. Chicago: University of Chicago Press, 1997.

El Edroos, Aboobaker. *Modern Indian Etiquette: Of Mixed Society, Describing Ancient Social Usages and Important Indian Manners and Customs, Aiming at Social Amity Between Indians and Non-Indians*. Surat: H.R. Scott at the Mission Press, 1922.

Guégan, Xavier. 'Visualizing Alienation: Symbolism and Duality in Samuel Bourne's Photographs of British India', *Visual Culture in Britain* 12 no. 3 (2011): 349–365.

Hall, Catherine. *Civilising Subjects: Colony and Metropole in the English Imagination, 1830–1867*. Chicago: University of Chicago Press, 2002.

Joshi, Priya. *In Another Country: Colonialism, Culture, and the English Novel in India*. Oxford: Oxford University Press, 2003.

Leask, Nigel. *British Romantic Writers and the East: Anxieties of Empire*. Cambridge: Cambridge University Press, 1993.

Lelyveld, David. 'The Fate of Hindustani: Colonial Knowledge and the Project of a National Language'. In *Orientalism and the Postcolonial Predicament: Perspectives on South Asia*, edited by Carol Breckenridge and Peter van der Veer, 189–214. Philadelphia: University of Pennsylvania Press, 1993.

Lester, Alan, Kate Boehme and Peter Mitchell. *Ruling the World: Freedom, Civilisation and Liberalism in the Nineteenth-Century British Empire*. Cambridge: Cambridge University Press, 2021.

Lester, Alan. 'Obtaining the "due observance of justice": The geographies of colonial humanitarianism', *Environment and Planning D Society and Space* 20, no. 3 (2000): 277–293.

Levine, Philippa and John Marriott, eds. *The Ashgate Research Companion to Modern Imperial Histories*. London: Ashgate, 2016.

Macfie, Alexander Lyon. 'Thuggee: An Orientalist Construction?' *Rethinking History* 12, no. 3 (2008): 383–397.

Magee, Gary and Andrew Thompson. *Empire and Globalisation: Networks of People, Goods and Capital in the British World, c. 1850–1914*. Cambridge: Cambridge University Press, 2010.

Mahmood, Syed. *History of English Education in India, Its Rise, Development, Progress, Present Condition and Prospects. Being a Narrative of the Various Phases of Educational Policy and Measures Adopted under the British Rule from Its Beginning to the Present Period (1781 to 1893)*. Aligarh: M.A-O. College, 1895.

Malcolm, John. 'Notes of Instructions to Assistants and Officers Acting under the Orders of Major-General Sir John Malcolm, GCB.' In *A Memoir of*

Central India: Including Malwa, and Adjoining Provinces, Vol. 2, edited by John Malcolm. London: Kingsbury, Parbury and Allen, 1823.

Mir, Farina. *The Social Space of Language: Vernacular Culture in British Colonial Punjab*. Berkeley: University of California Press, 2010.

Naregal, Veena. *Language Politics, Elites, and the Public Sphere: Western India under Colonialism*. New Delhi: Permanent Black, 2001.

Nayar, Pramod K. 'English Discourse and India'. *Oxford Bibliographies Online*. New York: Oxford University Press, 2021, https://www.oxfordbibliographies.com/view/document/obo-9780190221911/obo-9780190221911-0114.xml.

______. 'Civil Modernity: The Management of Manners and Polite Imperial Relations in India, 1880–1930', *South Asia: Journal of South Asian Studies* 39, no. 4 (2016): 740–757.

______. 'Moral Readership and Political Apprenticeship: Commentaries on English Education in India, 1875–1930'. In *The Edinburgh History of Reading. Vol. IV. Subversive Readers*, edited by Jonathan Rose, 138–161. UK: Edinburgh University Press, 2020.

______. *Colonial Education and India*, 5 vols. London: Routledge, 2019.

______. *Days of the Raj: Life and Leisure in British India*. New Delhi: Penguin, 2009.

______. *English Siege and Prison Writings: From the 'Black Hole' to the 'Mutiny'*. London: Routledge, 2016.

______. *Indian Travel Writing, 1830–1947*. 1830–1947, 5 vols.

______. *The Penguin 1857 Reader*. New Delhi: Penguin, 2007.

______. *Women in Colonial India: Historical Documents and Sources*, 5 vols. London: Routledge, 2013.

Ogborn, Miles. *Indian Ink: Script and Print in the Making of the English East India Company*. Chicago and London: Chicago University Press, 2007.

Orsini, Francesca. *The Hindi Public Sphere: Language and Literature in the Age of Nationalism*. Oxford: Oxford University Press, 2010.

Pinney, Christopher. 'Sepia Mutiny: Colonial Photography and Its Others in India.' In *Feeling Photography*, edited by Elspeth Brown and Thy Phu, 71–92. Durham, NC: Duke University Press, 2014.

Rao, Velcheru Narayana. 'Print and Prose: Pundits, *Karanams*, and the East India Company in the Making of Modern Telugu'. In *India's Literary History: Essays on the Nineteenth Century*, edited by Stuart Blackburn and Vasudha Dalmia, 146–166. New Delhi: Permanent Black, 2004.

Richards, Thomas. *The Imperial Archive: Knowledge and the Fantasy of Empire*. London: Verso, 1993.

Roy, Anindyo. *Civility and Empire: Literature and Culture in British India, 1822–1922*. London: Routledge, 2005.

Teltscher, Kate. *India Inscribed: European and English Writing on India, 1600–1800*. Delhi: Oxford University Press, 1997.

Tobin, Beth Fowkes. *Picturing Imperial Power: Colonial Subjects in Eighteenth-Century British Painting*. Durham, NC: Duke University Press, 1999, 110–138.

Trivedi, Harish. *Colonial Transactions: English Literature and India*. Calcutta: Papyrus, 1993.

Viswanathan, Gauri. *Masks of Conquest: English Literary Studies and India*. London: Faber & Faber, 1990.

Webb, William Trego. *English Etiquette for Indian Gentlemen*. 5th ed. 1895. Calcutta: S.K. Lahiri, 1915.

Williamson, Thomas. *Oriental Field Sports*. London: W. Bulmer, 1808.

INTRODUCTION

Domesticity, often a fraught exercise for the 'memsahib', carried on with the assistance of a retinue of Indian servants, meant tackling corruption, inefficiency and the all-pervasive social hierarchy of the colonised. Advice books were produced to aid the memsahib for this purpose. The Steel-Gardiner guide to housekeeping, which was a bestseller in its day and is excerpted here, was indispensable in the length and breadth of its coverage, from the care of children to the right wages for the servants. Diver's text, likewise, also demonstrates how running the home was difficult and has a resonance with the (male) dominion of running the Empire. These texts exhorted the Englishwoman to practise thrift, control and managerial skills, to be aware of the natives' penchant for dirt and indolence and the caste-community dynamics that inform the servant-class.

Entertainments of various kinds, from the 'nautch' that the men were particularly fond of to the shikar (of pigs, bison, tigers) and polo, were introduced and assiduously cultivated by the British in India. The archive is full of accounts of such hunts and recreational activities, such as Thomas Williamson's and Stebbing's accounts here. The thrill of the chase and the tedium of the wait are all documented. Practical advice on weapons, tents and skills required, traps to be laid are made available for specific game as well. Advice on gardening, such as Frederick Pogson's excerpted here, was always available for the memsahib. The kitchen garden as an integral component of the domestic economy was often highlighted.

The social life of the English, whether in the camp, the hunt, the 'station' or the hills of Shimla, was vibrant and had its fair share of romance, social tensions and amusements, as Edward Buck's detailed account of the hill station demonstrates. Co-opting the natives as assistants was necessary, but playing with them was a social manoeuvre that required considerable tact and diplomacy, as the British discovered. To ensure that the wheels of social and interracial interactions moved smoothly, instruction manuals, such as John Malcolm's excerpted here, and etiquette books were published for both colonial masters and the colonised.

ACKNOWLEDGEMENTS

The Raj has been a perennial favourite when it comes to research and writing, and I cannot remember a year when I did *not* do some 'Raj work'.

Chandra Sekhar of Bloomsbury was very receptive to the project idea, and has been incisive and encouraging when it came to subjects like the volumes' organisation, content and final form—to him, this project owes much.

I express my thanks to journals and anthologies, and their editors and reviewers whose comments have enabled me to sharpen my thoughts on the Raj-topic-of-the-moment. Among journals, I acknowledge: *South Asia, South Asian Review, Anglo-Saxonica* and *Asiatic*. Among the anthologies, I acknowledge *Ireland's Imperial Connections*; *The Edinburgh History of Reading*; *The English Renaissance, Orientalism, and the Idea of Asia*; *Cultural Histories of India*. To Debra Johanyak and Walter S. Lim, Rita Banerjee, Daniel Roberts and Jonathan Wright, Mary Hammond and Jonathan Rose, editors of these fabulous anthologies, many thanks for your invitation to contribute and the work you put into the volumes of which I am now a part.

To Kate Teltscher, whose work *India Inscribed* showed me where to go way back in the mid-1990s, I owe an intellectual debt of enormous proportions.

I am also grateful to publishers and editors at Penguin, Bloomsbury, Palgrave-Macmillan, Edinburgh University Press, Orient BlackSwan, Wiley-Blackwell and Routledge for their comments, suggestions and, above all, interest in this area and my contributions to it.

To Soma Ghosh, Librarian (English) at the Salar Jung Museum, Hyderabad, and her constant efforts, all undertaken with cheer and grace, to obtain materials when I have worked there, immeasurable gratitude.

Many books germinate in conversations with Anna Kurian, who is always enthusiastic about any Raj-work I do, especially if they are multivolume projects. For the constant-traveller role that you assay with such commitment, solidarity and affection, it is my privilege, Anna, to acknowledge you.

Thank you, Molly ('Chechu'), for enquiring lovingly about her 'little one'.

Nandana Dutta has been unceasing in her interest in my work, and her always gentle and loving urging to think in certain ways, even as she tries to catch up with her reading of what I publish. To your attention, insights and perspicacity, Nandana—much, much gratitude.

Professor K. Narayana Chandran established, for some of us willing ones, the standards in academic scholarship and publishing—that he sustains these standards even now, after four decades, is nothing short of the marvellous. To KNC's indomitable spirit of inquiry and work ethic, and showing us the way to do things, I am very grateful.

Friends who drop in 'WhatsAppingly', regularly, to check on me—Neelu, Bhalla, Ajeet, Kulsoom, Om, Archana, Ashish, Krishna Ram, Sai Jawahar, Savita, Vaishali, Soma and Zahid—thank you.

To Nandini, Pranav, my parents and parents-in-law, I owe unquantifiable gratitude, for never complaining at the volume of work I take on, my frequently distracted state of being and, more importantly, for creating an extraordinarily supportive environment.

And thank you, Shubha, for obtaining, wizard-like, essays and journal articles in minutes, and for your enthusiasm for my work.

To the works of P.G. Wodehouse, Agatha Christie, Stephen King, the comics around Batman—my regular reading—many of which unwittingly capture the horror, the abyss and the comedy of academia, I can never express enough gratitude.

It is a pleasure to thank Atul Nair who compiled many of the materials meticulously.

I am grateful to the Institution of Eminence (IoE) project's Professional Development Fund.

Thomas Williamson

Oriental Field Sports. London: W. Bulmer, 1808. 2 vols.

No 1.

PLATE I.

GOING OUT IN THE MORNING.

THERE being no inns, nor houses of a description suited to the accommodation of Europeans, in any part of India, it is usual for each gentleman to be provided with one or more tents, to which a suitable conveyance, either of elephants, camels, or bullocks, is usually attached. On account of the extreme heat of the climate, these tents are necessarily constructed on a large scale, with many apertures, and having a space of perhaps four or five feet between the inner shell or marquee, and the fly, which generally is three or four feet every way more extensive than the shell; making by this means a large awning or pavilion, for the accommodation of servants, and for the security of baggage.

The tents in question are made either of canvas, or of a narrow kind of coarse and cheap cotton, called *guzzee*. The former are for the most part lined with perpets, or baize. The latter being thin, is composed of many folds, perhaps four, five, or six, and lined either with the same kind of cloth dyed of any colour, with printed chintz, of which an immense quantity is manufactured in all parts of India, of beautiful patterns, or with a red cloth called *curroch*, which should be coloured with a dye made of shell lac, and receive its tint previous to being woven; the same as what are in England termed cloths-in-grain. The ropes are usually of cotton; and if made of the new material, are extremely durable. The rope makers, however, if not closely watched, are apt to mix a large portion of decayed cotton, collected from old tents, quilts, &c.; the tapes are also of cotton, and the quantity used would surprise an European tent builder. They are laid in the middle of the folds of guzzee which may be in any direction liable to strain. A tape proceeds from the peak of the tent, to every place where a rope is affixed, as well as all around the edge, and accompanies every bamboo, or lath, inserted in the walls for the purpose of sustaining the exterior of the shell, or marquee, at its proper height; which is commonly from five feet ten inches, to six feet four inches perpendicular: so that a tall person may walk all around within the area of the tent with his hat on. The walls lace on by means of loops of cotton line, which passing through eylet holes made in the upper edge of the walls, and being looped through each other in succession, brace them up to the shell very close and firm. Wherever there is a bamboo in the wall, a short loop is affixed to the bottom, secured to the work by a strong piece of leather, stitched on with great neatness and strength, for the purpose of receiving a wooden pin, of about a foot long; which being driven into the ground, prevents the walls from being blown in by the violent gusts of wind that generally prevail for many hours daily.

The peaks or caps at the top, are made of two or more layers of strong leather, manufactured in India; of late years to great perfection. All the leather work is covered with guzzee, if on the outside of the tent; but all within the tent is covered with the same colour or pattern as the lining. By this means great neatness is preserved.

Most tents are furnished with *veraudahs*, or flat projections, proceeding from the edges of the shell in two or more parts, so as to encrease the interior of the tent. They do not project beyond the fly, as they would thence be subject to wet from rain; which from their horizontal position they could not throw off. The doorways are made either in an arched form, or with square corners above as well as below. Some contrive them to shut by means of extra length in the walls; which, being brought to lap over, close them perfectly. This is certainly the securest mode, as well as the most comfortable; but the most convenient method is to have *purdahs*, which are hangings composed of the same materials as the tent, rather larger than the doorways, and kept extended to their due breadth by horizontal bamboos, which also prevent them from being blown in by the wind. These *purdahs* are rolled up when the doors are required to remain open, and are tied up by means of cords fixed to their centres for that purpose.

The tents are mostly furnished with *cheeks*, which are

applied to the doors in the same manner as *purdahs*, and are usually hung upon the edge of the shell or marquee between the wall and the *purdah*. These *cheeks* are made of small strips of bamboo, about the thickness of a crow quill; they are kept together by threads worked in various patterns, but commonly in checquers, and are sometimes bound round at their edges with tape or coloured cloth. *Cheeks* are extremely useful; they admit a moderate portion of air; keep out the glare, which is highly distressing during the heat of the day in every situation; render the interior private, though a person within can distinctly observe all that passes without; and serve to keep out a large number of the insects, frogs, &c. which, during the rainy season in particular, become an excessive nuisance after sunset. *Cheeks* roll up in the same manner, but in much less compass than *purdahs*.

Many circumstances render it expedient that all Europeans who travel, or go on parties of pleasure, should be accompanied by small guards of seapoys. The habits of all the natives of power or opulence have created in the minds of the inferior classes an opinion, that to be without such a retinue proceeds from a want of dignity, or from a want of importance, and produces, on many occasions, very unpleasant dilemmas. Frequently the head of a village, who is supreme within his own limits, will deny himself; will refuse to furnish supplies, though the money be tendered; and will behave with the greatest insolence. He will, perhaps, refuse to protect the party in the usual manner, by *chokeydars*, or nightly watchmen; while on the other hand, he will, not unfrequently, send some of his own gang to plunder the camp during the night.

However, the presence of a small guard, nay, even of a single seapoy, generally obviates these difficulties, and proves the means of not only protecting, but of amply providing the party with every requisite the country affords.

The guards usually sleep under shelter of the fly; in fair weather, under a tree; or occasionally in the open air; one or more sentries are stationed, which with the aid of the *chokeydars*, for the most part prevent the approach of thieves, belonging to other villages; though this profession is brought to such perfection in India, as to completely eclipse the feats of our European sons of Belial! If, however, the weather be not of the best, the guard, as also the servants, who partake of the same shelter, throw their small *Satringes*, or carpets used to sleep on, empty pin-bags, &c. over the ropes of the fly, and thus keep off the rain, or the heavy-dews; and in the day time, skreen themselves by the same means from the scorching rays of the sun. Some, perhaps, are accompanied by their *goorgahs*, or menials, who carry their quilts, and cooking apparatus, consisting in general of a *lootah*, or water pot, containing about a quart, a *deckchee*, or boiler, equal to nearly a gallon, and a *tussilah*, or flat platter, of about a foot or fifteen inches in diameter, with a side or rim about an inch high, and nearly perpendicular: the use of this last is to contain victuals when dressed, which the natives all eat with their right hands; taking up their viands with their fingers, and thrusting them into their mouths with their thumbs. It is remarkable that although there are appropriate terms for knives, forks, and spoons, in the Hindostanee language, yet the natives never use them at their meals; and in fact, appear to have neither of those articles, if we except the *chuckoo*, or clasp knife, and the *choory*, or butcher's knife. Till Europeans visited India, spoons, and forks in particular, were unknown there.

With regard to culinary apparatus, as well as liquors, &c. the usual mode of conveyance is by *bangies*. These are baskets or boxes, slung in net-work of coarse twine, at each end of a split bamboo, from four to five feet long, and balanced on a man's shoulder. The pace of these *bangies* may be from three and a half to four miles in the hour, which; considering that they will occasionally carry a dozen of wine in each basket, though eighteen bottles is a fair load for both, for eighteen or twenty miles, perhaps in very hot, or in rainy weather, will afford a sufficient proof of the vigour of this class of servants.

As to supplies of meat, they must be obtained from the cantonments whence the party proceeded; unless, as is often the case, sheep are driven out for the purpose. Most gentlemen have a small flock fed on grain: this arises from the custom prevalent throughout India of killing goat mutton, which, though generally fat, is very strong, and unpalatable to Europeans. Poultry can only be obtained among the Mussulmans, of whom numbers are interspersed in the villages; though they bear a very small proportion to the bulk of the inhabitants, who are Hindoos, and will not tolerate the existence of poultry on their premises. Such indeed is their detestation thereof, that a Hindoo would sooner forfeit his life than wear a fowl's feather. Milk and butter are to be had in plenty throughout the country. The former, if obtained from a village, cannot be used, unless the precaution be taken of having *it milked* into a clean vessel; owing to the invariable practice adopted by the natives of smoaking the insides of their milk *pots* before milking. The butter in use among the natives is generally made from the milk of buffaloes; it is rich, but white; and is never applied to any purpose until it be melted, when it becomes granulated, and unpleasant *to* Europeans. It is in fact only suited to culinary purposes, for which it answers as well as the best. The natives of opulence frequently drink off a pint or more in the morning, deeming it a wholesome delicacy, tending much to pinguefaction, which throughout India is esteemed a great blessing, and in a manner commands respect. Europeans, however, not only consider this kind of butter, which is called *ghee*, as nauseous, but find corpulency to be, on many accounts, both unpleasant and expensive. Good butter and bread are to be found in every Presidency, or civil station, and at all military posts; where bakers and buttermen are established, who provide those articles, manufacturing them in the English manner.

Cooking is carried on in the open air by means of embers; coals being unknown in India, except in the *Rainghur* country, where the *Soobanreeka* river runs for some miles through a mine of excellent quality. The country being extremely mountainous, and no navigable river within at least a hundred miles, though small streams abound, added to the vast abundance of fuel, occasions that valuable commodity to be neglected. The India Company, indeed, find it easier to send coal from England, as ballast, to their arsenals abroad; where quantities are occasionally used in fusing metals for casting ordnance. Iron spikes armed with hooks, are driven into the ground at proper distances, and serve as racks for the spits, which are placed over the centre of the embers formed into a long ridge, and are turned by hand, as in Scotland, and other parts. Pots are placed to boil on ranges of holes dug out of the ground; the turfs being placed as rests under their bottoms, so as to admit a free draught of air: or they are placed on *cheolas*, constructed of dried mud, which, though made to contain only one or two boilers, have the advantage of being portable, and can be turned to whatever quarter the wind may shift.

Under such circumstances, dinners are dressed which might vie with the best cookery in Europe; a circumstance the more extraordinary, as the natives, except of the lowest and most degraded casts, or sects, will not touch any viands that have been at the table of an European, or that may have been defiled by his touch, even though he should but enter the area made for the purpose of cooking the victuals!

The vast numbers of plantations made of mango trees,

especially throughout Bengal and the northern provinces, by the natives, chiefly through ostentation, afford considerable convenience to persons inhabiting tents. Some of these plantations or *topes* are of such extent, that an army of ten or twelve thousand men might encamp under shelter: a circumstance which to the native soldiery, with whom tents are not in use, is of great moment. In the hot season, the shade is both pleasant and salutary; in the cold months, these woods afford warmth by keeping off the bleak wind; and in the rainy portion of the year, those trees which have the thickest foliage contribute to the comfort of the troops, by throwing the water off from certain spots, and rendering them habitable. Sporting parties are benefited in a similar manner: such places are chosen as are well shaded, and near to wells or tanks. Some trees, however, are avoided, as having a baneful influence; the tamarind, for instance, under which nothing will vegetate. The *burghut*, or banian tree, exhibited in Plate II. has a similar effect on plants, but is not, like the tamarind, injurious to animals. The *kuntaul* or *kuttaul*, commonly called the *jack*, is the Indian fig. Its fruit grows like large pendant bulbs, from the stem or main branches. Some of these weigh from twenty to thirty pounds; they rarely ripen on the tree, requiring a stick smeared with a thick solution of fresh lime to be run through them, and to remain until the coat shall change colour and become soft. The kernels or fruit are numerous, and by some are much admired; but the smell of a jack when first opened is almost as offensive as carrion. When the fruit is nearly perfect, the scent is strong at times from the tree; but otherwise there is no inconvenience in being under its shade; which, from the opakeness of its foliage, much resembling the laurel, effectually precludes the sun. The mango tree being most common, is usually resorted to; the more so, as it is a general practice that when a plantation is made, a well should be dug at one of its sides. The well and the tope are married; a ceremony at which all the village attends, and in which often much money is expended. The well is considered as the husband; as its waters, which are copiously furnished to the young trees during the first hot season, are supposed to cherish and impregnate them. Though vanity and superstition are evidently the basis of these institutions, yet we cannot help admiring their effects so beautifully ornamenting a torrid country, and affording such general convenience.

Having premised thus much, I shall proceed to state the manner in which a party usually repairs to the hunting ground.

To those who have but one horse, which is a common case, especially among gentlemen of the army, it is an object of moment to keep him fresh for the sport. This motive, added to the refreshment produced by change of seat and position, induces many to proceed to and from the field on elephants, which are variously accoutred for the occasion; some having only the pads used when carrying burthens; others, if of small stature, furnished with saddles, or cushions and stirrups; and others again with *howdahs*, or carriages, with or without hangings. These are respectively exhibited in the present Plate, and their construction will be found particularly detailed in the subsequent Numbers, in such parts as may require more complete elucidation. Suffice it for the present to state, that the carriage pad is formed of canvas, stuffed hard with straw, and lashed securely to the elephant's back by strong hempen cords. It is in general spacious enough to hold about four persons, though I have seen some so large, being in proportion to the elephant's bulk, as to carry eight or nine with ease. It requires a good spring to jump up; and those not possessed of such active powers are aided by servants, or avail themselves of the benefit of a chair, &c. to facilitate their mounting. Saddles are appropriate to such elephants as may be of rather low stature, that is about six feet or less; they are placed on pads lined with cotton or wool, and are girted on as with horses. In this manner only one person can ride each elephant; it is, however, in my mind, the most pleasant mode. Some, instead of a saddle, have a long cushion fastened on with one or two pair of stirrups. These are certainly convenient and easy; besides which they possess the advantage of carrying double. The howdah being made on a strong frame, and of a heavy construction, requires not only to be very effectually secured to the pad, but should be borne by elephants of good stature; that is from seven feet upwards. They are of various forms. That exhibited in this Plate is an *Hindostanee*, such as has been ever in use among the natives, and was at first the only form adopted by Europeans, who have since considerably varied this conveyance. All howdahs, however, require a ladder to ascend into them; after which the ladder is slung at the side of the elephant, in a horizontal position, by means of rope-loops made for that purpose. The iron rails in the front were introduced by gentlemen for the purpose of supporting their fire arms; and some have added a similar guard all around the back, filled up with cord or wire netting, as a security against falling out. The *coosah*, or back division of the howdah, behind the front seat, is usually allotted to a servant, who conveys either an umbrella or ammunition, or furnishes the sportsmen with refreshment. Into this the menials generally ascend by climbing up the elephant's rump, in which they are aided by the ropes that pass, like a crupper, under the insertion of its tail.

The elephant is invariably driven by a *mohout*, let the form of conveyance be what it may. He sits on the neck, with his legs behind the ears, and his feet within a kind of collar of loose cords passed ten or twelve times round the neck. With his toes he guides the elephant; pressing under the ear opposite the way he would proceed: thus, if he would turn to the right, he presses with his left toe; and *vice versa*. He governs the elephant by means of an iron instrument about two feet long, having a large hook affixed near the top. This is called a *haunkus*, literally a driver: with the pointed end of it he either accelerates, or causes the elephant to lay down: in the former case he urges the point forward; in the latter, he presses it perpendicularly on the centre of the skull; accompanying each mode with words of command in general use, and for the most part so well understood by elephants as to suffice without recourse to the *haunkus*. As many elephants are impatient while mounting, or loading, it is not only proper to keep a certain pressure on the head, but to cause a grass cutter, who ordinarily attends, provided with a spear, spiked at both ends, and used chiefly to goad the elephant forward, to stand on one of the fore legs; pressing, if necessary, the end of the spear, so as to deter the animal from rising prematurely.

Those who proceed on horseback, occasionally find some difficulty in mounting; for, exclusive of the vice predominant in the horse throughout India, many of those animals are so shy of Europeans, as not to allow one to mount without being hoodwinked; as is shewn in the Plate. Indeed it has often been my own lot to possess horses I could neither mount nor dismount, without being held by their own particular *syces* or grooms, lest I might become a victim to their ferocious dispositions. When mounted, they are for the most part tolerably governable, possess great spirit, and are excellent hunters; but being, with few exceptions, stone horses, they are peculiarly quarrelsome and impatient, especially when in sight of a mare. This renders it impossible to ride boot to boot, as is practised in England. Indeed from a dozen to twenty yards interval sometimes proves too little for the eagerness of horses to make battle. It is considered as quite an ordinary circumstance to see one or two engagements, between led horses in particular; often to the greatest injury of the animals, and seldom without a dismal report of the damage done to the saddles, and other accoutrements.

PLATE XIII.

A TIGER SEIZING A BULLOCK IN A PASS.

TIGERS very rarely make their attacks on open plains; though instances have occurred, within my own knowledge, where they have proceeded half a mile, or more, from any cover, and made dreadful havock among travellers and peasants; acting as if intent on destruction only. We must not conclude that such conduct is in their ordinary course of practice, but may, no doubt, fairly attribute such a deviation from the marked character of the animal, to momentary anguish, or to resentment induced by an unsuccessful skirmish with one of its own species; when, being chased from the jungles, the defeated party bends its course towards any living object, teeming with revenge, and eager to give loose to its rage. For I have already observed, that the tiger is of all beasts of prey the most cowardly; its treacherous disposition induces it, almost without exception, to conceal itself until its prey may arrive within reach of its spring, be its victim either bulky or diminutive. Size seems to occasion no deviation in the tiger's system of attack, which is founded on the art of

surprising. We find, accordingly, that such as happen to keep the opposite side of a road, by which they are somewhat beyond the first spring, often escape injury; the tiger being unwilling to be seen before he is felt. Hence it is rarely that a tiger pursues; but, if the situation permit, his cunning will not fail to effect his purpose: he will steal along the road's side among the bushes parallel with the traveller's course, until one of the many chances which present themselves, of finding him within reach, induces to the attack. Often, where the country is rather too open to allow his proceeding in this manner, the tiger will take a sweep among underwood, or through ravines, in order to meet the traveller again at a spot whence he may make his spring.

Tigers are extremely partial to such sites as command a road, selecting one rather less frequented, in preference to one that is much in use. In the former they are certain of finding as much as will answer their daily wants. If, however, the haunt be on a public road, it is usually at some spot with grass or bushes, especially the *prauss*, and in the vicinity of some ample cover, supplied with water, to which the prey can be dragged. There, in some low, opake spot, the sanguinary meal is consummated in gloomy silence.

It should be observed that, for the most part, the tiger chooses his station on that side of the road which is opposite his haunt; so that when he seizes his prey, he proceeds straight forward, without having occasion to turn; and thus drags it across, mostly at a trot. If he misses his aim, he will rarely return, unless attacked; but in a sullen manner either skulks through the cover, or if the country be not sufficiently close to conceal his motions, he moves on at a canter; a pace in which a tiger appears very awkward; as with him it is not unlike the gait of a large heavy calf.

A large portion of the soil in India is of a reddish hue, and the grass during the summer heats being deprived of the sap proper to create a verdure, becomes of a dusky colour, very similar to the brighter parts of a tiger's coat. These circumstances are peculiarly favourable to the animal's concealment; so much so, that a tiger is often roused where there does not exist any cover adequate to sheltering half his bulk: the colour of the animal so perfectly corresponding with the surrounding objects, as to conceal the danger; or, if the animal be seen, he is mistaken for a mound of earth, or something equally innocent.

The tiger's fore paw is the invariable engine of destruction. Most persons imagine that if a tiger were deprived of his claws and teeth he would be rendered harmless; but this is a gross error. The weight of the limb is the real cause of the mischief; for the talons are rarely extended when a tiger seizes. The operation is similar to that of a hammer; the tiger raising his paw, and bringing it down with such force, as not only to stun a common sized bullock, or buffalo, but often crushing the bones of the skull! I have seen many men and oxen that had been killed by tigers, in most of which no mark of a claw could be seen; and where scratches did appear; they were obviously the effect of chance, from the paw sliding downwards, and not from design.

It often takes some labour for a tiger to remove a bullock he has killed, from any open situation to a safe retreat, where he can glut himself undisturbed; but he will convey away a man with as much ease, and in the same manner as a cat drags away a rat. I once witnessed an instance, which gave me a very complete idea of a tiger's proceedings, and of his powers. I was travelling post in my *palankeen*, through the Ramghur district, which is mountainous and little cultivated, being for the most part in a state of nature, and every where abounding in jungles, when a *baugy-wollah*, who conveyed two baskets of linen and refreshments, and who preceded the *palankeen* about an hundred and fifty yards, set down his load, and seated himself on the side of the road to rest awhile. About two yards behind him was a small bush, not much larger than a good sized currant tree, round which a small quantity of jungle grass was growing to the height of about three feet. There was not another twig to be seen for at least half a mile, on that side of the road. No sooner had the poor fellow seated himself, than a tiger sprang from behind, or rather from within the bush, and, after giving the fatal blow with his paw, seized the man by the shoulder, and dragged him off, with the utmost ease, at a round pace into a thick cover, which had formerly skirted the road, but which had, by order of government, been cut away to the distance of about a hundred yards, for the safety of travellers.

The most dangerous spots are the crossings of *nullahs*, where, if there be cover, tigers should ever be expected to lurk. The heat of the climate inducing much thirst, and the habits of the natives being in various respects much connected with water, cause most travellers to stop in these situations, where the tiger with very little trouble may select such objects for destruction as he may prefer. In such places it sometimes happens that a man, or a bullock, &c. is carried off daily; yet it will appear extraordinary, that rarely any means are adopted for removing the evil; though it is well known that tigers are easily made to quit haunts, if proper measures be resorted to. But it being the business of every body, nobody attends to it; especially as the people of India are predestinarians, and conceive they cannot avoid their respective fates! Nevertheless, we find them having recourse to charms, and to many superstitious devices to avert danger. A contradiction by no means singular, nor confined to any particular part of the universe.

It must appear remarkable, that tigers often quit the most advantageous haunts without the least apparent cause; for as to checking or destroying them, even where practicable, the natives never think of it, except under European influence; and in many parts of the country it is impossible to do any thing effectual. I am strongly inclined to think, that tigers are peculiarly subject to some acute distemper, which carries off great numbers; or that they have some very powerful enemy, with which we are unacquainted; else, if we admit that a tigress bears two cubs annually; nay, if we calculate that she rears but one in three years, during a period of twelve years, we should find the increase so prodigious, as to leave no chance against being overrun with them in every direction! In some districts, the rewards held forth by government and by individuals, have without doubt produced benefit; but such efforts must be confined to particular spots, and never could affect those immense jungles, stretching along the boundaries of Bengal for at least a thousand miles on each side, and extending in many places two or three hundred miles in breadth. These grand depots, to which neither man, horse, nor elephant can have access, and in which deer, &c. abound, supplying the superior beasts of prey with ample sustenance, could not fail, but for some powerful curb, to cause such an augmentation as must, in time, annihilate not only every animal a tiger could destroy, but ultimately the tigers themselves must perish of hunger. As to the *Dhole*, or wild dog, it is never seen but in the countries lying between south *Bahar* and the *Maharattah* frontier, towards *Nagpore*. For a description of the *Dhole*, which indeed is but little known in India, the reader is referred to plate XXI. of which that remarkable animal is the subject.

I have before observed, that tigers are not always to be checked by fire. However popular the opinion may be, and although we may consider it as an axiom, that a tiger may generally be driven away by noise, and especially by fire, yet so many instances are perpetually occurring, where neither the one nor the other has had the desired effect, that we may perhaps not be very wrong in judging, that, though a tiger, when in a state of satiety, may be easily alarmed, he is not easily repelled, by such means, when seriously in want of a meal! Nor on such occasions do we find that numbers operate as a defence. In the year 1792, a merchant, who was proceeding by the new road to Calcutta, with a large string of valuable horses for sale, was taken off his steed, as he was going through the *Katcumsandy* pass, at mid-day; though in the midst of a numerous retinue of servants, and in spite of the noise necessarily attendant on a large cavalcade. The tiger leaped down from a knob at the road's side, covered with small bushes and grass, about ten feet high, and dragged the unfortunate merchant to the opposite side; where, however, he was intimidated by the shouts of the horsemen, who pursued him as closely as they could get their horses to approach. The corpse was on the same day brought to our station at *Hazary-bhaug*, where it was interred.

When travellers find themselves benighted, and in camps, where either from the situation being suspected as abounding with tigers, or from being pitched in underwood jungles, it is usual to keep a good fire during the night. I doubt not but such a measure, added to other precautions, proves occasionally serviceable; but knowing as I do, that it has frequently happened during a succession of many nights, that the persons conveying the *dawks*, or posts, have been carried away in spite of the *mosauls*, or flambeaus, and of the continual beating of the *tom-toms*, or drums, by which they are ever accompanied at night, my opinion has long since been made up very completely on the subject; and some strange alteration must take place in the conduct of tigers in general, before I can bring myself to believe, that one half-famished, can be deterred by any means from making an attack. That tigers are often very capricious I will admit, and indeed that, in some instances, their conduct appears unaccountable; but I must assert, that where hunger is the motive, they are at least as consistent, and as persevering, as any other animals.

Mr. PAUL, of *Daudpore*, who has been spoken of in the preceding Number, and who, I doubt not, has killed as many tigers as any hundred persons in India, used often to remark, that he could instantly, at sight of a tiger, decide whether or not it had been in the habit of attacking the human race; or whether its devastations had been confined to cattle, &c. He observed, that such as had once killed a man, ever after cared but little for any other prey; and that they could be distinguished by the remarkable darkness of their skins, and by a redness in the cornea, or whites, of the eyes. PAUL was assuredly a competent judge; but, I apprehend, this assertion partook more of hypothesis than of reason. At all events, it must be considered as a very nice distinction. Many circumstances seemed to corroborate his opinion as to their predilection for human flesh; it having been observed in various instances, that such tigers as had been in the habit of seizing travellers, rarely did much mischief among the neighbouring herds. We can readily conceive, that the ease with which a human body may be dissected by a tiger, might cause him to give it a preference; but with regard to the physical effects of such diet, we may, without being accused of scepticism, require something more than bare assertion, or an individual opinion, ere we cease to doubt.

It is said that many strong, bold persons, have killed tigers by catching, or rather by receiving them, in their spring, by means of a broad substantial shield, covered with a thick net work, in which the claws become entangled, and afford an opportunity to the hazardous adventurer to plunge a sharp knife, somewhat similar to those in use among pork butchers, once, or oftener, into the chest or ribs of the animal, as he stands on his hind legs on such occasions. My own observation as to the weight and powers of a tiger, teach me to consider this as mere fable; for I am fully convinced, that no man, however robust, could sustain the weight of a tiger for one moment on his left arm; much less resist the violent spring of an animal, whose whole strength is collected for the occasion, and whose paw falls with such inconceivable force as to fracture the skull of an ox. We all know that, in various parts of the world, divers are furnished with knives for the purpose of stabbing sharks, which often attack them. Those unacquainted with the form of that fish's mouth, may doubt whether any man could defend himself from a ground shark of, perhaps, twenty feet or more in length; but the case is widely different between the two animals. The shark's mouth is placed so far back, being perhaps a foot behind his nose, that before he can seize his prey, he must turn on his side; thus giving the diver time to avoid the bite, and, at the same moment, presenting to his aim the only vital part susceptible of the fatal instrument.

The method of destroying tigers, said to be common in Persia, and towards the north of Hindostan, appears far more reasonable, as well as more concordant with the genius of the people. This device consists of a large semi-spherical cage, made of strong bamboos, or other efficient materials, woven together, but leaving intervals throughout, of about three or four inches broad. Under this cover, which is fastened to the ground by means of pickets, in some place where tigers abound, a man, provided with two or three short strong spears, takes post at night. Being accompanied by a dog, which gives the alarm, or by a goat, which by its agitation answers the same purpose, the adventurer wraps himself up in his quilt, and very composedly goes to sleep, in full confidence of his safety. When a tiger comes, and, perhaps after smelling all around, begins to rear against the cage, the man stabs him with one of the spears through the interstices of the wicker work, and rarely fails of destroying the tiger, which is ordinarily found dead at no great distance in the morning.

The most curious, and indeed the safest method except the poisoned arrow, is in use in some parts of the Nabob Vizier of Oude's dominions. I never saw it practised, though it has repeatedly been described to me by the natives in that quarter, and particularly by a Mussulman gentleman, who was for many years a public character at the Nabob's court, and who lately paid a visit to this country. Though it is probable that many a smile will be excited by the recital, yet, as I have a confidence in the fact, and do not perceive any thing improbable in the matter, I hesitate not to present it to my readers.

The track of a tiger being ascertained, which though not invariably the same, may yet be known sufficiently for the purpose, the peasants collect a quantity of the leaves of the *prauss*, which are like those of the sycamore, and are common in most underwoods, as they form the larger portion of most jungles in the north of India. These leaves are smeared with a species of bird-lime, made by bruising the berries of an indigenous tree, by no means scarce, but of which I cannot at present call to mind the name; they are then strewed with the gluten uppermost, near to that opake spot to which it is understood the tiger usually resorts during the noon tide heats. If by chance the animal should tread on one of the smeared leaves, his fate may be considered as decided. He commences by shaking his paw, with the view to remove the adhesive incumbrance; but finding no relief from that expedient, he rubs the nuisance against his face with the same intention, by which means his eyes, ears, &c. become agglutinated, and occasion such uneasiness as causes him to roll, perhaps among many more of the smeared leaves, till at length he becomes completely enveloped, and is deprived of sight. In this situation he may be compared to a man who has been tarred and feathered. The anxiety produced by this strange and novel predicament soon discovers itself in dreadful howlings, which serve to call the watchful peasants, who, in this state, find no difficulty in shooting the mottled object of detestation.

I am given to understand, that some exceptions have been made to the great bulk of the tiger pourtrayed in the Plate attached to this Number, most probably by gentlemen who have only seen the menageries at the Tower and at Exeter Change. If we were to take such as are there exhibited for a standard, the criticism would be just; but there is a wide difference indeed between the wild parent, and the cub reared in a cage. Even among buffaloes, in their savage and in their domesticated states, we perceive a wondrous disproportion in stature; notwithstanding that the latter, from the complete liberty they have as to extent of range, and in regard to enjoyment in their favourite element, the water, can scarcely be said to be reclaimed. Farther, let it be understood, that, at the moment of seizure, as also when exasperated, a tiger raises his fur in the same manner as a cat; and, exclusive of the magnifying powers of fear, appears far more bulky than when in a calm and passive state. Nor should it be unnoticed, that the cattle of India are rather of a small stature; so much so, that a bullock four feet six inches at the shoulder, is deemed fit for all the purposes of the ordnance department, in which they are invariably employed. All these considerations combined will reconcile the apparent disproportion, and should satisfy the reader of the correctness of the Plate in every particular.

The cattle throughout India are mostly white. They are generally very vicious; and being reared among the natives, are so alarmed and irritable in the presence of an European, as to require much skill and firmness in the management. When used for draught, they are worked with a single yoke, fixed by an iron bolt across the head of the beam, or pole, and are kept in their places by two straps of leather, passing under their throats respectively. The pads, of such as are employed to carry burthens, are of the same materials as those for elephants. The upper pad is of a narrow kind of canvass called *taut*, stuffed with straw: the under pad is ordinarily lined with blanket, and filled with cotton or wool. These pads are kept on by a strong kind of tape, going completely round them, and under the animal's belly, having at each end a loop of iron, or of wood, through which a strong cord being passed many times, the pads may be braced on to any degree of tightness. A bullock may carry from three to five maunds, of eighty pounds each, according to size and other circumstances. Grain is generally laden in two *taut* bags, laced together and suspended one on each side; but, to prevent the pressure from galling, a few pieces of small round bamboo are stitched to each side of the upper pad, longitudinally, and serve to render the weight uniform. Oil and *ghee*, or granulated buffalo butter, are carried in *dubbahs*, or carboys, made of green ox hide, containing about eight or ten gallons each. The cattle of Bengal are, in general, of the short-horned kind; those of Madras, that is to say of the Carnatic, have them more upright and straighter; somewhat similar in form to the horns of the antelope. All cattle in India are extremely skittish, and rarely make a journey without throwing their loads every four or five miles. Indeed were it not that the natives adopt the precaution of boreing the noses of all calves intended to be reared for work, and pass a rope through the *septum*, or division between the nostrils, tying it behind the horns so as to become a rein, it would be utterly impossible to manage them. The bags are rarely tied down, but are left to balance themselves. The red or black threads, running the whole length of the pieces of *laut*, give them a lively appearance; and though singular, are by no means displeasing to the eye.

The *bamboo* is so often noticed in this work, that some description of it may prove useful. It is of the reed kind, growing to the height of sixty feet, or more, and may be often seen six inches in diameter near the root from which it tapers up gradually to the top, the joints becoming longer and more hollow. The branches are very strong, but small, having little or no cavity, and are furnished with handsome spear-shaped leaves of about four inches long, by less than one inch in breadth at the widest part. It bears neither blossoms nor fruit, and is propagated either by the suckers it shoots up around its roots in the rainy season, and which are then excellent for pickling, or by cutting into staves of three or four joints each, when being buried half way in the ground, during dripping weather, or in wet situations, they soon vegetate, and in the course of a few years become both useful and ornamental fences. The hill bamboos, which are used for making *latties*, or staves, rarely grow to more than two inches in thickness. They are amazingly tough, having in general an inconsiderable cavity; and after being dressed with oil while hot, retain their suppleness for many years. They form excellent shafts for spears; and the lightest answer admirably for inserting into the walls of tents, purdahs, &c. They are in general use as walking sticks among the natives.

In windy, dry weather their friction often causes them to take fire; occasioning the hills on which they grow to assume a beautiful appearance at night.

PLATE XIX.

THE DEAD TIGER.

It has been repeatedly remarked, that the elephant invariably puts his trunk, as far as possible, out of danger. He seems to consider it as the instrument which supplies him with food; and in case of blindness, relies upon it to save him from falling into pits, &c.; accordingly we find he does not use it as a weapon; though, from a knowledge of its great powers, one would be apt to conclude, that it would be brought to its aid on all occasions. As I lately mentioned, the trunk is extremely tender, and an attack upon it never fails to defeat the most undaunted of the race. The male seems to rely chiefly on its teeth, which in some are very large; and frequently, when attacking a tiger, will suddenly kneel, making an effort to transfix its opponent. This mode of attack seems to be an innate principle; in fact, we can scarcely imagine how a male elephant should act with the hope of success if deprived of his tusks. Yet we find the generality of them to be extremely timid, and, that ordinarily, they would rather avoid than engage in a contest. Some have attributed the extreme aversion, so obvious in elephants, to engaging with animals far beneath them in bulk, and even their submission to the human race, to some magnifying power, with which they pretend the eye of the elephant is constructed, and by which their ideas of their own comparative superiority are completely subverted. This however is mere hypothesis, and would stand confuted by the evidence they must have of each other's bulk; which of course must be in a similar ratio increased, even were nothing else to be opposed to so vague a conjecture. As yet we are little acquainted with the anatomy of the elephant: Certainly we are not ignorant as to its osteology; but that is saying little. It is to be lamented that the heat of the climate precludes our practitioners from dissecting so particularly as to afford a complete acquaintance with the whole structure, and pathology, of so noble, as well as so useful, an animal.

I once saw an elephant use her trunk: a boar we were hunting made towards her, when she curled her trunk inwards, and, as he approached, turned rapidly to one side, applying her elastic weapon most forcibly against his side. The boar was knocked over by the blow, which resounded afar, and for a few seconds appeared to be much hurt: but the chase and defence we afterwards experienced gave us to understand, that he was not much the worse for the repulse. Elephants will frequently throw clods, or stones, at objects they may either fear or dislike. I have, on several occasions, seen them pick up lumps in ploughed land, and throw them with considerable force, and tolerable precision, at hogs that have been near them, and from which they expected an attack. When elephants find hogs intent on getting under their bellies, with the intention to rip, they sometimes lay down with astonishing quickness; thereby not only protecting their intestines from injury, but often crushing the hog; at least giving a squeeze such as few animals could endure. I had once a little elephant which had been repeatedly charged by hogs, and used, whenever she got one under her belly, to hustle it with all four legs; kicking in such a manner as rarely failed to deprive it of the means of escape.

Though, in general, elephants being once trained to work become perfectly tractable, excepting males at the rutting season, when they are sullen and vicious, yet many are somewhat treacherous, and have a trick of flinging out a hind leg at objects they chance not to like: these kicks, from the size of the limb, and its apparent unwieldiness, one would think might be sustained without any great injury. Such is by no means the case: the strength of the animal is not more conspicuous in any act than in kicking. They do not lash out like a horse, nor with the motion of an ox; but, poising themselves on the opposite hind leg, throw out that which is next to the object of vengeance, almost in a right line; much the same as if a paviour's rammer were swung from the same situation.

Those of the natives who wish to have elephants completely qualified for tiger-hunting, take the greatest pains to have such as promise well trained by the most expert *mohouts*. Few females are deemed fit to be employed in this way; on the other hand, such males as have long teeth, with a good curve, are considered most eligible. Nor can an elephant well be too large for encountering a tiger. It is to be observed, that, although a prince will obtain the finest animals that can be found, and go to great expence in having them fully instructed, yet that such are not selected for his own use in the field. At least the most powerful will generally be seen without any rider but the *mohout*; who perhaps may be provided with a spear. Such elephants are urged to attack the tiger with their teeth; on which they will receive the charge sometimes with great dexterity; causing the assailant to transfix, or at least to wound himself in his spring. There are, however, very few elephants that can be brought to perfection: nine in ten of them being disgusted with the sport, and giving way to very ordinary attacks. Hence a really staunch one is of considerable value.

It is worthy of remark, that such elephants as are newly caught, possess far more courage than those long domesticated. Probably, this superiority arises from their often falling in with tigers in their wild state, and being compelled to stand on their defence; or, that, from the frequency of such rencontres, they acquire a habit of indifference. Add to this, it is observable in all animals, that domestication assuredly breaks the spirit; rendering them passive, and causing a certain degree of timidity, operating greatly to their disadvantage in many respects. Nothing more completely illustrates the truth of this position, than the certainty, that a jungle cock, which has been born and reared in a wild state, though far smaller than the general run of game cocks, will, from its superior keenness, and activity, in all instances be found victorious! The natives of Hindostan, I mean the Mussulmans, are, like the Malays, wondrously attached to cock fighting; and in both countries the above experiment has been tried, where jungle cocks could be obtained; which is very seldom indeed.

The common method of training an elephant to attack tigers is with a stuffed skin; which being laid in his way, as he proceeds through a grass jungle, at first usually excites some alarm; but the elephant speedily becomes reconciled to the object, and, after a few trials, may be brought, not only to view it with indifference, but to put his foot on the supposed carcase; rolling it backwards and forwards, as it were for amusement; and occasionally bearing his whole weight thereon. When sufficiently reconciled to the complexion and feel of the fictitious enemy, the elephant is taught to receive it on his teeth, when thrown towards his head by one or two men. After this he is made to kneel, and press his teeth through the stuffing; so as to fix it to the ground. During all these parts of the tuition, the *mohout* uses every soothing means; caressing the elephant, and supplying him liberally with such dainties as he seems to prefer: thus, not only rendering him sensible of the advantage attendant upon his acquiescence and docility of disposition, but creating a regard for his keeper, which in the sequel is often found to contribute much to his safety.

Thus far elephants, in general, may be led without shewing much disinclination: some, however, take fright in the course of training, and become so invincibly obstinate, that neither force nor coaxing can induce them to proceed. Such, ordinarily, prove far worse than they were previous to any measures being taken to instruct them. But the severe part of the trial is yet to come. The inanimate object has, perhaps, been viewed with indifference; but when a boy is put within the skin, stuffed to its utmost dimensions, and caused to proceed, at first with silence, and afterwards with loud howlings, the elephant generally in following will shew some uneasiness. In this stage, however, he is not required to assault; but when a calf, or other animal, is substituted in lieu of the human stuffing, then the elephant is urged to the attack, and in every instance to shew his learning. I have before informed the reader, that elephants are extremely jealous of all small animals running near, but especially behind, them; and I may here add, that all, in general, would rather confront, or follow, a large beast than a small one. Most, indeed, feel the greatest uneasiness when dogs are near them, and move sideways so as to avoid them when approaching. The old topic of magnifying optics, mentioned in the last number, will perhaps be revived in behalf of such apprehensions; not however to my conviction.

During the time that an elephant is in training, it is held

prudent to accustom him to the sight and smell of any tiger which may be kept in a cage, &c.; and, especially, to debar him the sight of such tigers as, during the course of hunting, may be in an irritated state. When a tiger is killed, the elephant should then be brought up to roll, press, and transfix him, as before specified; and, if the noble animal shew no distrust, the carcase may be laid on his back. This part of the ceremony is, however, the most difficult of the whole; and if not managed with great delicacy and caution, may ruin the speculation completely. It is astonishing with what jealousy even the best trained elephant will tolerate the brindled burthen! Their anxiety becomes extreme; and in proportion to their knowledge of the tiger's nature and prowess, so do they become tenacious of allowing even one, in the death of which they have been instrumental, to be placed on their pads. It is not less curious, that some elephants, which never can be brought to approach a live tiger, will without hesitation allow themselves to be laden with a dead one; and exhibit no symptoms of apprehension, or of distrust, on the occasion. But I recollect seeing a tiger, which had been insufficiently secured on the back of an elephant of this description, fall off on the way home; thereby agitating the elephant so much, as to defeat every endeavour to replace the carcase; which, after all, we were compelled to convey on a *hackery*, or cart: no other elephant in the field would submit to be its bearer!

Horses are highly alarmed at both the smell and sight of a

tiger. They generally become so terrified as to lose their presence of mind; and, in a trembling state, exhibiting even more than Mr. Stubbs ever pourtrayed in his excellent paintings, seem to have lost the power to escape. It sometimes happens, that a bold horse is the means of saving not only himself and rider, but many others; and of this an instance occurred where four of us following a hog, close, the one after the other, our leader pushed through a small thick patch of grass; his horse, however, when in its centre, suddenly started, and flew off at a tangent; the next in succession would, in all probability, have felt the force of a tiger which lay concealed, had he not, in lieu of stopping short, as was to have been expected, sprung over the beast, which partly rose and shewed himself; giving a hint to us who were following, to avoid the danger. Some others of the party, who were amusing themselves with shooting from elephants, there being abundance of black partridges, obeyed our summons; and we had the pleasure of seeing the object of our terror changed into an innocent burthen for one of the elephants.

I never yet heard of a tiger infesting a country, nor indeed of one being killed, but what he was "*the largest ever seen!!!*" However, in spite of such frequency of monstrous growth, I will venture to assert, that nine in ten do not measure ten feet, from the tip of the nose to the tip of the tail. I am sensible, that, when in a state of provocation, they swell themselves greatly; for which the bristling up of their furs would account sufficiently. Many persons, however, think they possess the power of inflating their skins, in the moment of attack; and I am rather disposed, from my observations both in respect to tigers and their epitome, the cat, and indeed other animals, to join in such a belief. Those who have not seen the difference, would hardly believe the change which takes place, almost instantaneously, after the tiger's last gasp! His alarming appearance in some measure remains; the grim savage look being unchanged; but the sides fall in, and would lead to the supposition of the animal having died a natural death. I have known one or two exceptions from this; but then the tigers were remarkably fat, and had fallen with little opposition to the hunters.

Whether it be, that we are conscious in regard to a tiger's disposition; or, that there be something expressive of it inseparable from his figure and appearance in general, I know not; but, even when dead, men as well as animals feel much affected in their presence: a certain creeping, shuddering sensation pervades all. Dogs take a tour on seeing the carcase, and horses shew the most fixed antipathy! The efforts of the *syces* to bring their steeds to the spot where a tiger lays dead, generally avail nothing; but, for the most part, by agitating their minds, cause them to rear and kick, in that high style for which the horses of Hindostan are famous. The *syce* generally contents himself with keeping hold of the *bhaughdure*, or halter; observing, however, rather to let go altogether than to run the least risque of self-injury, whatever accident may thence occur to others.

It is not less curious, that an elephant keeps his trunk as scrupulously from too close an approach to a dead tiger, as he does from a living one. There is a certain instinct about this semi-rational animal, that seems to pervade every act of its life, and causes it to secure a member on which its whole dependance for sustenance is rested. Nor can we but admire the wondrous use to which it applies it, when no danger as to its safety is to be apprehended. In describing the method of extricating an elephant from a slough, its importance is exhibited; without such means, indeed, all the powers within the scope of human exertion, in many situations would be of no avail! To a blind elephant, exclusive of the circumstances attendant on the supply of food, the trunk becomes invaluable. It is a curious but well known fact, that such as are unhappily deprived of sight can proceed at a good pace over very unequal ground, avoiding lumps and hollows, stepping over ditches, and appearing to far less disadvantage than we should be apt to think must attend so serious a privation. They very rarely touch the ground with the trunk; but projecting it forward as far as it can be extended, they let the tip, which is a little curled inwards, so as to prevent straws, &c. from running into the nostrils, as it were skim along the surface; and thus regulate their steps by an exquisite sense, with which that organ must indisputably be endued!

The innumerable small streams that water Bengal, forming in the rainy season deep and rapid courses, but becoming at other times insignificant, render it necessary, during the hot weather, when perhaps only a muddy stagnate puddle is left, to throw over many small temporary bridges, or causeways; generally constructed of brush-wood and grass brought from the neighbouring jungles. These not being very firmly compacted, though covered perhaps near a foot deep with earth, vibrate very sensibly, even when trod by foot passengers; and often feel as if utterly unequal to sustain a man and horse. Many such bridges may be found during a morning's march; they must be crossed; even though there be but little water, and that the banks present no difficulty. To attempt riding through, or to cross an elephant even unladen, would be hazardous in the extreme; the generality of these small rivulets, especially such as are within reach of the tides, having such very loose muddy beds, as would swamp the largest animal.

The elephant possesses a nice discrimination; and, previous to venturing himself on a bridge of such a construction, invariably feels with his trunk. If he be satisfied, from the first trial, of the sufficiency of the structure, he will proceed to cross on it, with a slow, cautious pace; obviously sensible of his own weight, and watchful as to the effect of every step. If, by chance, he should feel cause for alarm, he either recedes with precipitation, in spite of every opposition, or wheeling suddenly round, abruptly flies the danger; without any deference for whatever may chance to be in his way back to *terra-firma!* We cannot but admire this principle of self-preservation in an animal which, in passing through the streets, is often seen to remove children with its trunk, that, being in its way, would, but for such tender care, be subjected to injury from its footsteps! The elephant is not, however, frightened by the vibration of the bridges, and causeways, above described. He may be seen to pass, with sufficient confidence, over many that tremble extremely under his pressure. He nicely discriminates between the elasticity of strength, and the tottering of weakness. Nay, he will often discover insufficiency where heavy carriages may have passed in safety; and, notwithstanding all the means resorted to by his impatient, and perhaps too confident *mohout*, will persist in his objections to cross, until, by some additional supports, his fears of being injured may be completely removed!

It is the same on arrival at the temporary piers constructed at the crossings of great rivers; as also when urged to enter a platformed boat; for the purpose of being conveyed across. If the boat be not sufficiently large to bear the pressure of the elephant's first steps, without inclining too much, and causing apprehension in the animal's mind, it proves sometimes absolutely impossible to get him on board. On such occasions, if there be other elephants at hand, one should be embarked before him; when, probably, the obstinate gentleman may follow. If, however, he should still persist, in spite of the fireworks, camels, &c. urging him forward, recourse must be had to floating him over between two large boats; or he may, eventually, be induced to swim over in company with other elephants.

In the preceding Plates I have given the position of howdahs variously; so as to enable the reader to form a complete idea in respect to their shape, &c. In the Plate annexed to this Number, the form of that kind shaped like a phaeton or gig-body is conspicuously exhibited. The position of the elephant which is kneeling, with its teeth goring the tiger, cannot fail to afford satisfactory intelligence on that head. The trappings have been varied according to the most common patterns and contrasts; while, on the whole, there will be found in each Plate somewhat either novel, or, in some measure, different from what may have been formerly represented. In this Plate I have introduced an ornament called the *surpaish*, which is rarely used by Europeans, but among the natives is considered as an indispensable part of the paraphernalia. This is a kind of skull-cap made of the same stuff as the other mountings, and, invariably, of the same colours as the *jolah* and *punkey;* the former of which covers the elephant in general, while the latter, which is suspended from rings fastened to the lower edge of the body of the howdah, serves, by its position, to conceal the ropes and beams that fasten the machine to the pad.

The native princes, and sometimes their *vaqueels* or ambassadors, as well as their great officers, have a number of sumpter elephants, which convey refreshments, and attend the chief closely throughout his journey. Sometimes men of rank imitate the sovereign, by having very large kettle drums, called *nagarahs*, slung across elephants or camels; these are beaten the whole length of the journey. I know nothing more tiresome than the perpetual jingling of large bells, suspended from the pads of elephants preceding the great man, two or three hundred yards from each other, to announce his approach. The motion of the elephants occasions the bells to strike at every step. This may be music in the estimation of the natives, who have no idea of our perfection in that science. A whimsical story is related of the late Nabob Asoph ul Dowlah; who, having been invited to a grand concert, on being asked how he liked the music, after the needful approbationary *wau! wau!* observed, that it was all very fine, but that he was in particular delighted with the first part; alluding to that abominable jargon, which ever attends the tuning of instruments: "a custom" which the great Handel thought "more honoured in the breach than in the observance," and accordingly so regulated the bands over which he presided, that all entered the orchestra completely in tune, and thus annihilated that part of the performance which so exquisitely gratified his Highness the Nabob of Oude!

John Malcolm

‘Notes of Instructions to Assistants and Officers Acting under the Orders of Major-General Sir John Malcolm, GCB’. In *A Memoir of Central India*, edited by John Malcolm. London: Kingsbury, Parbury and Allen, 1823. Vol. 2.

No. XVIII.

Notes of Instructions to Assistants and Officers acting under the orders of Major-General Sir John Malcolm, G.C.B.

THESE instructions are grounded upon principles which it has been my constant effort to inculcate upon all officers acting under my orders; and, at a period when I am leaving Central India, (perhaps not to return,) I feel it a duty I owe to them, to myself, and to the public service, to enter into a more full explanation of my sentiments upon the subject of our general and local rule, than could have been necessary under any other circumstances.

General Observations.

Almost all who from knowledge and experience have been capable of forming any judgment upon the question, are agreed that our power in India rests on the general opinion of the Natives of our comparative superiority in good faith, wisdom, and strength, to their own rulers. This important impression will be improved by the consideration we shew to their habits, institutions, and religion, by the moderation, temper, and kindness with which we conduct ourselves towards them; and injured by every act that offends their belief or superstition, that shews disregard or neglect of individuals or communities, or that evinces our having with the arrogance of conquerors forgotten those maxims by which this great empire has been established, and by which alone it can be preserved.

The want of union of the Natives appears one of the strongest foundations of our power; it has certainly contributed, beyond all others, to its establishment. But, when we trace this cause, we find it to have originated in the condition in which we found India, and the line we adopted towards its inhabitants; that it will continue to operate when the condition of that country is changed, and under any alteration in our course of proceedings, is more than can be assumed. The similarity of the situation of the great proportion of the people of this continent now subject to our rule, will assuredly make them more accessible to common motives of action, which is the foundation of all union; and the absence of that necessity for conciliation, which changes have effected, will make us more likely to forget its importance. Our power has hitherto owed much to a contrast with misrule and oppression; but this strength we are daily losing:—we have also been indebted to an indefinite impression of our resources, originating in ignorance of their real extent; knowledge will bring this feeling to a reduced standard. We are supported by the good opinion of the lower and middling classes, to whom our government is indulgent; but it has received the rudest shocks from an impression that our system of rule is at variance with the permanent continuance of rank, authority, and distinction in any Native of India. This belief, which is not without foundation, is general to every class, and its action leaves but an anxious and feverish existence to all who enjoy station and high name: the feeling which their condition excites exposes those who have left to them any portion of power and independence, to the arts of the discontented, the turbulent, and the ambitious: this is a danger to our power, which must increase in the ratio of its extent, unless we can counteract its operation by a commensurate improvement of our administration.

Our greatest strength, perhaps, and that which gives the fairest hopes of the duration of our rule over India, arises out of the singular construction of the frame of both the controlling and the executive Government. Patronage in all the branches of the local government of India is exercised under much limitation and check; favour effects less in this country, and competency more, than in any other scene of equal magnitude. There is an interminable field for individual exertion; and though men high in station are almost absolute, (and the character of our rule requires they should be so,) there is, in that jealousy of such power which belongs to our native country, a very efficient shield against its abuse. This keeps men from being intoxicated with their short-lived authority, and the fundamental principles which discourage colonization prevent public servants taking root in the soil, and make them proceed to the duties of government, as they would in other countries to the routine of an office, which employs their talents without agitating their personal feelings and interests, in any degree that can disturb or bias their judgment. This absence of baneful passions, and of all the arts of intrigue and ambition which destroy empires, produces a calmness of mind that can belong alone to the rulers of a country situated as the English employed in India now are, and gives them an advantage, which almost balances the bad effects of their want of those national ties that usually constitute the strength of governments.

Our success and moderation, contrasted with the misrule and violence to which a great part of the population of India have for more than a century been exposed, have at this moment raised the reputation of the British Nation so high, that men have forgotten, in the contemplation of the security and prosperity they enjoy under strangers, their feelings of patriotism; but these are feelings which that very knowledge that it is our duty to impart must gradually revive and bring into action. The people of India must, by a recurring sense of benefits, have amends made them for the degradation of continuing subject to foreign masters; and this can alone be done by the combined efforts of every individual employed in a station of trust and responsibility, to render popular a government which, though not national, has its foundations laid deep on the principles of toleration, justice, and wisdom. Every agent of government should study and understand the above facts. He should not content himself with having acquired a knowledge of the languages, and of the customs, of those with whom he has intercourse. All his particular acts (even to the manner of them) should be regulated by recurrence to the foundation of our rule, and a careful observation of those principles by which it has been established and can alone be maintained. Of the importance of this I cannot better state my opinion, than by expressing my full conviction, that, independent of the prescribed duties which every qualified officer performs, there is no person in a situation of any consequence who does not, both in the substance and manner of his conduct, do something every day in his life, which, as it operates upon the general interests of the empire through the feelings of the circle he controls or rules, has an unseen effect in strengthening or weakening the government by which he is employed. My belief that what I have assumed is correct, will be my excuse for going into some minuteness in my general instructions to those under my orders.

Manner towards the Natives.

The first and one of the most important points, is the manner of European superiors towards the Natives. It would be quite out of place, in this paper, to speak of the necessity of kindness, and of an absence of all violence; this must be a matter of course with those to whom it is addressed: there is much more required from them than that conciliation which is a duty, but which, when it appears as such, loses half its effect. It must, to make an impression, be a habit of the mind, grounded on a favourable consideration of the qualities and merits of those to whom it extends; and this impression, I am satisfied, every person will have, who, after attaining a thorough knowledge of the real character of those with whom he has intercourse, shall judge them, without prejudice or self-conceit, by a standard which is suited to their belief, their usages, their habits, their occupations, their rank in life, the ideas they have imbibed from infancy, and the stage of civilization to which the community as a whole are advanced. If he does so, with that knowledge and that temper of mind which are essential to render him competent to form an opinion, he will find enough of virtue, enough of docility, and disposition to improvement, enough of regard and observance of all the best and most sacred ties of society, to create an esteem for individuals, and an interest in the community; which, when grounded on a sincere conviction of its being deserved, will render his kindness natural and conciliating. All human beings, down to the lowest links of the chain, inclusive of children, are quick in tracing the source of the manners of others, and, above all, of their superiors :—when that is regulated by the head, not the heart; when it proceeds from reason, not from feeling, it cannot please; for it has in it, if at all artificial, a show of design which repels, as it generates suspicion. When this manner takes another shape, when kindness and consideration appear as acts of condescension, it must be felt as offensive. Men may dread, but can never love or regard, those who are continually humiliating them by the parade of superiority.

I have recommended those foundations of manner, towards the Natives of India, upon which I feel my own to be grounded. I can recollect (and I do it with shame) the period when I thought I was very superior to those with whom my duty made me associate; but as my knowledge of them, and of myself, improved, the distance between us gradually lessened. I have seen and heard much of our boasted advantages over them, but cannot think that, if all the ranks of the different communities of Europe and India are comparatively viewed, there is just ground for any very arrogant feeling on the part of the inhabitants of the former: nor can I join in that common-place opinion which condemns in a sweeping way the Natives of this country as men, taking the best of them, not only unworthy of trust, and devoid of principle, but of too limited intelligence and reach of thought, to allow of Europeans, with large and liberal minds and education, having rational or satisfactory intercourse with them. Such impressions, if admitted, must prove vital as to the manner of treating the Natives of India : I shall therefore say a few words upon the justice of the grounds upon which they rest. The man who considers them in this light can grant little or no credit to the high characters and the eulogies which are given to individuals and great bodies of men in their own histories, traditions, and records. He must then judge them by his own observations and knowledge, and his opinion will in all probability be formed not comparatively with Europeans of their own class of life, but with the public servants of government: a class of men who are carefully educated, whose ambition is stimulated by the highest prospects of preferment, and whose integrity is preserved by adequate salaries through every grade of their service. Before this last principle was introduced, (which is little more than thirty years,) the European servants of government were in the habit of making money in modes not unsimilar to those we now reproach the Natives in our employ with doing; and it may here be asked, if the same endeavours have been made to alter the habits of the latter as the former. I believe the exact contrary to be the fact, and that the system since introduced has not operated more to elevate the European, than to sink and depress the Native character; but this is not the place for the discussion of this large question.

Many of the moral defects of the Natives of India are to be referred to that misrule and oppression from which they are now in a great degree emancipated. I do not know the example of any great population, in similar circumstances, preserving, through such a period of changes and tyrannical rule, so much of virtue and so many good qualities as are to be found in a great proportion of the inhabitants of this country. This is to be accounted for, in some degree, by the institutions of the Hindu, particularly that of Caste, which appears to have raised them to their present rank in human society, at a very remote period; but it has certainly tended to keep them stationary at that point of civil order to which they were thus early advanced. With a just admiration of the effects of many of their institutions, particularly those parts of them which cause in vast classes not merely an absence of the common vices of theft, drunkenness, and violence, but preserve all the virtuous ties of family and kindred relations, we must all deplore some of their usages and weak superstitions: but what individuals or what races of men are without great and manifold errors and imperfections, and what mind that is not fortified with ignorance or pride can, on such grounds, come to a severe judgment against a people like that of India.

I must here however remark, that I have invariably found, unless in a few cases where knowledge had not overcome self-sufficiency and arrogance, that in proportion as European officers, civil and military, advanced in their acquaintance with the language and customs of the Natives of India, they became more sincerely kind to them; and, on the contrary, ignorance always accompanied that selfish pride and want of consideration which held them light, or treated them with harshness.

I am quite satisfied in my own mind that if there is one cause more than another, that will impede our progress to the general improvement of India, it is a belief formed by its population, from the manner of their English superiors, that they are viewed by them as an inferior and degraded race: but, on the contrary, if the persons employed in every branch of the administration of this great country, while their conduct marks those rigid principles of virtue and justice, under the check of which they act, comport themselves towards the people whom it is their duty to make happy with that sincere humility of heart which always belongs to real knowledge, and which attaches while it elevates, they will contribute by such manner, more than any measures of boasted wisdom ever can, to the strength and duration of their government.

It is of importance, before I conclude this part of the subject, to state my opinion, that in our manner to the Natives, though it is our duty to understand and to pay every proper deference to their customs and usages, and to conform to these as far as we can with propriety, particularly on points where the religious prejudices or the rank of those with whom we have intercourse require it, yet we should always preserve the European; for to adopt their manners is a departure from the very principle on which every impression of our superiority that rests upon good foundation is grounded. We should take a lesson on such points from what we see occur to Native Princes and others, who ape English habits and modes: they lose ground with one class—that to which they belong, without gaining with the other—that to which they wish to approximate. The fact is, they ultimately lose with the latter, for even their attachment is useless, when they cease to have influence with their own tribe. The European officer who assumes Native manners and usages may please a few individuals, who are flattered or profited by his departure from the habits of his country; but even with these, familiarity will not be found to increase respect, and the adoption of such a course will be sure to sink him in the estimation of the mass of the community, both European and Native, among whom he resides.

Intercourse.

The intercourse to be maintained with the Natives within your circle is of two kinds,—Private and Official.

Private Intercourse.

The first should extend as much as possible to all ranks and classes, and be as familiar, as kind, and as frequent, as the difference of habits and pursuits will admit.

There is a veil between the Natives of India and their European superiors, which leaves the latter ignorant, in an extraordinary degree, of the real character of the former. He can only judge his own domestics by what he sees of their conduct in his presence; of the manner in which they perform their other duties in life, he is, if not ignorant, but imperfectly informed: so many minute obstacles, grounded upon caste, usages, and religion, oppose an approach to closer acquaintance, that it can never be generally attained; but in private intercourse much may be learnt that will facilitate the performance of public duty, and give that knowledge of the usages and feelings of the various classes of the Natives, which will enable its possessors to touch every chord with effect. In joining with them in field sports, in an unceremonious interchange of visits with the most respectable, and in seeking the society of the most learned, the European public officer will not only gain much information, but impart complete confidence, and lay the grounds of that personal attachment which will ever be found of the greatest aid to his public labours. He will also obtain by such habits of private intercourse the means of elevating those he esteems by marks of notice and regard; but in pursuing this course he must beware, lest he lose his object by falling into the weaknesses or indulgences of the persons with whom he thus associates. It is in the performance of this part of his duty, when all the pride of station is laid aside, that he must most carefully guard that real superiority, which he derives from better knowledge and truer principles of morality and religion; for it is from the impression made by the possession, without the ostentation, of those higher qualities, that he must expect the benefits I have described as likely to result from a familiar and private intercourse with the Natives under his direction and control.

Official Intercourse.

In all official intercourse with the Natives, one of the first points of importance is, that these, whatever be their rank, class, or business, should have complete and easy access to personal communication with their European superior. The necessity of this arises out of the character of our rule, and of those over whom it is established. It is sufficiently galling for the people of India to have foreign masters; the impression this feeling must continually excite can only be mitigated or removed by a recurring sense of the advantages they derive from the wisdom and

Importance of direct communication in Intercourse.

justice of their European superiors, and this can alone be effected by direct communication with them. Though Native servants must be employed and trusted, and though it is quite essential to behave to all with kindness, and to raise the higher classes of them by a treatment which combines consideration and respect, yet they can never without hazard be used as exclusive mediums of communication: their real or supposed influence will, under whatever circumstances they are allowed frequent approach to an European officer in the exercise of authority, give them opportunities of abusing his confidence if they desire it; and as our servants, who are seldom selected from the higher classes, cannot be supposed to have even the same motives with those of Native rulers for good conduct, much less the same title to regard, men under our power will have, in aggravation of the feeling arising out of subjection to foreign rule, that of being to a certain extent at the mercy of persons of their own nation whom they neither trust nor respect. There is no remedy for such an evil except being completely easy of access; but this, however much the superior may desire it, is not to be established without difficulty and perseverance. It affects the interest and consequence of every man in his employ from the highest to the lowest; but in proportion to their efforts to counteract it, so must his be to carry this important point on which, more than all others, the integrity of his personal administration and the good of the country depend. No Native servant, high or low, must be allowed the privilege of either introducing or stopping an applicant or a complainant; all such must come with confidence to the European superior, or to such assistant as he may specifically direct to receive or hear them. It requires much temper and patience, constant activity, and no slight sacrifice of personal comfort, to maintain an intercourse with the Natives upon this footing; but unless it be done, (I speak here from the fullest experience,) the government of control now established in Central India cannot be carried on for any period, and the changes which must ensue from relaxation in this particular will be brought about in the manner most unfavourable to our character and reputation.

In establishing this direct personal intercourse, it is perhaps better, when the habits are so formed as to admit of it, that Natives of all classes and ranks should have admission and be heard at whatever hour of the day they come, except those of meals; but where such constant intrusion is found to interrupt other business, as it may be with many, certain portions of every day must be set aside to hear representations and complaints, and to see those who desire to be seen. The establishment of direct intercourse is, in my opinion, a primary and indispensable duty, and one no more dependent upon the inclination or judgment of the individuals to whom the charge of managing or controlling these countries is intrusted, than it is to an officer whether he shall attend his parade, or to a judge whether he shall sit a certain number of hours in his court: indeed, I consider that late events have so completely altered our condition in India, that the duties of almost every officer in the political department have become in a great degree magisterial, and, as such, must be more defined, and subject to more exact rules, than they formerly were.

Our right of interference (as will be shewn hereafter) is so limited, that it is not in one case in a hundred, of those that are brought forward, that an officer can do more than state calmly and clearly, to the party who seeks redress, the reasons and principles which prevent him from attending to his representation or complaint. He will have to repeat this perhaps fifty times in one day; but he must, in contemplating the good that will be ultimately produced, be content to take this trouble. The Natives of India cannot persuade themselves that, possessing, as we do, the means of establishing our direct rule, we shall long refrain from doing so. This impression weakens those Princes, Chiefs, and Ministers, whom it is our policy to support, in a degree that almost unfits them for being instruments of government. We can only counteract its bad effects by making ourselves understood by all, even to the lowest, upon this point; it is one on which they will never trust to a communication from any Native agent or servant, nor indeed will they be convinced of our sincerity till they observe for years that our words and actions are in unison; and they must, to satisfy them that there is no prospect of those fluctuations to which they have been so habituated, see that every thing originates with, and is known to, the superior: this knowledge, added to the right of approaching him at all moments, will gradually tranquillize their minds, and place them, as far as they can be placed, beyond the power of being made the dupes of artful or interested men.

It has been before said, that Native servants of all classes should be treated with that attention and respect to which they were from their station and character entitled. These will, of course, have at all times the freest intercourse with the superior, but they should never have the privilege of coming to any conference between him and other Natives to which they were not specifically called. But these servants (whatever might be their inclinations) will have little power of doing harm, when a direct intercourse (such as has been described) is well established, and its principles and objects generally understood. Indeed, one of the best effects of that intercourse is the check it constitutes on all nefarious proceedings of subordinate agents, and persons of every description; as such must act in hourly dread of discovery, when every man can tell his own story to the principal at any moment he pleases.

Importance of Publicity in Intercourse.

The next important point, to be observed in official intercourse with the Natives, is "Publicity." There can be no occasion to expatiate, here, upon the utility of this principle. It is the happy privilege of a state so constituted as that of the English in India, to gain strength in the ratio that its measures, and the grounds on which they are adopted, are made public; and this is above all essential in a quarter of India where we are as yet but imperfectly understood. There are and can be no secrets in our ordinary proceedings, and every agent will find his means of doing good advanced, his toil lessened, and the power of the designing and corrupt to misrepresent his actions or intentions decreased, in the proportion that he transacts affairs in public. He should avoid, as much as he possibly can, private conferences with those in his employ or others. These will be eagerly sought for; they give the individual thus admitted the appearance of favour and influence; and there is no science in which the more artful among the Natives are greater adepts, than that of turning to account the real or supposed confidence of their superiors. I know no mode of preventing the mischief which this impression, if it becomes general, gives men the power of effecting, but habitual publicity in transacting business. This will, no doubt, be found to have inconveniencies, which will be purposely increased by those who have their game to play, and indeed others; for Natives of rank and station, even when they have no corrupt views, are from habit and self-importance attached to a secret and mysterious way of conducting both great and small affairs.

A public officer placed in your situation must always be vigilant and watchful of events likely to affect the peace of the country under his charge; but no part of his duty requires such care and wisdom in its performance. He cannot rest in blind confidence, nor refuse attention to obvious and well-authenticated facts; but he must be slow in giving his ear, or in admitting to private and confidential intercourse, secret agents and informers, lest these make an impression (which will be their object) upon his mind; for there is no failing of human nature to which the worst part of the Natives of India have learnt (from the shape of their own government) so well to address themselves, as any disposition to suspicion in their superiors. From the condition of Central India, abounding as it must with discontented and desperate characters, intrigues, treasonable conversations, and papers, and immature plots, must for some time be matters of frequent occurrence and growth; but such will, in general, be best left to perish of neglect. Established as our power now is, men cannot collect any means capable of shaking it without being discovered; and it is, I am convinced, under all ordinary circumstances, wiser and safer to incur petty hazard, than to place individuals and communities at the mercy of artful and avaricious agents and spies, or to goad unfortunate men to a state of hostility by continually viewing them with an eye of torturing and degrading suspicion.

In the intercourse with the Natives of your circle, it is hardly necessary to advert to the subject of giving and receiving presents. The recent orders upon this subject, which have been communicated to you, are very defined and strict; but there is a necessity in this government of control for every agent to maintain on a high ground, not only the purity, but the disinterestedness of the English character, and you will avoid, as much as you possibly can, incurring any obligation to local authorities. These will sedulously endeavour to promote your convenience and comfort, and will press favours upon you both from design and good feelings; but there is a strength in preserving complete independence on all such points that must not be abandoned. Our political superiority, to be efficient, must be unmixed with any motives or concerns, either connected with our personal interest or that of others, that can soil or weaken that impression on which its successful exercise depends.

Forms of Intercourse.

The forms of the official intercourse between European agents and Natives of rank were, before we obtained paramount power, a matter of mere moment, and one on which we could less relax than at present, because our motives were at that period more liable to be mistaken. Though it is essential in our intercourse with nations who are attached to, and give value to, ceremonies, to understand such perfectly, and to claim from all what is due to our station, that we may not sink the rank of the European superior in the estimation of those subject to his control; it is now the duty of the former to be much more attentive to the respect which he gives than what he receives, particularly in his intercourse with men of high rank. The Princes and Chiefs of India may, in different degrees, be said to be all dependent on the British government: many have little more than the name of that power they before enjoyed; but they seem, as they lose the substance, to cling to the forms of station. The pride of reason may smile at such a feeling; but it exists, and it would be alike opposite to the principles of humanity and policy to deny it gratification.

In official intercourse with the lower classes, the latter should be treated according to the usages of the country, as practised by the most indulgent of their Native superiors. It will be found that they require personal notice and consideration in proportion as their state is removed from that knowledge which belongs to civilization; and it is on this ground that the Bheel must have more attention paid him than the Ryot. It is more difficult to give confidence to his mind, and to make him believe in the sincerity and permanence of the kindness with which he is treated, because he is in a condition more remote from the party with whom he communicates, and, before he can be reclaimed, he must be approximated.

Interference.

The interference of agents employed in this country with Native Princes or Courts, or their local officers, cannot be exactly defined, for there will be shades of distinction in every case, that will require attention; but all must be subject, and that in the strictest degree, to certain general and well-understood principles, founded on the nature of our power, our objects, our political relations with the different states, the personal conduct of their rulers, their necessity for our aid and support, and their disposition to require or reject it in the conduct of their internal administration. The leading principle, and the one which must be continually referred to, is grounded on the character of our controlling power and its objects. It is the avowed, and I am satisfied it is the true, policy of the British State, while it maintains the general peace of the country, to keep, not only in the enjoyment of their high rank, but in the active exercise of their sovereign functions, the different princes and chiefs who are virtually or declaredly dependent on its protection. The principal object (setting aside the obligations of faith) is to keep at a distance that crisis to which in spite of our efforts we are gradually approaching—of having the whole of India subject to our direct rule. There is no intention of discussing here the consequences likely to result from such an event. It is sufficient for executive and subordinate officers to know, that it is the desire of the government they serve to keep it at a distance, to render it their duty to contribute their whole efforts to promote the accomplishment of that object; and on the manner and substance of their interference the local success of this policy will greatly depend.

On all points where we are pledged by treaty to support states, or to mediate or interfere between them and others, we must of course act agreeably to the obligations contracted; and in such case no instructions can be required. It may not, however, be unuseful to remark, that, on all occasions where they are referred to, treaties and engagements should be interpreted with much consideration to the prince or chief with whom they are made. There is often, from opposite education and habits, much difference between their construction and ours of such engagements; but no loose observation, or even casual departure from the letter of them, ought to lead to serious consequences, when it appeared there was no intention of violating the spirit of the deed, or of acting contrary to pledged faith. When any article of an engagement is doubtful, I think it should be invariably explained with more leaning to the expectations originally raised in the weaker than to the interests of the stronger power. It belongs to superior authority to give ultimate judgment upon all points of this nature which come under discussion, but that judgment must always be much influenced by the colour of the information and opinion of the local agent. My desire is to convey how important every subject is that connects in the remotest degree with that reputation for good faith, which can only be considered our strength, while it exists unimpaired in the minds of the Natives: and in this view the most scrupulous attention should be paid to their understanding of every article of the agreements we make with them, for no local advantage, nor the promotion of any pecuniary interest, can compensate for the slightest injury to this corner-stone of our power in India.

With the government of Dowlet Row Sindia (a great part of whose possessions are intermixed with those of our dependent allies in this quarter) we have only general relations of amity; and however virtually dependent events may have rendered that prince, we can (except insisting upon the exact performance of those settlements which we have mediated between him or his delegated officers and some of his tributaries) claim no right of interference in any part of his internal administration; nor should there, unless in cases of unexpected emergency which threatened the general peace of the country, be any disposition shewn to interference, except on specific requisition from the resident at Gualior. Without interfering, however, we have hitherto, and shall continue to exercise a very salutary control both over Dowlet Row Sindia and his local officers by the terms on which we communicate and act with the latter. When these are men of good character, and study the happiness of the inhabitants, and the improvement of the country, we can, by the cordiality and consideration with which we treat them, and the ready attention we give to the settlement of every petty dispute they have with the subjects of our allies, as well as other friendly acts, grant them a countenance and aid which greatly facilitate their success in their local administration. The same principle leads to abstinence from all communication, and to our keeping aloof (except where the general peace is at hazard) from all intercourse with those of Sindia's managers who are noted for misrule or bad faith. This line of conduct towards the latter, grounded as it publicly should be on the avowed principle of keeping our character free of

Interference with Sindia's Government.

soil from their proceedings, locally increases our reputation; while it has the effect of rendering the employment of such men inconvenient and unprofitable to the state, and thus constitutes one of the chief means we have of working a reform in its internal administration: nor is it a slight one, for the impression of our power is so great, that the belief of a local officer possessing our good opinion and friendship is of itself sufficient to repress opposition to his authority, while his forfeiting our favour is sure to raise him enemies, both in his district and at Gualior.

With the courts of Holkar, Dhar, Dewass, and almost all the petty Rajpoot states West of the Chumbul, our relations are different. These have been raised from a weak and fallen condition to one of efficiency, through our efforts. But, though compelled at first to aid them in almost every settlement, we have, as they attained the power of acting for themselves, gradually withdrawn from minute interference on points connected with their internal administration, limiting ourselves to what is necessary for the maintenance of the public tranquillity.

There is so strong a feeling in the minds of princes and chiefs above alluded to, and in those of all their officers, (from their prime minister down to the lowest agent,) of their actual dependence upon the British government, that it is almost impossible to make them understand that they are, in the conduct of their internal administration, desired and expected to act independently of it. Their difficulty of comprehending and trusting the policy which dictates our conduct in this particular, arises out of its being opposite to all their habits and knowledge. Time alone, and the most minute care of every European agent employed, can impart to them that confidence which is essential to their becoming competent functionaries of rule. To effect this object, the principles hitherto inculcated and acted upon must be steadily pursued, and we must decline all interference, except in cases where Grassiahs, Bheels, or other plunderers are concerned. These, from their situation or strength, can only be kept in order by the power of the British government; and we must in such cases even have the limits of our interference exactly defined, that no belief may exist of our possessing the power of departing from the restrictions we have imposed upon ourselves; for on such impressions being general, and being confirmed by scrupulous consistency of action, depends our success in giving that efficiency to the various Native authorities subject to our control which is necessary to enable them to perform the different duties allotted to them.

In cases of interference with lesser rulers, such as the reformed Rajpoot plunderers and Bheel chiefs, we may be compelled to enter more minutely into their affairs; but the principles observed should be the same; and while we take care to repress every disposition to a return to predatory habits, and see that men who have long cherished such possess themselves of honest means of livelihood, we must respect their prejudices, and not hastily break in upon the rude frame of their internal rule; but leave (down to the Turwee or head of the Bheel Parah or cluster of hamlets) the full exercise of his authority over those under him, according as that is grounded on the ancient prejudices and usages of the tribe to which he and his family or followers belong.

The feelings of irritation and hatred with which

almost all the Princes and Chiefs of this quarter regard the Grassiahs and Bheels, and the total want of confidence of the latter in their nominal superiors, have and will continue to render calls for our interference very frequent; but however high the character and condition of the one party, and however bad and low that of the other may be, we must never grant our name or support to measures of coercion or violence, without fully understanding the merits of the case, nor without having had direct communication with the party or parties inculpated; otherwise we may be involved in embarrassment, and become unconsciously the instruments of injustice and oppression.

Many questions will occur deeply connected with our reputation for good faith which cannot be decided by any exact rules; but, whenever that is concerned, the tone of our feeling should be very high. It is the point upon which the moral part of our government of this great empire hinges; and in these countries where our rule and control are new, and in which the inhabitants cannot yet understand any explanations that do not rest upon broad and obvious grounds, the subject requires much attention. There are many cases in which our faith, though not specifically, is virtually pledged to individuals: Ministers, for instance, of minor or incompetent Princes or Chiefs, who have been brought forward or recognised by us in the exercise of authority, have a claim upon our support and consideration, which nothing but bad conduct on their part can forfeit. We should, no doubt, be most careful in any interference that leads to such obligations. They are only to be incurred when a necessity that involves the peace and prosperity of the country calls for them; but they must be sacredly observed; for, with a people who look in all questions of government more to persons than systems, the abandonment, except from gross misconduct, of any individual who had been raised or openly protected by us, would excite stronger feelings than the breach of an article of a treaty, and locally prove more injurious, as it weakens that reliance upon our faith which is the very foundation of our strength.

We may rest satisfied, while we pursue the course I have stated, (and it is the one to which our faith is almost in every case, either directly or by implication, pledged) that we have from our paramount power a very efficient check over states and tribes, whose rulers, officers, and chiefs, will soon discover that they can only gain our favour and support by good conduct, or forfeit it by bad. With such knowledge, and with means comparatively limited, we cannot expect they will be disposed to incur displeasure, when the terms on which they can gain approbation are so easy; at least no men possessed of common sense and discernment (qualities in which the Natives of India are seldom deficient) can be expected to act in such a manner;—but we must not conceal from ourselves, that their conduct in this, as in all other particulars, will rest chiefly on the value of that condition in which they are placed or rather left; and in proportion as we render it one of comfort and dignity, so will their care be to preserve our good opinion and to merit our confidence. It is, indeed, upon our success in supporting their respectability, that the permanence of a system of control over great and small Native states, such as we have established in this quarter of India, will depend. We have no choice of means in the performance of this delicate and arduous part of our duty. Though the check must be efficient, it should be almost unseen: the effect ought to be produced more by the impression than the exercise of superior power. Our principal object must be to elevate the authorities to whom we have left the administration of their respective territories: we must, in all cases of interference, bring them forward to their own subjects as the prominent objects of respect and obedience; so far from the agent attracting any to himself, he should purposely repel it, that it may be given to the quarter where it is wanted, and to which it belongs. When we aid any Prince or Chief against his own subjects, his name should be exclusively used; and we should be most careful in making our Native agents and servants pay the full measure of respect to every branch of his administration, and continually be on the watch to check that disposition which is inherent in them, to slight local authorities, that they may in the name of their master draw that attention to themselves, which it is quite essential should belong to the officers of the Native government. It is evident that our control can only be supportable, to any human being who has the name and appearance of power, so long as it is exercised in a general manner and regulated by the principles above stated. When it descends to minute checks and interference in the collection of revenue, the administration of justice listens to the complaints of discontented, or even aggrieved individuals, and allows upon system its own Native agents to interfere and act in the name of the paramount state,—the continuance of independent power, in any shape, to either Prince or Chief, is not only impolitic but dangerous, as his condition must be felt by himself, and by all attached to his person or family, as a mockery and degradation; and the least effect of such feelings will be the extermination of all motive to good or great actions. For when control is divested of its large and liberal character, and takes a more minute shape, whatever merit belongs to the administration becomes the due of the person by whom it is exercised, or his agents, and the nominal Prince and his officers are degraded into suspected and incompetent instruments of rule.

In this general outline of our interference with the rulers, great and small, of this part of India, I have dwelt much upon the political considerations upon which it is grounded; because I am convinced that there is no part of the subject that requires to be so deeply studied, and so fully understood, as this should be by every subordinate agent; for there is no point of his duty which is at once so delicate and arduous, or in which success or failure so much depends upon individual exertion. He will be prompted to deviate from the course prescribed, by the action of his best feelings, and by hopes of increasing his personal reputation; but he will be kept steady in that course by a knowledge of the importance of those general principles on which the present system rests. It is in the performance of this part of his duty that all which has been said regarding manner and intercourse must be in his memory; for men in the situation in which those are, with whom he must, in all cases of interference, come in contact, are not to be conciliated to their condition, nor kept in that temper towards the paramount authority which is necessary for its interest they should be, by mere correctness or strict attention to justice. The Native state must be courted and encouraged to good conduct, and the earnest endeavour of the British agent must be to give their rulers a pride in their administration, to effect which object he must win to his side not only the rulers themselves, but the principal and most respectable men of the country. In his efforts to gain the latter, however, he must beware of depriving the local authority of that public opinion which is so essential both as a check to misrule and a reward to good government; but which would cease to be felt as either, the moment the ties between Prince and subject were seriously injured or broken.

Where the public peace, of which we are avowed protectors, has been violated, or where murders or robberies have been committed, we have a right to urge the local authorities (whom we aid both with means for the prevention and punishment of such crimes) to pursue, according to their own usages, the course best calculated to preserve the safety of persons and of property. In other cases connected with the administration of justice, though there is no right of interference, it will be for their interest, and for our reputation, to lose no opportunity of impressing generally the benefit and good name that will result from attention to ancient institutions, particularly to that of the popular courts of Punjayet, which have never been discontinued but in periods marked by anarchy and oppression.

The practice of Suttee is not frequent in Malwa, and that of infanticide is, I believe, less so. The first is a usage, which, however shocking to humanity, has defenders among every class of the Hindu community. The latter is held in abhorrence by all but the Rajpoot families, by whom it is practised, and to whom it is confined; for many of the most respectable chiefs of that tribe speak of this crime with all the horror it merits. You cannot interfere in the prevention of either of these sacrifices, beyond the exercise of that influence which you possess from personal character; indeed to attempt more would be at the hazard of making wrong impressions, and of defeating the end you desired to attain. Praise of those who abstain from such acts, and neglect of those who approve or perpetrate them, is the best remedy that can be applied. It is the course I have pursued, and has certainly been attended with success.

That the line of interference which has been described is difficult, will not be denied; but what course can we discover for the future rule and control of the different Native states in India, which does not present a choice of difficulties? Men are too apt, at the first view of this great subject, to be deluded by a desire to render easy, and to simplify, what is of necessity difficult and complicated. Moral considerations come in aid of the warmest and best sentiments of the human mind to entice us to innovation: we feel ourselves almost the sharers of that crime and misrule which we think our interference could mitigate or amend; and in the fervour of our virtue we are too apt to forget, that temporary or partial benefit often entails lasting and general evil,—that every plan, however theoretically good, must be practically bad, that is imperfectly executed. We forget, in the pride of our superior knowledge, the condition of others; and self-gratification makes almost every man desire to crowd into the few years of his official career, the work of half a century. Thus measures have been, and continue to be brought forward, in advance of the community for whose benefit they are intended. Of what has passed it is not necessary to speak; the future is in our power, and I cannot conclude this part of the subject, which relates to an interference that is calculated, according as it is managed, to hasten or retard the introduction of our direct rule, without impressing upon every officer employed under my orders the importance of a conduct calculated to preserve, while it improves, the established governments and native authorities of the country. To these it is his duty to give such impulse as he can without injuring their frame, towards an amendment suited to their situation, to the character of the rulers, and to that of the various classes under their rule. I consider, and the opinion is the result of both experience and reflection, that all dangers to our power in India are slight in comparison with that which is likely to ensue from our too zealous efforts to change the condition of its inhabitants, with whom we are yet, in my opinion, but very imperfectly acquainted. A person who entertains such sentiments as I do upon this question, must appear the advocate of very slow reform; but, if I am so, it is from a full conviction that any thing like precipitation in our endeavours at improvement is likely to terminate in casting back those we desire to advance;—on the contrary, if, instead of over-marching, we are content to go along with this immense population, and to be in good temper with their prejudices, their religion, and usages, we may gradually win them to better ways of thinking and of acting. The latter process, no doubt, must be one of great time; but its success will be retarded by every hasty step.

Employment of Servants. There are few points on which more care is required than the selection and employment of Native servants for the public service. The higher classes of these, such as Moonshees, Mootsuddies, and Writers, should be men of regular habits of life, intelligent, and of good characters in their own tribes. There is no objection to an officer continuing to keep in service a person he has brought from a distant province, who has been long with him, and on whose fidelity and competence he can repose; but, generally speaking, it is much better to entertain respectable Natives or old residents of the country in which he is employed; such may have looser habits and be less attached, but the former his vigilance will check and correct, and attachment will soon be created by kindness and consideration. Their advantages over foreigners are very numerous. The principal are, their acquaintance with the petty interests of the country, and their knowledge of all the prejudices and the jealousies of the different classes of the community to which they belong. On all these points the superior should be minutely informed, and, if he employs men not personally acquainted with the disposition and condition of those under his charge or control, his information on such subjects must come through multiplied mediums, which is in itself a serious evil. But, independent of this, the employment of the Natives of a distant province is always unpopular, and they are generally viewed with dislike and suspicion by the higher and more respectable classes of the country into which they are introduced. This excites a feeling in the minds of the former, which either makes them keep aloof from all connexion with the inhabitants, or seek the society, and use as instruments, men who are discontented or of indifferent character. It is difficult to say which of these causes has the worst effect. The one gives an impression of pride, if not contempt, and the other of design and an inclination to intrigue; and both operate unfavourably to the local reputation of the master.

I have observed, that the Natives who are least informed of the principles of our rule, are ready to grant a respect and confidence to an English officer, which they refuse to persons of their own tribe; but they are apt to form an unfavourable opinion of his disposition and character from any bad conduct of his Native servants, if foreigners; on the contrary, when the latter are members of their own community, the exposure of their errors or crimes, while it brings shame and conveys a salutary lesson to the class to which they belong, is attended with the effect of raising, instead of depressing, the European superior in their estimation. To all these general reasons might be added many, grounded on the particular condition of Central India. The oppression the inhabitants of this quarter have recently suffered, both from Hindu and Mahomedan natives of the Deckan and Hindustan, makes them naturally alarmed at these classes. There is, also, in the impoverished state of many of the best families of the country, a strong additional reason for our giving them, in preference to strangers, what little we can of salary as public servants.

In the above observations there is no desire to exclude any member of Deckan or Hindustan families, who have settled for life, or for several generations, in Malwa; such objection would proscribe from our employ some of the most intelligent and respectable inhabitants of that province.

It has been before mentioned, that publicity in our transaction of business is most essential, chiefly as it puts at repose an alarmed and agitated population, and, beyond all, their Princes and Chiefs. We may greatly promote this object by the selection of servants. I early observed a very serious uneasiness, if not alarm, in Holkar's ministers, regarding the course I meant to pursue towards that court; and as one means of removing it, I chose as a principal Native writer an intelligent Brahmin, whose family was attached to that of Holkar, in whose employ I found him, and who could, I knew, from his connexions, have no permanent interests separate from his duty to that State. I was conscious of having nothing to conceal, but I knew the importance of Tantia Jogh and others being satisfied that this was the case. No measure I have adopted has tended more to tranquillize their minds; and I state the fact because its application may be suited to cases of daily occurrence.

In the employment of the higher classes of Native servants, they should, as much as possible, be restricted to their specific duties, and no one should be allowed to take a lead, or mix (unless when directed) in the occupation of another. The keeping of these persons in their exact places will be found difficult, from the habits of the Natives being opposite to such rules; but it is essential; for errors, if not guilt, will be the certain consequence of a confusion of duties, which destroys that pride which good men feel from possessing confidence, and enables bad to evade that personal responsibility which constitutes the chief check upon their conduct.

The employment of the lower classes of public servants requires much attention. These should be selected on the same principles that have already been stated, with reference to the duties they are to perform, which ought always to be exactly defined;

and their conduct vigilantly watched. It will indeed be found useful to render as public as possible the nature of their employment, and to call upon all local authorities to aid us in the prevention of those unauthorized and odious acts of injustice and oppression towards the inhabitants of the country which this class will, in spite of all our efforts, find opportunities of committing. I speak from the fullest experience when I state, that, though the Natives of India may do full justice to the purity of our intentions and the excellence of the principles of our rule, they are undisguised in their sentiments regarding those parts of our administration in which the very dregs of their own community are employed. They cannot, indeed, but see with feelings of detestation and resentment a man raised from the lowest of their own ranks, and decorated with the official badge or stick of a civil or political English officer, become the very next moment insolent to persons to whom he and his family have been for ages submissive, or turn the extortioner of money from those tribes among which he has before lived as an humble individual.

The power of this class of servants to injure our reputation is every where great, but more so in the proportion that the Natives of the country are ignorant of our real character, and where their dread of our power is excessive. Of the mischief they have done, or rather tried to do, in Malwa, I can speak from a perfect knowledge. I have endeavoured with unremitting solicitude to counteract their impositions and oppressions, by publishing proclamations and giving high rewards to all who informed against or seized any of my servants when attempting the slightest interference in the country, or affecting to have any business beyond that of carrying a letter, or some specified or limited duty; but I have, nevertheless, been compelled within three years to punish publicly, and discharge, one Moonshee, two Mootsuddies or writers, three Jemadars, and upwards of fifty Hircarrahs; and almost an equal number of the same class belonging to other public officers have been taken and punished, or banished the country. These examples will shew the danger of being tempted, by any convenience of service, or a desire to accelerate the accomplishment of our objects, to employ such instruments with any latitude of action.

The importance of encouraging the dependent States of India to do their own work, and to lean, on points of internal administration, as little as possible upon us, has been before noticed; and as long as we manage to keep clear of that species of interference which weakens and unsettles, without any proportionate good to balance its evil effects, we shall have credit in general opinion for all the good measures which the State under our protection adopts, and our reputation will be benefited (from the comparisons that are drawn) even by its acts of folly and injustice. But the latter advantage will be lost by any half and impolitic mixture in its concerns, and there is no mode in which this will be found so injurious as that of granting it the aid of Native servants in our employ. Allowing the higher classes of these to enter into the affairs of such governments in any shape, would be destructive of every principle that has been inculcated; but the giving their rulers, ministers, or local officers, the aid of our lower servants, would be still more to the injury of our reputation; for among the higher classes we might find men of virtue and firmness of character beyond what could be expected from the others when exposed, as they would be, to much temptation. They would be used for purposes of coercion, if not oppression,. and there would be sufficient art in those who thus employed them to throw, when that was their object, the odium of what these instruments did upon the English government. But, in general, their desire would be limited to have the aid of the British name to alarm into compliance with their demands, individuals or communities. They would be aware that the Hircarrah or servant sent to assist their authority was a check upon their proceedings, and this would lead to his being bribed; and, if he did not become an instrument of violence, it would only be because he received higher wages from the party he was sent to oppress. I have seen such manifold instances of the bad effects resulting from the employment of this class in the manner described, that I have for more than three years peremptorily refused any such aid to Native chiefs, and must require all those under my orders to do the same. The best answer to all applications upon this subject is, that compliance is at variance with the system ordered to be pursued, and that the usage of granting such aid, though it might be found convenient, and in some cases accelerate the accomplishment of good measures, must in the end produce much evil, and be attended with loss of reputation to the British Government, whose good name could not be intrusted to low agents and menials acting beyond the strict and vigilant observation of the European officer.

Maintenance of the public peace.

The right we have to act, when the public peace is threatened or disturbed, has been generally noticed under the head of Interference; but it will be useful to say a few words on the mode of exercising that right, particularly as it relates to points which are connected with the internal administration of police and criminal justice.

In countries which have been long in the condition of Central India, there is a connexion, formed between the most powerful and the most apparently insignificant of the disturbers of the public peace, which will for some time require a vigilant attention to every act of the latter to prevent the revival of a disorderly or predatory spirit. In common cases we shall only have to prompt the local authority to exertions. But when our aid is required, and troops or any persons acting under our orders apprehend delinquents, they should invariably be given over to the ruler or chief in whose countries the crimes were committed, by whom they will be examined and punished according to the established custom. I have usually limited my interference in this part of the administration of the Native States of Malwa to two points. The first is, that in cases of robbery, but particularly cattle (the common booty of Bheels and other plunderers), there should be restitution to the owners the moment the property was proved, leaving those persons through whose hands it has passed by real or pretended sales, to have their disputes and recriminations settled, and to recover from each other, according to usage. This practice is now general, and its enforcement for the last two years has done more to put an end to Bheel and other robberies, than all the other measures that have been taken. The second point on which I have endeavoured to make a change in practice of the administration of Justice in the Native States of Malwa, is that of preventing the crime of wilful murder being commuted for the payment of a pecuniary fine; but in all cases of this nature where circumstances compel us to interfere, it is desirable that no execution should take place till guilt has been clearly proved. The observance of this rule is more necessary, as in cases where the criminals are of a plundering tribe, such as Bheels and Baugries, the Native ruler or chief will be disposed to deem the mere accusation enough to warrant the punishment; whereas it is exactly with such classes that it is of importance to us to be most particular, lest we lose the impression we desire to make upon them, by becoming in any way accessaries to acts of violence or injury.

On all occasions when the local power is sufficient, it is most desirable to bring it into action, that it may cease to be dependent upon us for the maintenance of the internal peace. This is particularly advisable where excesses are committed, that have either as their real or professed causes, superstitious or religious feelings. In such cases, except where the mixture of political motives is manifest and avowed, or the danger imminent, we should call upon the Native government, by its duty and allegiance to the paramount state, to put down all disturbers of the peace, particularly when fanatics, like those lately at Pertaubghur*, combine with their atrocities the avowal of sentiments hostile to our rule. The actual condition of Central India makes it likely that such efforts as that above alluded to may be repeated, and they will always (however contemptible they may seem) require to be treated with much delicacy. It should be deemed a guiding principle not to act if we can avoid it; and when absolutely compelled to do so, it is

* Vide Letter to Captain Macdonald, dated 18th June, 1821.

essential that we should appear not as principals, but in support of the local government; for the spirit that engenders such excesses, whether they proceed from intrigue or fanaticism, will only attain strength by opposition; and any violent measures on our part, however justified by crime or outrage, might make the most unfavourable impressions upon an ignorant and bigoted population, who, while they confess all the benefits of our general rule and control, are easily excited to a dread of our success ultimately leading to attempts at changing the religion and institutions of their forefathers.

In cases of rebels or plunderers collecting in such force as to require British troops to suppress them, you will (if the emergency prevents reference to superior authority) make a requisition for aid from the nearest commanding officer that can furnish it.

The rules for such requisitions have been generally notified: the political agent will give the fullest information of the service to be performed, the nature of the country, the character of the enemy and his resources, leaving the military officer, when possessed of such knowledge, the selection of the force, both as to number and equipment, that is to be placed at his disposal. But it is to be strongly impressed upon both, that in a country like Central India, the means employed should always be above the object to be accomplished, as failure or defeat in any enterprise or action would be attended with very bad consequences.

It is almost superfluous to repeat what has been sedulously inculcated upon you as a primary duty during the last three years, the adoption of every preventive measure to avert the necessity of the employment of force. Its appearance has hitherto been almost in all cases sufficient to produce the required effect; and in the few instances where it has been employed, the moment of success has been seized for that of conciliation. To act differently, and to pursue those wild tribes who are the common disturbers of the peace, with retaliation of outrages, beyond what is necessary to evince our power, is to confirm them in their habits, and to add to their other motives of hostility those of resentment and despair. When engaged in warfare with such classes, we should be cautious how we inflict summary punishment on the individuals who fall into our power. These are often the mere instruments of crime, and act in its commission under as strong an impulse of duty to their superiors, as the soldier in our ranks; and it is as unreasonable to expect their habits can be changed by making examples of such men, as it would that we could subdue the spirit of a nation by putting to death every soldier belonging to it that we found fighting against us in action. The increased danger in which this placed individuals, would only strengthen that powerful feeling by which they were attached to their leaders, while it added that of revenge against those who treated them with what they deemed cruelty and injustice. It is the duty of all agents of the British government to direct their efforts to effect a change in the frame of these savage communities, instead of commencing, in imitation of unprincipled and despotic Native rulers, an unprofitable and interminable warfare upon individuals, who can hardly be termed guilty when they act by the express order of chiefs to whom and their predecessors they and their fathers have given implicit obedience for centuries. The nature and strength of the ties which subsist in these societies were fully discovered in the trial of Nadir Singh*, the celebrated Bheelalah chief of the Vindhya range. No one has questioned the justice of his punishment; but that of the persons who committed by his order the barbarous crime for which he was exiled, would have been deemed an act of oppression.

One of the most effectual means that you have to maintain the peace, is that of exerting yourself to render all (even the poorest and wildest classes) sensible of the benefits they derive from your protection. There is no point in which this is more required than against the excesses of our troops, camp-followers, merchants who have passes, and, in short, all who on any ground use the British name. The governments of the different Presidencies have been long sensible of this evil, and have endeavoured by the strictest orders and proclamations to correct it. The pressing of begaries and hackeries has been positively forbidden; but these orders must be enforced with a rigorous and uncompromising spirit by the civil and political authorities, otherwise they will prove unavailing. This is a point of duty in which I consider those under my orders to have no option or latitude; in the present condition of Central India it is one of too much importance, both as it relates to the temper of the inhabitants, and the reviving prosperity of the country, to warrant any deviation, either for the accommodation of individuals or the public service. The former, when no longer encouraged by improper or unwise indulgence to trust in any way to the country, will soon learn to be independent of its aid; public

---

* Vide Letter to Government, dated 9th May, 1820.

departments will in like degree become, from providing for their own wants, more efficient; and when the inhabitants are satisfied that it is not in the power of any person, whatever be his rank, to press them or their cattle, they will be inspired with a confidence that will lead to their furnishing more resources to troops and travellers, from a desire of profit, than has ever yet been extorted by an oppressive system; which, according to all Natives I have heard speak upon the subject, has been carried to as great, if not greater lengths in countries subject to our rule and control, than in the worst of their own governments.

There are, I fear, many omissions in these notes of instructions, but an anxiety to render them complete has already made them far longer than was at first intended. One of my chief objects has been to impress in the most forcible manner the great benefits which are to be expected from a kind and conciliating manner, and a constant friendly intercourse with those under your direction and control. It is the feelings and knowledge which such habits on your part will inspire, that can alone give effect to the principles of action that have been prescribed for your observance. You are called upon to perform no easy task: to possess power, but seldom to exercise it; to witness abuses which you think you could correct; to see the errors, if not crimes, of superstitious bigotry, and the miseries of misrule, and yet forbear, lest you injure interests far greater than any within the sphere of your limited duties, and impede and embarrass, by a rash change and innovation that may bring local benefit, the slow but certain march of general improvement. Nothing can keep you right on all these points but constant efforts to add to your knowledge, and accustoming your mind (as I have before urged you) to dwell upon the character of the British power in India, and that of the empire over which it is established. The latter, comprehending numerous tribes and nations, with all their various institutions and governments, may truly, though metaphorically, be viewed as a vast and ancient fabric, neither without shape nor beauty, but of which many parts are in a dilapidated state, and all more or less soiled or decayed; still it is a whole, and connected in all its parts, the foundations are deep-laid, and to the very summit arch rests upon arch. We are now its possessors, and if we desire to preserve, while we improve it, we must make ourselves completely masters of the frame of the structure to its minutest ornaments and defects: nor must we remove the smallest stone till another is ready, suited to fill the vacant niche, otherwise we may inadvertently bring a ruin on our own heads, and those of others, on the spot where we too eagerly sought to erect a monument of glory.

(Signed) JOHN MALCOLM.

Camp Dhooliah,
28th June, 1821.

J. Frederick Pogson

Indian Gardening. Calcutta: Wyman, 1872.

INDIAN GARDENING.

THE KITCHEN GARDEN.

In the plains of India, almost every house has either a Kitchen Garden, or sufficient land attached to it which may be converted into one. In the hills, the want of land prevents many a landlord and public-spirited tenant from making and keeping up a garden. The Kitchen Gardens already in existence are capable of very great improvement; and our object is to point out how this may be best and most economically effected.

We have explained the important part which lime plays in the economy of flowers and fruits, and we now wish to draw attention to the fact of its being present in all cereals and culinary vegetables, in greater or lesser quantity; and as it is very much needed in every Indian garden soil, we would recommend, as the first step towards improvement, that the soil of the entire Kitchen Garden be properly limed. The quantity of sifted lime to be allowed to the square yard should not be less than 3 chittacks, or 2,700 grains, which gives 300 grains of lime per square foot. For certain vegetables double this quantity will have to be used. At the lesser rate, a plot of garden land measuring 24 feet in length by 6 feet in breadth, will require exactly 3 seers of sifted bazar *chunam,* and this quantity should be mixed up with twice as much sand, or finely pulverised earth, and applied by hand to the surface of the soil. This done, the land should be trenched, or well dug up with the mattock or *phowrah,* the clods broken, and the soil prepared for manuring and sowing.

In the plains, European vegetables are, as a rule, grown in the autumn and winter months; consequently all preliminary operations will have to be commenced on the cessation of the rains, or, say, any time between the 15th of August and the 15th of September: but in the Himalayas gardening is carried on throughout the year, the Pea, Cabbage, and Cauliflower not being affected by the snow or frost.

It is not our intention to notice in succession the large number of vegetables indigenous to India, many of which are not used by Europeans; but we shall select the best, and as all English vegetables will be fully dwelt upon, ample information will be supplied to enable the amateur to grow them to perfection.

When possible, we purpose giving a simple analysis of the vegetable under notice, as by this means the amateur will be enabled to judge what substances he should use or add to farm-yard manure to ensure the best produce.

It should be remembered that the manure obtained from the stall-fed cow, ox, and sheep, are very different, as regards quality and composition, from that produced by the grass-fed animal: hence, if the latter be used, the mineral deficiencies will have to be made good by artificial means. The value of the dog as a regular supplier of assimilated phosphate of lime cannot be overrated, and when we consider his faithfulness and general usefulness, the trifle spent on his food is amply repaid.

The fresh manure of the grass-fed cow contains in 100 parts as follows, viz. :—

Water	69·58
Woody fibre	26·39
Animal matters	2·58

Of mineral matters—

Salt	0·08	
Sulphate of potash	0·05	
Sulphate of lime	0·25	
Carbonate of lime	0·24	
Phosphate of lime	0·46	
		1·08
Carbonate of iron		0·09
Sand and waste		0·28
	Total ...	100·00

—*Dr. Ure.*

The manure of the Indian grass-fed cow probably does not contain half the above quantity of mineral matters, hence the absurdity of expecting superior crops from the use of such manure.

A supply of manure obtained from a stall-fed cow* was dried and burned, and 100 parts of the ashes were found to contain as follows, viz. :—

	Cow.	Horse.
Potash	17·15	9·33
Soda	6·30	0·61
Lime	7·31	5·22
Magnesia	4·50	2·03
Peroxide of iron ...	3·34	2·03
Sulphuric acid	3·23	3·92
Silicic acid	41·00	59·96
Phosphoric acid ...	17·05	7·92
Total ...	100·00	100·00

* For the sake of comparison the analysis of horse-dung has also been given. The horse was fed upon oats, rye-bread, hay, and straw,—total 22 lb daily; and the cow consumed 80lb of mixed food per diem.

The urine of the stall-fed cow is of considerable value as manure, containing 56·74 of potash, 1·74 of lime, 4·09 of magnesia, and 4·63 of sulphuric acid in 100 parts; and the same quantity of horse urine contained, of potash, 28·97; of lime, 27·75; of magnesia, 4·22; and of sulphuric acid, 6·48.

It is the custom in India to waste these valuable liquid manures; the amateur gardener will however, at once, see their value, and will preserve and utilize both. Thus, crops requiring lime and potash would be very greatly benefited by solid and liquid horse-manure, whilst that of the cow would be of considerable value for succulent vegetables, such as Spinach, Cabbage, Lettuce, Celery, &c. Horse-manure, owing to its richness in lime, if applied to cotton, would produce an increased supply of cotton wool; but if cow manure was applied thereto, a most abundant supply of wood and leaves would be secured, with a very insignificant yield of cotton wool.

The manure of the camel, goat, and sheep is remarkably rich in ammonia and its salts; hence they should be mixed with finely pulverised earth and charcoal dust, and kept under cover apart from the preceding manures. The vegetables which contain a large percentage of nitrogen will thrive and flourish when treated with such manures. Peas, Beans, Linseed, the Poppy, and Tobacco, contain nitrogen in abundance, and, as a consequence, are greatly benefited by the application of either of the above.*

---

* The fossil bones so abundantly met with in the Sewallicks, Nerbudda Valley, and other parts of India, is a manure of the very highest value, and would be worth £4 per ton in the London market. India is capable of supplying all Europe with this valuable mineral. But as it is Government property it may not be touched; and as it would be presumption on our part to point out how it might be brought into use without the aid of the costly sulphuric acid, we are obliged to be silent.

With a little practice, the amateur will in a short time be able to make up all kinds of composts, and to apply them at his discretion.

The Chinese, who are great gardeners, as a rule manure each individual plant, and as the system is economical and effective, we would recommend its adoption.

The amateur gardener should understand something about the rough analysis of soils, and the following instructions will be found of considerable use :—

1*st.*—Weigh a given portion of soil, heat it, and dry it : the loss is water.

2*nd.*—Burn whatever remains : the loss is chiefly vegetable matter.

3*rd.*—Add hydrochloric acid to the residue, and thus the quantity of lime may be determined, its presence being indicated by effervescence ; and the longer it continues, the richer the soil in lime.

4*th.*—Wash a fresh portion of soil to determine the quantity of insoluble silicious sand.

5*th.*—To determine the presence of humic acid, dissolve a little common soda in water, add some of the soil thereto (previously reduced to a pulvurent form), and give it a good boil. Pour the solution into a glass and let it settle, and then pour off the coloured solution (without any sediment) into another glass. If vinegar or diluted hydrochloric acid be added to the clear brown or brownish coloured liquid, brown flocks will fall, which are humic acid. 36lb of carbon and 27lb of water form 63lb of humic acid. All black and dark-coloured soils are rich in this fertilizing substance ; poor soils contain little ; and sandy soils absolutely none. The manure of the elephant is very rich in this substance, because he eats the entire Sugarcane, the dried stalks of Maize and Millet and, in addition, goodly-sized branches of trees, with their leaves, twigs, and bark. He assimilates their nourishment, and passes their woody or cellular fibre, 81℔ of which contain 36℔ of carbon and 45℔ of water. We have mentioned this circumstance to show the value of elephant-manure, which can always be procured in military stations in the plains; it being of no use to the Department of Public Works, whose subordinates collect and burn bricks with stable litter, and horse and cow or bullocks' dung. These manures also contain much cellular fibre, derived from the oats, barley, hay, and grass consumed by these quadrupeds.

6th.—To determine the presence of phosphate of lime, or bone-earth, weigh out 209 grains of soil and place it in a glass, and pour half an ounce of diluted hydro-chloric acid over it. Stir and mix with a glass rod, and allow it to stand for thirty hours; after which add half an ounce of distilled water, stir as before, and run through filter-paper. If to this clear solution liquid ammonia be added, a pale amber-coloured liquid will float (like oil on water) on its surface: this is phosphate of lime in solution, and it may be precipitated by further additions of liquor ammonia.

7th.—To determine the presence of iron, treat the soil, as before, with the acid, and to the filtered solution add a grain or two of prussiate of potash; stir as before, and in a few minutes the solution will become of a beautiful blue colour, owing to the presence of the iron present in the soil.

8th.—To determine the presence of nitrate of potash, or saltpetre, boil 500 grains of soil in two ounces of distilled water. When cold, run through filter-paper; evaporate this clear solution (over sand or water, as most convenient) till reduced to a tea-spoonful. In it dip a slip of unglazed paper (the margin of a newspaper will supply the material needed), and dry it in the sun. If nitre be present, this slip of paper, on being fired, will behave exactly like touch-paper.

By these simple tests the presence of the substances named will be determined; but if the amateur desires to obtain a quantitative analysis of the soil, he will have to proceed according to the lucid instructions given in Professor Johnston's handbook on the analysis of soils.

The value of lime in the soil is so very imperfectly understood in India, and its use as a manure so little known, that we invite especial attention to the following, viz.:—"Lime is an essential ingredient in all fertile soils. In 1,000lb of such soil there are 56lb of lime, while barren soils contain only 4lb."—*Professor Johnston.* To apply fresh lime to such soils would be simple waste; but to withhold it from the majority of Indian garden soils is false economy. In like manner, if salt be present in the soil, the quantity prescribed as an addition to certain manures, will have to be lessened, otherwise not.

The following information on the subject of soils will be found of practical value by others besides the amateur gardener:—

"Soils have been divided in the following way, according to the proportion of clay, sand, and lime which they possess:

"1*st.*—Argillaceous soils, possessing little or no calcareous matter, and above 50 per cent. of clay.

"*2nd.*—Loamy soils, containing 20 to 50 per cent. of clay, with a little lime.

"*3rd.*—Sandy soils, containing not more than 10 per cent. of clay.

"*4th.*—Marly soils contain from 5 to 20 per cent. of calcareous matter.

"*5th.*—Calcareous soils contain more than 20 per cent. of carbonate of lime.

"*6th.*—Humus soils are those in which vegetable mould abounds."—*Professor Balfour.*

We give below a list of vegetable seeds of the best description, as supplied by Messrs. Carter & Co., seedsmen, London, and we purpose following the list in giving the necessary instructions for their cultivation:—

VEGETABLE SEED LIST.

1. Peas of all kinds.
2. Beans, broad.
3. French Beans and Runners.
4. Beet.
5. Kale.
6. Brussels Sprouts.
7. Albert Sprouts.
8. Broccoli.
9. Cabbage.
10. Savoy.
11. Carrots.
12. Cauliflower.
13. Celery.
14. Cucumbers.
15. Endive.
16. Leek.
17. Lettuce.
18. Onion.
19. Parsley.
20. Parsnip.
21. Radish (long) & Turnip.
22. Spinach, summer and winter.
23. Turnips (best for succession, including Six Weeks.)
24. Tomato.
25. Vegetable Cream and Marrow.
26. Pot Herbs.
27. Melons.
28. Potatoes, all choice kinds.

Flora Annie Steel and
Grace Gardiner

The Complete Indian Housekeeper and Cook.
London: William Heineman, 1909.

Indian Housekeeper's Guide

CHAPTER I

THE DUTIES OF THE MISTRESS

HOUSEKEEPING in India, when once the first strangeness has worn off, is a far easier task in many ways than it is in England, though it none the less requires time, and, in this present transitional period, an almost phenomenal patience; for, while one mistress enforces cleanliness according to European methods, the next may belong to the opposite faction, who, so long as the dinner is nicely served, thinks nothing of it being cooked in a kitchen which is also used as a latrine; the result being that the servants who serve one and then the other stamp of mistress, look on the desire for decency as a mere personal and distinctly disagreeable attribute of their employer, which, like a bad temper or stinginess, may be resented or evaded.

And, first, it must be distinctly understood that it is not necessary, or in the least degree desirable, that an educated woman should waste the best years of her life in scolding and petty supervision. Life holds higher duties, and it is indubitable that friction and over-zeal is a sure sign of a bad housekeeper. But there is an appreciable difference between the careworn Martha vexed with many things, and the absolute indifference displayed by many Indian mistresses, who put up with a degree of slovenliness and dirt which would disgrace a den in St. Giles, on the principle that it is no use attempting to teach the natives.

They never go into their kitchens, for the simple reason

that their appetite for breakfast might be marred by seeing the *khitmutgâr*[1] using his toes as an efficient toast-rack (*fact*); or their desire for dinner weakened by seeing the soup strained through a greasy turban.

The ostrich, who, according to the showman, "*'ides 'is head in the sand and thinks as 'e can't see no one, as nobody can't see 'e*," has, fortunately, an exceptional faculty of digestion. With this remark we will leave a very unpleasant subject.

Easy, however, as the actual housekeeping is in India, the personal attention of the mistress is quite as much needed here as at home. The Indian servant, it is true, learns more readily, and is guiltless of the sniffiness with which Mary Jane receives suggestions; but a few days of absence or neglect on the part of the mistress, results in the servants falling into their old habits with the inherited conservatism of dirt. This is, of course, disheartening, but it has to be faced as a necessary condition of life, until a few generations of training shall have started the Indian servant on a new inheritance of habit. It must never be forgotten that at present those mistresses who aim at anything beyond keeping a good table are in the minority, and that pioneering is always arduous work.

The first duty of a mistress is, of course, to be able to give intelligible orders to her servants; therefore it is necessary she should learn to speak Hindustani. No sane Englishwoman would dream of living, say, for twenty years, in Germany, Italy, or France, without making the *attempt*, at any rate, to learn the language. She would, in fact, feel that by neglecting to do so she would write herself down an ass. It would be well, therefore, if ladies in India were to ask themselves if a difference in longitude increases the latitude allowed in judging of a woman's intellect.

The next duty is obviously to insist on her orders being carried out. And here we come to the burning question, "How is this to be done?" Certainly, there is at present very little to which we can appeal in the average Indian servant, but then, until it is implanted by training, there is

[1] The object of this book being to enable a person who is absolutely unacquainted with India, its language and people, to begin housekeeping at once, the authors have decided on adhering throughout to purely phonetic spelling. The only accent used will be the circumflex.

very little sense of duty in a child; yet in some well-regulated nurseries obedience is a foregone conclusion. The secret lies in making rules, and *keeping to them*. The Indian servant is a child in everything save age, and should be treated as a child; that is to say, kindly, but with the greatest firmness. The laws of the household should be those of the Medes and Persians, and first faults should never go unpunished. By overlooking a first offence, we lose the only opportunity we have of preventing it becoming a habit.

But it will be asked, How are we to punish our servants when we have no hold either on their minds or bodies?—when cutting their pay is illegal, and few, if any, have any real sense of shame.

The answer is obvious. Make a hold.

In their own experience the authors have found a system of rewards and punishments perfectly easy of attainment. One of them has for years adopted the plan of engaging her servants at so much a month—the lowest rate at which such servant is obtainable—and so much extra as *buksheesh*, conditional on good service. For instance, a *khitmutgâr* is engaged permanently on Rs. 9 a month, but the additional rupee which makes the wage up to that usually demanded by good servants is a fluctuating assessment! From it small fines are levied, beginning with one pice for forgetfulness, and running up, through degrees of culpability, to one rupee for lying. The money thus returned to imperial coffers may very well be spent on giving small rewards; so that each servant knows that by good service he can get back his own fines. That plan has never been objected to, and such a thing as a servant giving up his place has never been known in the author's experience. On the contrary, the household quite enters into the spirit of the idea, infinitely preferring it to volcanic eruptions of fault-finding.

To show what absolute children Indian servants are, the same author has for years adopted castor oil as an ultimatum in all obstinate cases, on the ground that there must be some physical cause for inability to learn or to remember. This is considered a great joke, and exposes the offender to much ridicule from his fellow-servants; so much so, that the words, "*Mem Sahib tum ko zuroor kâster ile pila dena hoga*" (*The Mem Sahib will have to give you castor oil*), is often heard in the mouths of the upper servants when new-comers give trouble In short, without kindly and reasonable devices of this kind, the usual complaint of a want of hold over servants *must* remain true until they are educated into some sense of duty. Of course, common-sense is required to adjust the balance of rewards and punishments, for here again Indian servants are like children, in that they have an acute sense of justice. A very good plan for securing a certain amount of truthfulness in a servant is to insist that any one who has been caught out in a distinct falsehood should invariably bring witnesses to prove the truth of the smallest detail. It is a great disgrace and worry, generally producing a request to be given another chance after a few days. These remarks, written twenty years ago, are still applicable, though the Indian mistress has now to guard against the possibility of impertinence. This should never be overlooked for an instant.

To turn to the minor duties of a mistress, it may be remarked that she is primarily responsible for the decency and health of all persons living in her service or compound. With this object, she should insist upon her servants living in their quarters, and not in the bazaar; but this, on the other hand, is no reason why they should turn your domain into a caravanserai for their relations to the third and fourth generation. As a rule, it is well to draw a very sharp line in this respect, and if it be possible to draw it on the other side of the mothers-in-law, so much the better for peace and quietness.

Of course, if the rule that all servants shall live in quarters be enforced, it becomes the mistress's duty to see that they are decently housed, and have proper sanitary conveniences. The bearer should have strict orders to report any illness of any kind amongst the servants or their belongings; indeed, it is advisable for the mistress to inquire every day on this point, and as often as possible—once or twice a week at least —she should go a regular inspection round the compound, not forgetting the stables, fowl-houses, &c.

With regard to the kitchen, every mistress worthy the name will insist on having a building suitable for this use, and will not put up with a dog-kennel. On this point the authors cannot refrain from expressing their regret, that where the power exists of forcing landlords into keeping their houses in repair, and supplying sanitary arrangements, as in cantonments, this power has not been exercised in regard to the most important thing of all; that is, to the procuring of kitchens, where the refuse and offal of ages cannot percolate through the mud floors, and where the drain water does not most effectually apply sewage to a large surrounding area. With existing arrangements many and many an attack of typhoid might be traced to children playing near the kitchen and pantry drain, and as in large stations the compounds narrow from lessening room, the evil will become greater.

In regard to actual housekeeping, the authors emphatically deny the common assertion that it must necessarily run on different lines to what it does in England. Economy, prudence, efficiency are the same all over the world, and because butcher meat is cheap, that is no excuse for its being wasted. Some modification, of course, there must be, *but as little as possible.* It is, for instance, most desirable that the mistress should keep a regular storeroom, containing not merely an assortment of tinned foods, as is usually the case, but rice, sugar, flour, potatoes, &c.; everything, in short, which, under the common custom, comes into the *khânsâmâh's* daily account, and helps more than larger items to swell the monthly bills. For it is *absolutely impossible* for him to give a true account of consumption of these things daily, and so the item must in every case be a nominal charge far above actual expenditure. With regard to the best plan for keeping this storeroom, the next chapter must be consulted.

A good mistress in India will try to set a good example to her servants in routine, method, and tidiness. Half-an-hour after breakfast should be sufficient for the whole arrangements for the day; but that half-hour should be given as punctually as possible. An untidy mistress invariably has *untidy*, a weak one, *idle* servants. It should never be forgotten that—though it is true in both hemispheres that if you want a thing done you should do it yourself—still, having to do it is a distinct confession of failure in your original intention. Anxious housewives are too apt to accept defeat in this way; the result being that the lives of educated women are wasted in doing the work of lazy servants.

The authors' advice is therefore—

"Never do work which an ordinarily good servant ought to be

able to do. If the one you have will not or cannot do it, get another who can."

In regard to engaging new servants, written certificates to character are for the most part of no use whatever, except in respect to length of service, and its implied testimony to honesty. A man who has been six or seven years in one place is not likely to be a thief, though the authors regret to say the fact is no safeguard as far as qualifications go. The best plan is to catch your servants young, promoting them to more experienced wages on the *buksheesh* theory above-mentioned. They generally learn fast enough if it is made worth their while in this way. On the other hand, it is, as a rule, a mistake to keep servants *too long* in India. Officials should be especially careful on this point, as the Oriental mind connects a confidential servant with corruption.

To return to written certificates. Their total abolition is impossible in India where the society is so fluctuating, but it would certainly be advantageous if a stand against them was made, except in certain cases. There is no reason whatever why further personal reference should not be requested. In the majority of cases this request *could* be complied with, to the great benefit of distracted house-keepers who, having engaged a cook adorned apparently by the seven cardinal virtues, find that the only merit he possesses is being the son of a father who, having died in the odour of sanctity, left his certificates to be divided amongst his children! But in this, as in all the difficulties besetting Indian housekeeping, *combined* effort is wanting. For instance, it may safely be said that if Indian servants found cleanliness necessary in every service they took, the present abominations would soon disappear, for they are naturally obedient.

It is always advisable to give neat, durable, livery coats for wearing when on actual duty in the house. Broadcloth is a mistake, being hard to keep clean, and apt to get fusty. Good washing serge, such as that to be got at the Elgin Mills, is best, made to fit well, but loosely, with sleeves of proper length and width. These coats, in the case of table servants, should hang on pegs in the pantry, and only be put on for actual attendance. If carefully brushed and put away as the warm season comes on, they will last for two years. For camp work, &c., a commoner washing suit may be given, and in the hot weather, cotton liveries of dark blue, which can be washed regularly every week. Any little extra expense is better than having a servant behind your chair who reeks of dirt and smoke; or, what is worse, a whited sepulchre, whose outside snowiness conceals warm clothes which have been slept in for months.

Finally, when all is said and done, the whole duty of an Indian mistress towards her servants is neither more or less than it is in England. Here, as there, a little reasonable human sympathy is the best oil for the household machine. Here, as there, the end and object is not merely personal comfort, but the formation of a home—that unit of civilisation where father and children, master and servant, employer and employed, can learn their several duties. When all is said and done also, herein lies the natural outlet for most of the talent peculiar to women. It is the fashion nowadays to undervalue the art of making a home; to deem it simplicity and easiness itself. But this is a mistake, for the proper administration of even a small household needs both brain and heart. A really clever woman always sees this, and, like George Eliot, the greatest of modern women, prides herself on being an excellent housekeeper. It was written of her that "*nothing offends her more than the idea that her exceptional intellectual powers should be held to absolve her from ordinary household duties.*" In regard to expenditure, the mistress of a house has it in her power to make debts, as to prevent them, for. she, and she only, has the power of preventing that extravagance in small things, which is but the prelude to a like recklessness in greater matters.

It is astonishing how few women know how to keep accounts; yet this is the first step towards economy, and a little method and care in this point saves infinite friction. One special fault which the authors believe besets most women is the habit of not showing all transactions on paper. For instance, in paying a minor bill, some *annas* or *pice* are allowed to remain as an advance to be deducted from the next payment, which must then either be written down less than it is, or paid less than it is written down. This is absolutely a false system, and is the cause of more dispute and hopeless addings up of balances than a novice can well imagine. So if you have two or more funds you nominally wish to keep separate, do not borrow from one and pay back to the other without showing the transaction; above all, do not receive small items of money and keep them off the paper altogether by saying, "Ah, I paid that to So-and-so, therefore it is all square." Accounts, in fact, do not come under the head of *Cookery*.

But on this subject we refer the reader to the special chapter on Accounts; here we may only warn young housekeepers not to descend to wrangling over prices or items. Make up your mind as to the fair price. Do not take an article at an exorbitant one simply because you want it. Some housekeepers in India nowadays cheerfully give the equivalent of one and sixpence per pound for bad beef, and by so doing are ruining the poor. Accept past deceit or fraud as *past*; tell the offender quietly that you do not intend to pay such a price again, and in cases of extravagance, give the order that in future the ingredients are to be brought to you before being put into use. If meat is bad, or dear, resort for a week to doing your own marketing, but do not sit for half-an-hour and squabble over it with your *khânsâmâh*. Make it a rule that all food which is to be used that day shall be personally inspected by the mistress, otherwise you may pay good prices for bad things. It must be remembered that half the faults of native servants arise from want of thought and method, and that mere fault-finding will never mend matters. A mistress must know not only where the fault lies, but how to mend it. So, in keeping accounts, a mistress *must* take the lead, and, knowing the proper prices of the different articles, and the amount which ought to be consumed, set aside all objections with a high hand.

Having thus gone generally into the duties of the mistress, we may detail what in our opinion should be the daily routine.

The great object is to secure three things—smooth working, quick ordering, and subsequent peace and leisure to the mistress. It is as well, therefore, with a view to the preservation of temper, to eat your breakfast in peace before venturing into the pantry and cookroom; it is besides a mistake to be constantly on the worry.

Inspection parade should begin, then, immediately after breakfast, or as near ten o'clock as circumstances will allow. The cook should be waiting—in clean raiment—with a pile of plates, and his viands for the day spread out on a table. With everything *en evidence*, it will not take five minutes to decide on what is best, while a very constant occurrence at Indian tables—the serving up of stale, sour, and unwholesome food—will be avoided. It is perhaps *not* pleasant to go into such details, but a good mistress will remember the breadwinner who requires blood-forming nourishment, and the children whose constitutions are being built up day by day, sickly or healthy, according to the food given them; and bear in mind the fact that, in India especially, half the comfort of life depends on clean, wholesome, digestible food.

Luncheon and dinner ordered, the mistress should proceed to the storeroom, when both the bearer and the *khitmutgâr* should be in attendance. Another five minutes will suffice to give out everything required for the day's consumption, the accounts, writing of orders, &c., will follow, and then the mistress (with a sinking heart) may begin the daily inspection of pantry, scullery, and kitchen. But before she sets foot in the back purlieus, let her remember that if a mistress will not give proper appliances, she cannot expect cleanliness. If, however, this excuse is not valid, the authors' advice is—*notice the least dirt quietly, with the order that before going for his mid-day recess the servant in fault shall come personally and report its removal.* Let the mistress then send another servant to see if this be true; but let her guard against giving herself the least trouble in the matter. For here, again, Indian servants are like children, gaining a certain satisfaction in the idea that at any rate they have been *troublesome.*

We do not wish to advocate an unholy haughtiness; but an Indian household can no more be governed peacefully, without dignity and prestige, than an Indian Empire. For instance, if the mistress wishes to teach the cook a new dish, let her give the order for everything, down to charcoal, to be ready at a given time, and the cook in attendance; and let her do nothing herself that the servants can do, if only for this reason, that the only way of teaching is to *see* things done, not to let others see *you* do them.

Another duty which must never be omitted, so long as copper vessels are used for cooking, is their weekly inspection to see that the tinning is entire. No more fruitful source of danger and disease can be imagined than a dirty copper saucepan; and unless proper supervision is given, we advise every mistress to use nothing but aluminium utensils. Apart from the fact that their lightness is of value when camping and travelling, personal experience shows that they are durable, absolutely safe, and peculiarly adapted to cookery, since their contents do not readily burn. Unless of the very best, enamelled pans are not safe owing to their tendency to chip. It is a significant fact that the appearance of appendicitis as a common disease is co-temporary with that of the common use of enamelled saucepans. In many jails, nowadays, glazed earthenware utensils may be had, which are invaluable for milk, fruit, and soups. In fact, a much larger variety of articles can now be had of native manufacture than was possible ten years ago, and it need hardly be said that it is clearly the Indian housekeeper's duty to encourage native industry.

In regard to other household questions. The bearer's account for odds and ends is apt to be a source of trouble; indeed, a well-known Indian story tells of a bachelor who with a smile paid 820 rupees at the end of a year for *soot-sooie-button* (needles and threads and buttons). This was a palpable extravagance; yet the usual price charged and acquiesced in for matches, even in the hot weather, when the mere thought of fires is offensive, is 8 annas a month; for which sum 4 dozen boxes can be bought. It is wise, therefore, to limit the number of odds and ends, for which this servant is responsible, to the lowest ebb. *Jhârans* (dusters) are another source of trouble. Some ladies give them out every day, others once a week. The latter is perhaps the best way, if it ends in inspection, as you can then see the dirt better, and impose a fine for the using of glass cloths as sink swabs, and so on; while in the daily plan, the dignity which doth hedge about a perfectly clean cloth, gives a fictitious virtue to the servant using it! As a rule, three and a half-dozen coarse kitchen cloths, two dozen glass, and two dozen tea-cloths per week should suffice to remove all possibility of excuse from the pantry.

CHAPTER VI

THE DUTIES OF THE SERVANTS

In the following chapter the authors have adopted the division of labour which obtains in Bengal and Northern India. In Bombay, Madras, Ceylon, and Burmah the manner of life is so different, that residents in these Presidencies will find it necessary to piece the duties of the various servants together into a new classification. Nevertheless, it is none the less certain that the work has to be performed, whether the worker be called by one name or another; also, that the majority of servants, from Himalaya to Cape Comorin, are absolutely ignorant of the first principles of their various duties. The *masaul* doing the lamps in Bombay is quite as likely to do them badly as his congener, the Bengali bearer, while the Madras butler's besetting sins are not far removed from those of the Oude *khitmutgâr*. The authors, therefore, believe that, given this slight difference in classification, the following brief outline of household duties will be found useful all over India. To facilitate this alteration, they give a comparative table showing the work assigned to each servant and the approximate wages demanded by good servants of each class at the present time in the various Presidencies.

BENGAL.	BOMBAY.	MADRAS.	CEYLON.	BURMAH.
1. Bearer, 10 rs. to 16 rs. Head of house, valet, housemaid.	1. Butler, 15 rs. to 30 rs. Head of house, valet, wait; does marketing.	1. Butler, 15 rs. to 30 rs. Head of house. As Bombay.	1. *Appu*, 20 rs. to 35 rs. Head of house. As Bombay.	1. Boy, or butler. Same as Madras. Double wage.
2. Cook, 14 rs. to 40 rs. As a rule caters also.	2. Cook, 20 rs. to 30 rs. Cooks.	2. Cook, 10 rs. to 25 rs. Cooks.	2. Cook, 25 rs. Cooks.	2. Cook. As Madras.

BENGAL.	BOMBAY.	MADRAS.	CEYLON.	BURMAH.
3. *Khitmutgár*, 10 rs. to 18 rs. Waits at table.	3. *Masauls*, 15 rs to 20 rs. Waits at table.	3. Mateys, 10 rs. to 15 rs. Waits at table.	3. Boys, 12 rs. to 15 rs. Waits at table.	3. Mateys, 20 rs. Waits at table.
4. *Khansamah*, 10 rs. to 20 rs. Housekeeper and head waiter. Head, as it were, of the commissariat department. A useless servant.	4. None.	4. None.	4. None.	4. None.
5. *Musolchi*, 6 rs. to 10 rs. Scullery man.	5. Cook's Boy, 7 rs. Do.	5. *Tunny ketch*, 6 rs. Cook's help; a woman generally.	5. Kitchen coolie, 5 rs. to 10 rs. Scullery man.	5. Cook's coolie, 12 rs. Kitchen help.
6. *Mehtar*, 6 rs. to 8 rs. Sweeps, underhousemaid.	6. *Humal*, 10 rs. to 15 rs. Does bearers's and superior sweeper's work.	6. *Musolchi*, 8 rs. to 10 rs. As Bombay.	6. House coolie, 10 rs. to 12 rs. Superior sweeper and inferior bearer's work.	6. *Humal*, or house coolie. As Madras, 16 rs.
7. *Bhisti*, 8 rs. Carries water.	7. Waterman, 8 rs. Carries water.	7. Waterman, 6 rs. Carries water.	7. None, except in country.	7. Waterman, 14 rs.
8. *Ayah*, 10 rs. to 20 rs. Lady's maid, nurse.	8. *Ayah*, 12 rs. to 20 rs. Do. do.	8. *Ayah*, 12 rs. to 18 rs. Do. do. Does needlework.	8. *Ayah*, 20 rs. Do. do. Does needlework.	8. *Ayah*, 12 to 18 rs.
9. *Dirzi*, tailor, 15 rs. Not kept in Calcutta.	9. *Dirzi*, 15 rs.	9. *Dirzi*, 10 rs.	9. *Dirzi*. Seldom kept.	9. *Dirzi*. Seldom kept.
10. *Dhobi*, washerman, 10 rs. for two persons, 16 rs. for a family.	10. *Dhobi*, 8 rs. each person.	10. *Dhobi*, 6 rs. each person.	10. *Dhobi*, 5 rs. each person.	10. *Dhobi*, 8 rs. each person.
11. *Syce*, or grooms, 8 rs. Does groom's work.	11. *Ghora wallahs*, 15 rs. Do.	11. Horsekeepers, 10 rs. Do.	11. Horsekeepers, 12 rs. Do.	11. *Syce*, 12 rs. Do.
12. Grasscutters, 6 rs. Seldom kept.	12. Grasscutters, 6 rs. Seldom kept.	12. Grasscutters, 6 rs. Seldom kept.	12. None kept. Women bring grass.	12. Grass generally bought.
13. Gardener, *Mâlee*, 6 rs. to 30 rs.	13. *Mâlee*, 6 rs. to 30 rs.	13. *Mâlee*, 6 rs. to 6 rs.	13. Gardener, 10 rs. to 12 rs.	13. Seldom kept.
14. *Gow wallah*, cow man, 6 rs. to 8 rs.	14. Seldom kept.	14. Cow man, 6 rs. to 8 rs.	14. Not kept.	14. Not kept.

It will be seen that the chief difference in the distribution of household work lies in the head man in Bengal being the bearer; and in Madras, Bombay, &c., the butler. The difference is greater than it seems on paper; for while the bearer is invariably a Hindu, the butlers are Christians or Mahomedans. In the former case the whole of the household goods, barring those connected with food, are placed in charge of one man; in the latter, everything, without any exception. In Bombay the various duties of the servants are not so marked as in Bengal; but most of the house-servants dust, sweep, wait at table, and cook, if required to do so. Roughly speaking, butler and *hamal* divide the bearer's duty in Bombay, while in Madras they are performed by the butler and *musolchi.* Both in Madras and Bombay an inferior sweeper, either male or female, is kept. Details regarding the duties of the Bengal servants will be found below, with a few recipes for things required in their work.

Duties of the Bearer.

The implements required by the bearer are—

- 12 Soft dusters per week.
- 1 Feather broom.
- 1 Bottle home-made furniture polish.
- 1 Clothes brush.
- 1 Corkscrew.
- 1 Pair scissors.
- 1 Chimney brush.
- 1 Tin Putz Pomade.
- 2 Funnels.
- 1 Bottle brush.
- 1 Ice breaker.
- 1 Salver for cards.
- 1 Bottle benzine.
- Hammer, tacks, glue, string, &c.

The bearer should be the head servant, and the greatest care should be exercised in engaging one who is honest and respectable. Being his master's valet, the other servants give weight to his opinion, and follow his lead, knowing that he has opportunities for private communication with the authorities. Ear-wigging, it must be remembered, is supposed by the Oriental to be all-powerful. The discipline and respectability of the servants' quarters depend to a great extent on the character of the bearer, who should be held responsible.

The bearer must be an early riser. He has charge of every single thing in the house, save those in the dining-room and pantry, and any loss or breakage has to be accounted for by him; therefore it is to his own advantage that he should keep an eye on the under-servants. In addition, one of the greatest alleviations of Indian discomfort lies in his hands; that is, keeping the house free of mosquitoes. To do this he must in the hot weather shut every window before dawn. They may be opened afterwards; but if they are not shut between four o'clock and six o'clock mosquitoes will come in.

His next duty is to remove the lamps used the night before to the lamp-room, taking those used in the bedrooms from the *ayah* or *khitmutgâr*, as the case may be, whose duty it is to bring them out to the bearer. This should be done at the opportunity afforded by the taking in to the bedroom of the early cup of tea. He should also call upon the *khitmutgâr* to remove coffee cups, tumblers, &c., that may have escaped notice. He should not remove them himself.

When the sweeper has swept the outer verandahs, the upper and lower windows should be thrown open, but not till then, or the dust will come in.

One day a week the drawing-room should receive a thorough cleaning, summer and winter; and after a dust-storm a complete turning out is also necessary; but on other days the sweeper should, with a soft brush and dustpan, sweep over the whole room, shaking mats, &c., outside, as they are apt to harbour vermin. The bearer meanwhile should remove the flower-vases and place them on a table in the verandah, fold up newspapers and put them in a certain fixed receptacle, replace books in the bookshelf, restore chairs to their proper place, and sort everything up as far as possible. It is a good plan to have a separate basket for all papers, envelopes, &c., found on the floor anywhere about the house, as it is then a sure find for lost letters or memoranda. Punkahs and thermantidotes often blow scraps of paper off tables.

When this is done the whole room should be carefully dusted.

The weekly turn-out should include a polish to all articles of furniture, a smart beating of the backs of the carpets, and a cleaning of windows. Dirty windows are the sign of a bad bearer. If the bearer is valet also, he should now attend to his master's room, brushing and folding the clothes used the day before, tidying the dressing-table, and not forgetting to dust the mirror.

As a rule, the gardener or the mistress arranges the flower vases, but it is the bearer's duty to take them back into the drawing-room when they are ready. He should remember that as he is responsible for all the ornaments and the many valuable things left lying about a drawing-room, it is to his interest *not* to let strangers in. On the weekly cleaning day the flower vases should be thoroughly washed out with soap and water, taking care to remove all sediment with a bottle brush. If soap and water fails to restore the polish of the glass, a few drops of sulphuric acid in the water is infallible.

After breakfast the bearer should be in attendance on his mistress at the godown, and report *openly* to her anything which has occurred in the compound during the last twenty-four hours which she ought to know. He need fear no enmity from other servants if he does this fearlessly, openly, and honestly.

If he has charge of the wine, he should ask for what is needed, and keep his mistress informed as to the supplies in his charge. He should see the grain weighed out for the horses, cows, and poultry, and should never fail to report anything unsatisfactory in their management.

The bearer should be ready to receive callers from twelve o'clock till two. Unless his mistress has told him to say "*durwâza bund*" (the Indian equivalent for not at home), he should *at once* usher the visitors into the drawing-room and present their cards to his mistress, wherever she may be. He must never do this with his fingers, and a small tray for receiving the cards should always lie on the verandah, or hall table.

One of the most important parts of a bearer's work is the charge of the lamps, and yet not one man in a thousand knows anything about it. Most lamps in India burn kerosene oil, and the great secret of making them give a good clear light is cleanliness. When a tin of kerosene has to be opened, it is only necessary to make a hole in two opposite corners of the top, about the size of a pea. This can be done with a round nail and hammer. As a full tin of oil generally runs twenty-five bottles, the bearer should have that number ready. He should then decant the whole tin into the bottles, and at once report any deficiency to his mistress. By this means fraud on the part of the supplier will be detected at once, and also the very common adulteration of the oil, as the bearer will be able to see if it runs clear and uniform in tint to the very bottom. To fill the lamps the reservoirs should be removed from their stands to a separate table and most carefully filled by means of a proper can or an old teapot. If any kerosene is spilt on the reservoir, it should be thoroughly removed. If it is necessary to remove the burners, before replacing them the loose ends of wick should be squeezed dry by drawing them downwards through the fingers over a basin or empty tin kept for the purpose. The burner should then be held to the light, to see that all air-holes are free from dust or dirt. Any clogging is fatal. When the burner is replaced, the wick should be very slightly turned up and *cleaned*, not cut, by gentle rubbing with a duster and a final squeeze between finger and thumb. If any threads or unevenness appear, they may be carefully removed with the scissors, but as a rule scissors should never *touch* the wick. If due care in filling the reservoirs at a different table is observed, and the chimneys and globes are never touched with greasy fingers, it is hardly ever necessary to use water in cleaning them, a chimney brush and dry duster being quite sufficient. The overpowering smell of most Indian lamp-rooms is simply due to wasteful carelessness in filling.

The wick of a lamp should *never* coil round in the reservoir. Even the best oil has a sediment, and when the wick lies in it for weeks and weeks, the fibres get clogged, and so the oil is prevented from rising through them. Therefore, when a new wick is put in, it should only just reach to the bottom of the reservoir; if the lamp is kept well filled, as it should be, it is surprising how long even this little bit of wick will burn brilliantly; and though this plan involves more frequent change of wick, and a slight excess in the amount used, this is more than compensated for by the satisfaction of clear white light. Once a week every reservoir should be completely emptied and wiped out with a rag. The oil from them should be put with that squeezed from the wicks, and filtered before it is used again.

Candlesticks must be cleaned every day, and every trace of grease removed with hot water.

In the evening, when the bearer lights the lamps, he should also see that each bedroom has its candle and box of matches; at the same time, he should satisfy himself that the sweeper, *bheesti*, and other servants have done their work. On bringing the lamps into the drawing-room he should tidy it up, remove bits of thread, torn papers, &c., from the floor, draw the curtains, and if there is a fire, see that the wood-box is full. If the bearer is also *âbdâr, i.e.*, serves the wine at table, it is his duty to inform the *khitmutgâr* what wine-glasses will be required, and satisfy himself that they are duly placed on the table. If the *âbdâr* has to serve a large number of people, especially in the hot weather, when guests are naturally in a hurry for something cool to drink, it requires method and preparation to be successful. The ice should be broken into pieces before dinner is announced, and wrapped in a napkin. The best way of breaking up ice is to use a short sharp steel skewer; a large darning-needle fixed in a handle answers well. No hammer is required, as the lightest pressure with the sharp point will split the ice. The soda-water should be ready to hand, champagne wire removed, claret uncorked, and the wines for dessert decanted in scrupulously clean decanters. The *âbdâr* should not dodge round the table in serving the guests, but go round methodically, beginning with the lady at the host's right hand.

The bearer should always be on guard against the ravages of white ants, fish insects, and other vermin; and in the rainy season he must not forget the periodical airing of all woollen clothes, blankets, rugs, &c.

Another important work of the bearer is making the beds, excepting, of course, those in the ayah's charge. It may generally be asserted that no native servant has the faintest idea how to make a bed, and therefore those mistresses who desire to make their guests comfortable will do well to give at least one practical lesson on this subject, insisting on the mattress being turned, the sheets evenly spread and separately tucked in, and the pillows well shaken up. An Indian bed too often consists of a hard felted surface, with more than a suspicion of crumbs, and covered by frantically crooked sheets and blankets, which the slightest movement reduces to chaos, while a sudden turn lets them loose in disastrous avalanche on the floor.

Recipes for the Bearer.

1. **Armenian Cement.**—Half oz. isinglass soaked in water till soft. Strain, add 2 oz. spirits of wine, and dissolve with gentle heat. Dissolve ¼ oz. selected mastic pearls in 2 oz. spirits of wine. Mix both solutions whilst warm. Powder 1 drachm gum-ammoniac, and mix on a slab with enough solution to damp it through. It will then incorporate with the rest of the solution if stirred over gentle heat. Strongest cement known. It will join polished steel.

2. **Ants, to keep from Tables, &c.**—Tie a rag dipped in castor oil round the legs of the table or cupboard.

3. **Ants, White, to keep away.**—Tar the floor with thin tar. Infallible, and cleanly. Indigo in the concrete is said to be efficacious.

4. **Brass Work, to clean.**—Cut a lime in half, rub over the brass, wash the article thoroughly in soap and water, dry and polish. One teaspoon of sulphuric acid mixed in quarter of a pint of water, and used instead of the lime, is still better. Sapolio and Brookes' soap also do well, but Putz pomade is the best.

5. **Brass Work, Benares, to restore the Gold Colour.**—Coat the ornament with a paste of powdered sal-ammoniac and water. Heat over, or rather in, a slow charcoal ash fire, rub dry, and polish with bran.

6. **Brass Work, to preserve untarnished.**—Coat lightly with pale paper varnish.

7. **Bottle Wax.**—One lb. resin melted with ¼ lb. suet and ¼ lb. shellac.

8. **Bottle Paste or Dextrine.**—Wet 2 oz. arrowroot with 2 oz. cold water. Soak 80 grains gelatine in 14 oz. water for one hour. Bring to the boil. When the gelatine is quite dissolved, add the arrow-root, and boil for four minutes. Pour into a bowl to cool. When nearly cold, add 1 oz. spirits of wine, in which 6 drops of pure glacial carbolic acid have been mixed. Stir well, bottle, and cork. It will keep for months.

9. **Carpets, to remove Ink Stains.**—Wash, if possible, while still wet, with fresh, hot boiled milk. Sponge again and again with hot water. Time and patience must be plentifully used. A weak

solution of oxalic acid may be tried if the stain is very dark, but the risk of injuring the colour is very great. It is, however, possible to re-dye the injured portion, with a result certainly preferable to a black spot.

10. **Chairs, to prevent the Leather from Cracking.**—Rub with white of egg beaten thin with water.

11. **Chimneys, to prevent Cracking.**—Set in a pan of cold water, and gradually heat to boiling point. Let the chimneys remain in the water till cold.

12. **Cloth or Velvet Embroidery, to clean.**—Bake a very thick *chapâtti* (unleavened cake) of coarse *atta* and water. When barely cooked through, take the inside doughy part, form into a roller, and with the palm of the hand roll in over the embroidery. The fluffs and hairs stick to and come away on the dough, which also acts, like bread, as a cleanser. Excellent for velvet.

13. **Dubbin for Boots.**—Melt 2 oz. mutton suet, 4 oz. black resin, and 1 pint fish oil. One of the best dressings for boots is plain castor oil. Vaseline is also good.

14. **Glue, Strong.**—Digest by gentle heat in a corked bottle 3 oz. rectified spirits of wine with 4 oz. of fine pale shellac. The Chinese use nothing else for all their wood-work. Excellent for pianos.

15. **Furniture Polish.**—Mix in a bottle equal parts of linseed oil, turpentine, vinegar, and spirits of wine; or half a teacup shredded beeswax dissolved in 1 teacup turpentine. The sanitary polish called Ronuk is very good.

16. **French Polish.**—Put into a bottle enough pale shellac slightly broken to fill it one-third, fill up with spirits of wine. Digest in the sun.

17. **Grease Spots, to remove.**—Rub with oil of turpentine and air in the sun; or place a double fold of blotting-paper over the spot, and rub with a moderately hot poker.

18. **Patent Leather, to preserve.**—Use plain boiled linseed oil. The easiest plan to make a good drying oil is to powder 2 oz. of litharge and 1 oz. oxide or sulphate of lead. Put into a pint bottle of linseed oil, agitate occasionally for ten days. Set in the hot sun for two more, then decant the clear portion.

19. **Scouring Drops.**—Mix 2 oz. rectified spirits of turpentine with 2 drachms essential oil of lemon or cloves. Rub on with a clean rag till the stain disappears.

Duties of the Sweeper.

The implements required by the sweeper are—

- 1 Native broom for verandahs.
- 1 Dust-pan and brush.
- 1 Carpet-switch.
- 1 Hearth brush.
- 1 Ash-pan.
- 1 Dust cloth.
- 1 Slop pail and cloth.
- 1 Bath-room basket.
- 1 House flannel.
- 1 Scrubbing brush.
- Soap.
- 12 Dusters of all sorts.
- Set boot brushes.
- 1 Turk's head for cleaning walls.
- 1 Carbolic or Phenyle bottle.
- 1 Wooden spud.
- 1 Tin whitewash and brush.
- 1 Comb and brush for dog.

In most houses the sweeper is engaged simply because he is the husband of the *ayah*. This is an immense mistake, as the whole cleanliness of the house depends upon him. Again, his duties give him the *entrée* to every room, therefore the trust reposed in him must necessarily be great. He is, in fact, the under-housemaid, and should never be allowed to degenerate into the dirty, unkempt drudge, whose sole notion of work is to raise a dust-storm with a broom, and try experiments on the relative fragility of your pet ornaments by flicking them with a greasy duster. Housekeepers will find a rupee or two more well expended in securing the services of a man who is presentable, and who is both fit to, and capable of, receiving orders direct. Care should also be taken that the sweeper is not imposed upon by every other servant; as a rule, he is simply hunted from pillar to post, and made to do odd jobs for everybody; the *khitmutgârs* being special offenders in this way, calling on the sweeper at all hours to clear up their messes, and generally to be the scapegoat for their dirty habits.

When a large number of servants are kept, making a full compound, and there are also dogs and poultry to be looked after, we *strongly* recommend the employment of an under or mate sweeper, who should do the outdoor work. So much of the cleanliness and consequent healthiness of a house and compound depends upon the sweeper, that it is *worth while* to make sure the work is not scamped; and the plan here advocated, of having two sweepers, will be found to be far more satisfactory in large establishments than the employment of an upper and under bearer, neither of whom will do any real cleaning. The under-sweeper (who will seldom require more than six rupees a month) should have the charge of the servants' houses, compound, and stableyard, look after the dogs and poultry, sweep the verandahs, remove the refuse from the cook-house, and be generally responsible for outside cleanliness. The upper sweeper should be virtually the under-bearer, leaving the head man available as butler and valet.

The sweeper's first duty in the morning is to see to the bath-rooms and empty the slops, taking care to observe all regulations as to the disposal of refuse, and to keep everything sweet and clean. His next is to sweep the verandahs, then the dining-room and hall, and lastly, the drawing-room. A damped brush or duster is best for Persian carpets. If there has been a fire, he should, after placing the dust-cloth over the rug, proceed to remove the ashes, and thoroughly clean the hearth. It will be found a good plan to make the sweeper keep a pot full of colour-wash to take the place of hearthstone. With this he should wash over the inside of the arched recess which in most Indian houses does duty as a fireplace; by thus removing the smoke and dust marks, the hearth has a much tidier appearance. Once a week, every room in the house should have a complete cleaning out, beginning with the upper windows and walls, and finishing with a rub down to all the doors and frames. Such of the boots and shoes as have not been cleaned over-night should now be attended to: in some houses the bearer cleans the boots, and he always remains responsible for their being ready when wanted, and should always keep clean the patent leather, and the finer kinds of shoes; but in many respects it is better to make the sweeper do the dirty work.

After each meal it is the sweeper's duty to go into the scullery, and, under the *khitmutgâr's* orders, remove all refuse to *its proper place*. In large stations there is generally a recognised place for the refuse heap, which is periodically cleared away by conservancy carts; but in other cases the best plan is to dig a long trench, three feet deep by two broad, in some convenient corner of the garden, piling up the earth on one side only. As the sweeper throws in the refuse he should cover it with dry earth from above, taking care not to use the trench in various parts, but work steadily from one end, and to fill it up only to about two feet, and after that to make it level with pure earth. When one trench is filled, another may be dug alongside. In this way all refuse becomes valuable manure for the garden.

The sweeper's last duty at night is to see that everything in his charge is clean, and to give both scullery and kitchen a final sweep-out. On this depends much of the health of the household. The sweeper should always have on hand a supply of some disinfectant, and should be instructed how to use it, or whitewash if that is preferred. His duties in regard to dogs and fowls will be found under those headings. The following recipes will be found useful for the sweeper :—

1. **Boots, to black.**—Remove every atom of dust or mud with the brush, or, if necessary, a damp cloth. Put on the smallest possible amount of blacking, and leave it to dry thoroughly, then polish as hard as you can. Do not forget to take the laces out before blacking laced boots or shoes. If the leather feels sticky, too much blacking has been used. For brown shoes, use one tea-cup shredded beeswax dissolved in one tea-cup turpentine, or the usual brown boot polish. Polish with a silk cloth.

2. **Chitai Matting, to clean.**—Wash with strong salt and water Dry at once with a soft cloth.

3. **Grey Wash for Fireplace.**—Make a *gharra* full of rather thick whitewash, colour with powdered charcoal, and add a little rice-water or glue.

4. **Iron, to clean.**—Use powdered bathbrick and oil, with plenty of elbow-grease.

5. **Red Wash for Fireplace.**—Mix one pice worth of *hirmchi* with one pice worth of *géru* in sufficient rice-water to make the whole to the consistency of whitewash.

6. **Rust, to remove.**—Take powdered polisher's putty (or crude peroxide of tin) mixed with a little oxalic acid and water. Apply on the rust spot as a paste for a few minutes. Wash off carefully, dry and polish. Both Brooke's soap and Putz pomade are excellent for metal work.

7. **Whitewash Marks on Wood, to remove.**—Mix 1 oz. salt with 1 oz. linseed oil and 4 oz. of water. Rub on with a damp duster till the spot disappears.

8. **Windows, to clean.**—Remove varnish or putty marks with spirits of wine. Wash with soap and clean water on both sides of

the pane. Polish with a dry rag. If the polish has gone, it may be restored by dry, powdered tripoli, and a very fine polish may be given by dusting powdered chalk, tied up in a piece of muslin, on to the glass, and then rubbing it off with a dry, clean rag. Greasy cloths will never clean glass.

9. **Windows, to preserve Glass from Paint.**—Make the painter or varnisher use a thin slip of glass as a guard. Put this close to the woodwork, when all surplus stuff will be smeared on it, not on the real window glass below.

Duties of the Cook.

The implements required are mentioned hereafter.

The first duty of the cook is to have a tidy cook-room, and for this his mistress is mainly responsible in the first place. We cannot insist too often on the folly of expecting cleanliness when there are no appliances rendering it possible to be clean.

The cook-house, then, must be airy and wholesome. The floor should be of broad, flat bricks, such as are used for mosques and public buildings, set close in really good mortar. There will then be no difficulty in getting it swept and *washed* out every day.

No better mode of open fire cooking exists than the *chûla* arrangement for charcoal, at present in use in most parts of India, and which closely resembles that seen on the Continent. It is convenient, economical, safe, and suitable in every way to the requirements of the climate. But it is *not* necessary that the whole erection should be made of mud and loose bricks, as is very generally the case. Good bricks, well set and surmounted by a strong sheet of iron clamped to the bricks, with holes cut to correspond to the round brick *chûlas* below, will make as good and as cleanly a kitchen range as any cook need desire. A hot case with an oven beneath it can be built on one side. Such an oven is very simply made; it is merely a framework of sheet iron with a door in front, let into the bricks with a place for charcoal below and above, and a space of about one inch left between the iron and bricks at the back to act as a flue.

The expense of such simple arrangements is trifling in the extreme, and no practical cook who has ever personally superintended the working of that diabolical invention, a native *tizâl* or oven, will ever allow one in her kitchen. The mischief it can do to the best made cakes is simply incredible; and it is impossible to say which is more difficult, to get the lid *on*, or, having succeeded in that, to get it *off* again. The mere sight of a *tizâl* with two crooked legs, the missing third supplied by a tottering pile of bricks, and three inches of dust and ashes inside to prevent the utter cremation of the wretched cake, is enough to dishearten any one. No one need be astonished if, in the frantic effort to get the lid full of burning coals off or on, the whole frail structure collapses, and *khitmutgâr*, charcoal, ashes, cake, and tins are mingled in hopeless confusion. If the initial expense is not a bar, we strongly recommend every housekeeper to have a kerosene oil stove with an oven on a table in a verandah, where she can use it for dainty cooking. We also strongly advise, where possible, the introduction of American stoves, simply for the sake of their ovens. No one who has not tried the effect of making stock, boiling vegetables, preparing stews, &c., in an oven has any idea of the saving of trouble and the vast superiority of the food so prepared. It is more nourishing and infinitely more palatable. In addition, it is more hygienic, the very high temperature of the air in the oven effectually sterilising it, and preventing the entrance of flies, &c. Such stoves as the Constantine, Empress, Victoress require no fixing, and burn wood or charcoal.

A point which must be insisted on in a cook-room is the raising of the washing-up place or sink so far from the ground that the refuse water will fall into a proper and movable receptacle outside, and *not* filter into the ground. It cannot be right that food should be cooked in a house whose very foundations are saturated with sewage. The sink, then, should be at least two feet from the ground, with a high ledge round, and a stand for water vessels on one side. These are best made of old kerosene tins with iron handles, and in each should be a tin-dipper—any empty tin will serve the purpose. Every kitchen should contain two tables—a dishing-up table, which is best close beside the range, if not part of it, and a working table. Beside the latter there should be another stand for two water vessels, as it is by no means advisable that water which has been standing, so to speak, in the *sink* should be used for cooking.

The cook should be provided with a cupboard which locks for his stores, and an open bunker for his charcoal. Shelves for saucepans, and a row of hooks for different utensils, are of course necessary.

With regard to the utensils themselves, the best and safest are the aluminium saucepans now so much used at home. Copper is a constant source of anxiety, any slight fit of indigestion rousing suspicions of the *dêgchies*; so that, if possible, it is best to use nothing but aluminium [1] and steel, especially when cooking for children. The number of utensils must, of course, vary with the style of establishment, but a small household, no less than a large one, requires the little conveniences and requirements which are so often conspicuous by their absence in Indian cook-rooms. The following list only gives absolute necessaries, if clean and wholesome cooking is expected. The Urdu name is given against each.

6 Stewpans or saucepans, of sizes, with covers	*Dêgchi*
2 Frying-pans	*Fry-pân*
1 Omelet-pan, enamelled	*Momlet-pân*
1 Large kettle with cock	*Kittli*
1 Colander	*Turkâri ke chulni*
1 Wire frying basket	*Tôkri*
1 Egg poacher	*Unda poach-dân*
1 Large boiler	*Dêgchâ*
2 Small tin saucepans	*Sârse-pân*
1 Mortar and pestle	*Imâmdusta*
1 Curry stone	*Sil*
1 Gridiron	*Gridârni*
2 Iron charcoal stoves	*Ungêthi*
1 Roaster	*Kubâb-dân*
1 Chopper	*Châppa*
1 Saw	*Âri*
6 Kitchen knives	*Chûri*
6 Forks	*Kârnta*
6 Metal spoons	*Chumchâ*
1 Gravy strainer	*Gravy ke chulni*
1 Potato muller	*Âlu mulne ke lukri*
2 Graters	*Grâte-dân*
3 Dredgers	*Mirich, âtta,* and *nimuk dâns*
2 Ladles	*Chumchâs*
1 Whisk	*Kûchi*
12 Bowls, of sizes	*Piyâle*
1 Coffee mill	*Câffê ke chukki*
1 Coffee roaster	*Câffê senk-dân*
1 Set scales and weights	*Turâzu*

[1] Aluminium saucepans are to be had in Madras and also in Cawnpore.

1	Meat safe	*Dûli*
1	Hair sieve	*Chulni*
2	Wire sieves	*Chulna*
1	Jelly-bag	*Jeli ki thaili*
1	Mincing board	*Mêz*
1	Paste board	*Crûs ke mêz*
1	Rolling-pin	*Bêlun*
24	Dusters and cloths . . .	*Jâhrun*
	Moulds *à discrétion* . . .	*Sâncha*
	Pie dishes	*Pi-deesh*

If high-class cooking is attempted, a *bain marie* becomes absolutely necessary for the sauces; but this can easily be made in any bazaar out of an old kerosene tin cut down to six inches, the edge turned over an iron wire, and handles put at each side. This, half filled with water, in which four small bazaar-made tin saucepans can be plunged, is all that is necessary, and the whole arrangement need not cost more than two rupees. In fact, a very little supervision and ingenuity suffices to fit up a cook-room properly at a small cost. Small enamel pans are now to be bought in most shops, and there are an infinity of labour-saving trifles which repay their cost in kitchen work, such as egg-beaters, bread crumb mills, vegetable slicers, &c., which it is well worth while to add to the above list.

Having thus placed the cook in a decent kitchen, with decent appliances, the harder task remains of getting him to keep it in a decent state. This will never be accomplished unless the mistress takes the trouble of seeing that her orders are obeyed. The sweeper should go into the cook-room twice a day—once before breakfast, and once after dinner—at both of which times every particle of refuse should be removed, and the sink swept and washed clean. The ashes must also be removed, and the whole place put into thorough order, saucepans hung up, waterpots re-filled, tables washed down. A little method is all that is required, for once the sweeper and the *bheesti* are on the spot, it is no trouble to the cook to insist on their doing their duty thoroughly.

Even supposing the kitchen is kept in a cleanly state, it by no means follows that the food will be cooked cleanly, and the mistress must always be on her guard against the dirty habits which are ingrained in the native cook. The strictest morning parade will not prevent him stirring the eggs into a rice pudding with his finger, but a practical illustration that the method is both troublesome and ineffectual may do some good. In the same way, once the saving of time resulting from proper appliances is brought home to the cook, you may trust him to use them; but not till then.

It would take page on page, chapter on chapter, to tell the many evil habits in which Indian cooks have been grounded and taught; but in the Cookery Book published as a companion to this volume, most of them are mentioned in the various recipes as things not to be done. There is therefore no need to detail them here.

In regard to catering, the authors much prefer the less common system of allowing the cook to do the marketings, without the intervention of the *khansâmâh.* If one man is responsible for the quality of the provisions, and another for the preparation of them, it is impossible to get a firm grip of blame on either, in the event of unpalatable food. One throws the fault on the other, and even if the *khansâmâh* is held responsible, it must always be with a mental reservation, if the mistress be herself a practical cook; for the best food will not stand bad cooking, any more than good cooking will take the place of good food. It is certainly a great satisfaction to be able to award praise or blame with a free hand, and for this reason alone divided responsibility is objectionable. Again, the man who is to do the cooking alone knows *what* he intends to make, and what sort, size, and quality of ingredients he requires. The bazaar is seldom so far away but that the cook can get to it before breakfast if he arranges his work methodically, while the commission he of course makes on every article is so much inducement for him to work well. As half the comfort of life depends on the actual cooker of food, it is as well to keep him pleased with himself and with his service. Yet for one mistress who makes a point of commending a well-cooked dish, how many are there who never dream of praise, and whose only criticism is unmeasured and often unreasonable blame?

There are certain delusions current in cook-houses in India, such as the belief that it is the *yolk* of the egg which clears soup, against which it is useless to argue. Autocratic high-handedness is the only weapon of any avail. As an instance in point, one of the authors ordered potted sheep's head several times, and in spite of minute instructions the result was failure. At last the head was ordered for inspection, and it was *skinned*. The reply to an indignant query as to why strict orders had been disobeyed, was that sheep's heads were always skinned—it was *dustoor, i.e.* custom; together with the remark that skinning or not skinning had nothing to do with the non-setting of the jelly, which every one knew came from *bones* and not skin. The offender was told to boil an unskinned head for twelve hours. He came next day with a new light on his face. "*Mem Sahib*," he said, "*do they by any chance make gelatine of skins, for, as the Lord sees me, I can hardly cut that jelly with a knife!*" Here was a case of sheer ignorance of facts well known to an English child; and it must never be forgotten that this is not the exception, but the rule. An Indian cook does not understand why eggs will not rise if whipped slowly, or why syrup will never crystallise unless stirred. He often stands confounded before his own failures, unable to tell *where* he has gone wrong, or how; and if his mistress is a practical cook, he will give a smile of wonder and relief when she points out what he must have done to have caused that specific result. The consequent testimony, "*Béshukk—âp such furmâta hai—aisa hua*" ("Without doubt, your honour speaks truth—it was so"), will go further to raise a mistress in his estimation than any amount of theoretical knowledge she may display. It must not be forgotten either that the best cooks are liable to failures. The fire may be too slack, and yet the delay of increasing it may be *worse* than making the best of what you have. Attention may be distracted for half a second, and lo! the custard curdles, the caramel burns. In cooking, as in other things, the charity born of sympathy covers a multitude of sins.

In regard to the actual duties of a cook in India, they are confined entirely to cooking. He has nothing whatever to do with the morning tea, boiling the kettle, making the toast, &c. That is the *khitmutgâr's* work, and even when poached eggs are taken it is best not to make the cook responsible, for the early morning is his marketing time. In the same way he is in no way responsible for the proper serving of breakfast, only with the dressing and dishing up of the hot dishes, whatever they may be. Tea, coffee, eggs, milk, toast, butter, &c., are in charge of the *khitmutgâr*; and so is the afternoon tea. Beyond this, everything which comes to table is in the cook's care, and he must arrange with the table servants how the various dishes and sauces are to be served.

A considerate mistress will always look a day or two ahead in her orderings, but the cook should be encouraged to act on his own responsibility in minor details, and be praised when he has contrived some fresh pudding or side-dish. This is an immense relief, especially in the hot weather, when one racks one's brains in vain to think of something new, and everything that comes to mind seems a Dead Sea apple of dust and ashes.

Never let a cook *run down* in his cooking, even when he is in camp; for it is a dead certainty that once the niceties of dishing up and dressing are disregarded, a general slackness will set in. *"I can't cook well'm,"* said an English servant to one of the authors; *"there ain't really enough cookin' to do; my 'and gets h'out."* This is still more true with an Indian servant. So insist on everything being done every day in the same style. Then, if a friend comes into dinner unexpectedly, you need have no anxieties. The dinner may be plain, even frugal, but it will be correct, even to the most minute details.

Between the Scylla of sheer pitchforking of viands on to the dish, and the Charybdis of what cooks call *"sujānut,"* or decoration, *simply as decoration*, the mistress will find it a little hard to steer a middle course; but the one fault is as bad as the other, and cutlets coloured pink with cochineal, and green with spinach, may in the opinion of some be as unappetising to the look as a heterogeneous mass of chops and garnishing swimming in a loose gravy, which shows by a high-water mark on the dish that it underwent a tide on its way from the cook-room. A good cook is not made, he is born; so if you are lucky enough to find one, do anything to keep him—short of letting him know that you are anxious to do so!

Finally, if in the hot weather the results of his hands are poorer than usual, and he shows a captious dislike to criticism, give him a blue pill, or present him with a bottle of Eno's Fruit Salt. It is very bilious work stooping over a hot fire with the thermometer above 100°. The use of English cooking stoves is gradually growing. If the cook has one he is to be encouraged to use the oven for every possible process of cookery. Soups, stews, vegetables, are all better done in the oven than on the top of the fire.

Duties of the Khitmutgâr.

The implements required by the *khitmutgâr* are numerous—

1 Set of plate brushes.	1 Knife board.
2 Chamois leathers.	1 Tin for washing knives.
1 Box plate powder.	1 Jug mop.
1 Box polishing paste.	1 Wooden butler's-tray.
1 Brazier or *angithi*.	1 Toasting fork.
1 Earthen butter cooler.	Kitchen paper for wrapping spare plate.
2 Galvanised iron pails.	1 Bread pan.
1 Decanter drainer.	Wire covers for jam, &c.
3 Wooden or tin tubs.	1 Silver basket.
1 Plate rack.	Endless dusters and tea cloths.
1 Scrubbing brush.	1 Pair butter spats.
1 Hot case.	

This servant is a curious mixture of virtues and vices. As a rule, he is a quick, quiet waiter, and well up in all dining-room duties; but in the pantry and scullery his dirt and slovenliness are simply inconceivable to the new-comer in India.

The best of them will, if put to it, give a final polish to your teacup with some portion of his own clothing; or place fresh-made mustard on the top of the old to save the trouble of cleaning out the pot. Much of this is, of course, due to heredity, all Mahomedans of the lower classes being apparently blind to dirt; but more is the result of almost every table-servant beginning work as what is called a *musolchi*—a nameless, abject, adjunct of the scullery, who washes up by the light of Nature. Dirty habits thus grow unchecked by the mistress's eye, and cling to the learner long after he has risen to higher things; whereas, if the sensible plan, advocated elsewhere, is adopted, of having no *musolchi*, the *khitmutgâr* would have to learn his work thoroughly from the beginning. But whatever may have been his training in the past, the mistress should insist on her *khitmutgâr* washing up, in the present, with his own hands. Plate, glass, teacups and breakfast cups, &c., should be washed in the pantry. Dinner plates and dishes should be washed either in another scullery, if available, or in the verandah; for if the pantry and scullery work are done together, there is no possibility of keeping the pantry as it should be—sweet, clean, and free from flies. In addition, there is a certainty that the same greasy water will be used for plates and cups alike.

The pantry should be provided with a washing-up table—King's patent washing-up table, price 16s., is a great boon—and at least three wooden or tin tubs. A supply of cold water can easily be secured by placing a cask against one of the outside walls with a few inches of leaden pipe, and a tap inside, while a sink below the tap is also easily made to connect with a removable zinc tub outside: cask to be filled and tub emptied every day. Even if this be not done, the usual habit of emptying the dirty water on the floor, to trickle away through a hole, should be sternly repressed. The scullery or verandah should also have a washing-up table, a plate-rack, and at least two wooden tubs, and a pail for scraps.

In regard to dusters, tea-cloths, &c., the supply must be much larger than is necessary for an English household. The best plan is to give out the week's supply to the bearer, and make him responsible for issuing the fixed daily number of clean cloths, and taking back the same number of soiled ones. Otherwise your fine glass cloths will be used for scrubbing the kettle, and being black with grease and dirt, will fall to pieces in a few washings from the manipulation necessary to remove the filth.

One thing must be fought against root and branch, and that is the extraordinary want of forethought, and desire to save themselves much washing-up, which leads every *khitmutgâr* to vary his waiting at table by constant dives into the pantry, whence he returns breathless with a hastily-wiped spoon or a forgotten butter-knife. Everything required for each meal should be in the dining-room before that meal is announced, and a running accompaniment of washing should be ruthlessly repressed. If milder measures fail, lock the pantry door before sitting down to meals for a few days, and fine one *pice* for every missing article. Good habits are quickly learned when there is no possibility of continuing bad ones. In regard to details of the *khitmutgâr's* duties, it will, perhaps, be as well to begin with the things he is to leave undone, since his offences are by no means of the negative order.

Therefore he should not lay the table for any meal more than one hour before that meal is to be served. He should not devise ingenious patterns with the spare silver. He should not attempt to fold up the cloth unaided, and so reduce it to creases. He should not make a separate journey to the pantry for each separate article, but use a tray, like a reasonable human being. He should not wash up glass, china, plates, and silver in one small *dêgchi* with a rag tied to a stick. He should not clear away the table and lay it for the next meal whilst the family are still at table. He should not use the table napkins as kitchen cloths. He should not conceal, or attempt to conceal, a dirty duster about his person when waiting at table. He should not leave things to be washed up till they are wanted. Finally, he should not say the kettle is boiling when it is not. This is an inexcusable offence, but universal.

The *khitmutgâr's* first duty is to send in the *chôta hâzri* to the bedrooms at the appointed hour. The tray should be covered with a tray cloth, and a cosy be invariably provided for the teapot. This done, the sweeper should be called to sweep the dining-room, and the *under-khit* should then throw open the windows, shake out the curtains, dust and polish chairs and tables, whilst the head *khit* turns his attention to the sideboards, burnishing up the set silver, if any, and putting everything in order. He should also remove the flower vases, see that they are clean, and place them ready for re-filling on the gardener's table on the verandah.

Before laying the table for breakfast or any meal, the *khit* must first inquire of the cook what dishes are to be served, otherwise he cannot know what articles will be required. This is rarely done, and is at the bottom of half the frantic dives into the pantry of which we have complained above.

The *khit* should then lay the table carefully, placing on the sideboard every extra which may be wanted, and he should satisfy himself that the *under-khit* has put a sufficiency of plates and dishes into the hot case. This can easily be made in the bazaar out of an old tin-lined packing-case. A few wire shelves and a pan of charcoal will turn it into a very efficient plate-warmer. These rules are to be observed at every meal. In regard to breakfast, specially, it may be noticed that every dish should be brought in at once on the butler's-tray and placed either on the sideboard or table, according to the custom of the house. If a person refuses one dish, another should be handed at once, as there are no set courses at breakfast. Nothing save meat dishes and plates should be removed from the table until the guests have risen, and butter, &c., taken from their places to be handed round, should be returned to the same spot. Washing up must never be commenced till the family have left the dining-room, as the pantry is generally close by, and the clatter is annoying. Everything should be cleared away at once; the cups put ready to wash in the pantry, the greasy plates outside; the jam, sugar, butter, bread, cruets, &c., returned to their places; the cloth brushed, folded, and placed in the press.

When all this is done comes the time for washing up.

Then the knives should be put to stand in an upright tin made for the purpose, and sufficient hot water poured in to cover the blades only. The silver should next be placed in one of the tubs in very hot water. The *under-khit* should meanwhile be scraping off the remains from the plates outside, and placing everything to be washed in a large tub of hot water. Cups, plates, dishes—every bit of china—should first be washed in clean hot water and then rinsed and well rubbed with *the hands* in clean cold water, and set to drain on the table or rack. When all are washed the tubs should be emptied and put aside, and then, and not till then, should drying be commenced. In this way one tea-cloth will do the work of six, which are used a little, then thrown on the floor, then taken to soak up greasy water, then perhaps used to rub down the table. Everything, as it is dried, should be put in its proper place.

The *under-khit* should follow the same rules with the meat plates, &c., except that they should be set to drain in the rack, and not wiped at all. He should then take the knives in hand and clean them, not forgetting to wipe the handles with a damp cloth. The *khit* meanwhile should be busy on the silver, putting each article as he washes it into a pan of clear, cold water, whence it should be taken piece by piece, wiped dry with a soft cloth, polished with another, finally rubbed with a chamois leather, and put, as it is done, into the plate basket. These rules for washing up apply to every meal. After breakfast the *khit* should attend his mistress to the storeroom and ask for everything he may want for the table.

Lunch should not be laid till half-an-hour before the time for serving it. If due method is observed in washing up, a good two hours' recess will have elapsed between the end of breakfast work and the laying of lunch. This is quite sufficient leisure for any but the idle. As at breakfast, the *khit* should inquire what dishes are to be served, and make arrangements accordingly. Washing up follows the same lines, the upper *khit* taking glass and silver. Between lunch and afternoon tea-time (which is often irregular in time) the *khit* should not leave the house, but should occupy himself with the spare silver, which cannot have too much elbow-grease. The *khit* will thus be at hand to bring tea at any time, should the advent of visitors require it to be brought, either earlier or later than usual; if the kettle is boiling, which it should be, on a charcoal brazier in the verandah, a sharp servant will appear with the tray, toast, cakes, &c., less than five minutes after it has been ordered. Yet how often has not every Indian visitor been kept wearisomely waiting for the tea, the offer of which he was unwise enough to accept.

When his mistress goes out, the *khit* is once more at leisure, if he has been wise enough to see to his preparations for dinner between lunch and tea-time. Dessert should then be arranged, and creased tablecloths or napkins taken to the *dhôbi* (washerman) for an iron. A *khit* should always be reminded that an untidy table, dull glass, and tarnished silver tell his character far more truthfully than his *chits* (certificates) tell it; and that even should he lose the latter, as *chits* through some fatality are always being lost, he need fear no difficulty in finding, and keeping, a good place if his glass, china, and silver attest his industry.

The procedure at dinner is much the same as at lunch; but special care should be taken to avoid delay between the courses. Vegetables, especially potatoes, should be handed with the joint, and not ten minutes after, when people have finished their meat. To facilitate carving at the side-table, the cook should never put sauce or gravy in the dish, but in a separate bowl. A servant should never put anything down, even for an instant, on the dinner-table, and he should never dodge round the table, but serve steadily from right to left.

Silver should receive a special cleaning twice a week, and once a week the pantry should be cleared out, and everything in it receive an extra wash. Water carafes must be emptied every night and set to drain in the decanter drainer. Silver should be counted over every night, and glass and china once a week. If a breakage is not reported, and the mistress discovers it, cut the *buksheesh* money remorselessly; not so if it is reported, since accidents will occur.

Dirt, illimitable, inconceivable dirt must be expected, until a generation of mistresses has rooted out the habits of immemorial years. Till then look at both sides of your plates, and turn up the spare cups ranged so neatly in order in the pantry. Probably one-half of them are dirty.

The following recipes will be found useful by the *khitmutgâr* :—

1. **Brass, to clean.**—Use Putz pomade, or rub with finely pounded bathbrick mixed to a paste with sweet oil, or powdered sal-ammoniac mixed in the same way with water. Polish with equal parts of bran and whiting.

2. **Bread, to freshen.**—Soak the loaf for one minute in boiling water, then bake till dry in a hot oven.

3. **Butter, to keep sweet.**—Press the butter into the bottom of an empty jam jar, then invert the latter in a soup plate of water. This keeps out the air effectually. If the butter is kept actually in the water, the latter should always have salt or boracic acid in it, and be changed every day.

4. **Coffee, to make Essence of.**—For every two tablespoons of ground coffee take one breakfast cup of cold water. Place in a wide-mouthed jar and stand all night. Place the jar in a *dêgchi* of water, and let the whole come to boiling point. Strain and bottle. It will keep for a week, the addition of an equal quantity

of *boiling* water making it hot enough to use. Similar essence may be made in any machine by adhering to the same proportions of coffee and water.

5. **Glass, to clean.**—Wash in warm water with *bâsun* (parched gram flour) mixed to a paste with water, and use like soap. Rinse well, and polish. The stains or rims in neglected water carafes, decanters, &c., are best removed by a few drops of strong hydrochloric, or, at a pinch, sulphuric acid in a tumbler of water. This should be poured into the carafe and well shaken. Rinse thoroughly in clean water, as the acid bites into the glass.

6. **Plate, to clean.**—Powder, mix, and bottle four ounces each of common salt, alum, and cream of tartar. Add a teaspoon of this mixture to every quart of water. Boil the plate in the water for five minutes. Remove and plunge in cold water. Dry and polish, using a little powdered chalk tied in a muslin bag, and dusted over the silver during the final polish. Elbow-grease is the only secret of bright plate. Every now and again wash with Sapolio.

7. **Table Linen, to remove Wine Stains from.**—Put a soup plate under the stain while wet and squeeze a lemon or pour boiled milk over it. After five minutes wash out with water. A careful servant will remove all small grease stains from table linen as they appear by rubbing bread on them, and see all creases ironed out.

8. **Tea, to make.**—Use boiling water, and warm both tea and teapot before the fire. Fill the pot at once with the amount of water required. Infuse for five minutes, and decant into another well-warmed teapot.

9. **Toast, to make.**—Cut *stale* bread into thin, even slices. Hold at some distance from the fire at first in order to dry it (or if there is an oven, place in that); then closer to give it a golden brown tinge. Toast should be crisp and yellow brown, not tough and dirty white, streaked with burnt black. Place the toast when made in the toast-rack at once. The Christy bread-knife enables any one to cut thin toast even out of new bread.

The Duties of the Musolchi or Scullion.

The implements required by the scullion are, as a rule, confined to a pail of greasy water and a rag swab. The wisdom of having such a servant at all is doubtful; but if the most prominent duty of a table attendant—cleanliness—is delegated to a nameless drudge on six rupees a month, a very great deal of supervision must be exercised by the mistress to ensure obedience to orders. In most houses the scullion is an unknown quantity, a gruesome ghoul of spurious cleanliness, bearing, as his badge of office, a greasy swab of rag tied to a bit of bamboo.

It is said that good *khits* will not work unless a *musolchi* is kept; but this is not the authors' experience, and one of them has never allowed such a servant in the house; though in the cook-room she acknowledges a drudge may be necessary in a large family. Indeed, it seems absurd that *khitmutgârs* should be above the washing of valuable glass and china; for it must be remembered that if *once* a *musolchi* is admitted to the pantry, he will be used for everything and anything. There is no objection whatever to his doing the preliminary clearing of the dinner-plates in the verandah, as elsewhere advised. Indeed, this *is* the scullery-maid's duty, and the *musolchi* should be a scullion, and nothing else; the pantry is a step above him, and on no pretence should he be allowed to flourish his swab there. Under the system, or no system, which obtains in most houses, the *musolchi* and the sweeper are the only two servants who ever condescend to clean anything. Curiously enough, in these cases they acquire a strange similarity in dress and demeanour; possibly because, being everybody's slave, they lose all spirit and self-respect. Both slink from sight, and become furtive even in *their* methods of work, and both contrive to assimilate an incredible amount of pure griminess around their own persons.

In many so-called good houses the *musolchi* is the motive-power underlying the simulated activity of the Mahomedan servants. He lights the early fire, makes the tea and toast, and prepares everything for the *khitmutgâr*, who is generally a lordly relative. It is he who washes up the early breakfast cups and saucers, and makes it possible for his real master, the *khitmutgâr*, to lay the table leisurely.

Breakfast over, the lordly one retires for recess, while the *musolchi*, left in sole possession of the pantry, proceeds to wash up everything in one poor pennyworth of water, with an intolerable amount of greasy cloth. *Jharans* (cloths) here, there, everywhere; all more or less filthy, all more or less capable of leaving a fine bold smear on your plates and dishes

The process, as patented by the unchangeable law of *musolchi*-dom, is simple :—

1. Plates are plates, and include cups and saucers, teapots, side-dishes, and milk-jugs.

2. Spoons are spoons, and include knives, forks, toast-racks, &c.

3. Water is water, so long as it is fluid.

4. Cloths are cloths, so long as they hold together. After that they are used as swabs.

5. The floor is a floor, and nature made it as a table.

6. Variety is pleasing; therefore always intersperse your stoneware plates with china teacups.

7. At the same time, union is strength; so pile everything together, use one water and one cloth, and do not move from your station till everything is dried and spread carefully in the dust.

8. Only one side of a plate is used by the *sahib logue ;* it is therefore purely unreasonable for them to cavil at the other side being dirty.

The cleaning of knives follows, and *musolchi*-dom has long ago reduced this to a science in the way of destruction. Given a little of his own productions in the way of broken china, and a slanting wooden board destitute of leather, and the *musolchi* will produce an Indian knife, *i.e.* a two-edged pliable spatula, out of the best shear steel, in an incredibly short space of time. In extreme cases he has been known to clean your silver with bathbrick ; and being invariably a slave to his work, he may be seen all day wiping and smearing, smearing and wiping, whilst the *khitmutgârs* lounge on their beds or smoke pipes in the kitchen. Such a state of affairs will, however, never be allowed by a good mistress. Even if a *musolchi* be kept, which is by no means advisable, he should be a responsible servant on good wages; indeed, it is an admirable plan, if *khitmutgârs* object to washing up, to keep one *khit* and put on a *musolchi* on higher wages; it generally settles the matter.

Where a *musolchi* is really needed is in the cook-room. There, just when clean hands are necessary, the scouring of a saucepan may become imperative; and some one to stand between the cook busy at his pastry board and the fire which requires fresh fuel, is a vast aid in preventing the thousand and one trivial accidents and dangers that beset the culinary art. Only those who have actually cooked a whole dinner know the immense relief it is to have some one at hand to prevent those sudden interruptions, which seem invariably to come at the most critical moment.

The *musolchi,* then, finds his proper place amongst the pots and pans, and the utmost he should have to do with plates and dishes should be the clearing away of bones and fragments from the dinner-plates, and, perhaps, a preliminary washing of the same,—the *khitmutgâr,* however, being held entirely responsible for the cleanliness of every dish, plate, cup, saucer, or article of any kind or sort which he puts on his master's table. By keeping the *musolchi* in the kitchen, and at the same time recognising him as your servant and *not* a general drudge, another advantage is secured. He can be trained as a regular cook, and should be taught to look forward to promotion during the time his superior may be on leave, or sick. It is an immense comfort to know that a sudden attack of ague in the kitchen need not result in starvation to the dining-room. Before leaving the subject of cook room and table servants, it is bare justice to say that a lengthier experience of England has made the authors admit that their blame of the East applies to the West also. They have seen an experienced parlour-maid use a whale-bone scrubbing brush to a silver tray, a cook boil her under-clothing in the stock pot, and a housemaid empty slops into the bath! In fact, Indian servants are no dirtier than, if as dirty, as those of other countries.

The Duties of the Bheesti.

With the implements required by the *bheesti* the mistress has little to do beyond providing him with a few clean dusters and seeing that he has a sufficiency of hot and cold water cans, and at least one filter.

Bheesties are, as a rule, the cleanest servants in an Indian household, and are, as a class, more ready to turn their hands to an odd job than any of the others. The duties, however, in which he comes absolutely under the mistress's eye are few. The first is to bring daily a supply of drinking water from some approved source, see it boiled in the vessel set apart for the purpose, and put it to cool in earthen pots beside the filter. These earthen pots should be emptied out every day, as also the filter and every receptacle of filtered water. As often as not, if this rule be not strictly enforced, filtered water is quite, if not more unsafe, than that drawn fresh from the well.

The *bheesti's* next duty is to keep a supply of fresh water in the bathrooms, and to heat the water required for the morning baths. It will be found a good plan to give out, or allow, the wood or charcoal for this purpose quite separately from the kitchen fuel; for complaints of stinting on the one side, or extravagance on the other, are sure to arise as an excuse for tepid baths, or large consumption. The water-jugs, carafe, sponge, and soap dishes are in the *bheesti's* charge, and it is his duty to keep them clean and duly filled with fresh water. We strongly advise the placing of an ordinary three-*gurrah* filter close to the servants' houses, so that those who desire it can always have a supply of fresh water. Such little evidences of care for their health are duly appreciated by the servants; and, in addition, the removal of one of the chief causes of epidemic disease—impure drinking-water—is a source of safety to the entire household.

In regard to the supply of water in bathrooms, the *bheesti* must be made to scrub out the earthen vessels at least once a week, and boiled water should be put in the carafes.

What is generally called a "Punjâb tub" will be found a great convenience for heating bath-water. It consists of an ordinary wooden cask, with a small iron cylinder fixed upright through it like a chimney. This has a grating slightly above its joint with the cask bottom. The cask, which is open at the top and raised on bricks, is then filled with water, and charcoal burned in the cylinder This is an inexpensive and rapid method of heating water. If the Punjâb tub be placed in the verandah near the pantry, it will be found an exceedingly useful aid to the *khitmutgârs* in heating water for washing up, and thus taking the place of the English boiler.

Filters are often a source of great trouble, and the following, recommended publicly by an authority, will be found excellent.

Cut the bottom neatly off a quart bottle. This may be done with an ordinary steel file well moistened by oil of turpentine, or by tying a hank of cotton thread dipped in turpentine round the bottle, setting light to it, and immediately dipping the bottle into cold water. Get a new cork, and through the centre put the glass tube of a Maw's feeding-bottle (to be had in any bazaar), pushing it well through and letting the indiarubber tube remain as in the feeding-bottle. Cork the bottle tight, place a bit of sponge in the neck to prevent the tube getting clogged, and fill the bottle with, if possible, animal charcoal finely pounded—but free from dust—and silver sand, in equal parts. Place another sponge at the open end of the bottle, and either close by tying a piece of muslin over, or get a tight fitting tin cover made in the bazaar; it must, of course, be perforated with small holes. If this filter be placed in an ordinary *gurrah* of water, and the indiarubber tube attached to the glass tube be allowed to hang over the side into a proper vessel, such as a *suráhi,* water will filter over rapidly when once it has started. This must be effected as with a baby's bottle, by squeezing the nipple or by sucking it. In this case, the nipple should be removed afterwards. The advantage of this filter is the ease with which it can be cleaned and renewed. The Berkefield Filter Co., Oxford Street, London, supply excellent filters. And the Gem Still provides a convenient method of obtaining absolutely pure water.

It has lately been discovered that the addition of even a few grains of alum to a gallon of water is almost the best filter there is. In fact, if the water is first boiled, then put to cool in a small-mouthed vessel in a clean place, with two grains of powdered alum to every gallon, it will, after an hour's settling, and carefully decanting to another vessel, be practically as pure as it is possible to get water undistilled.

Permanganate of potash added till the water is faintly pink is supposed to destroy most bacilli. It is also put into wells nowadays, about 2 oz. every week or so for a well in constant use.

The Duties of the Ayah.

Many ladies keep no *ayah;* the implements one requires are few, and consist chiefly of dusters, brushes, &c.

The *ayah's* duties naturally vary immensely with her situation. If there are no children, she is virtually a lady's maid, while if an English nurse is kept, her responsibilities are almost *nil.* On the other hand, when she is really head nurse, she is of all the servants the most important.

In the latter case, again, her duties would vary very much

according to the part taken by her mistress; so that it is hardly worth while treating of the *ayah* simply as a nurse. We may only remark that with very few exceptions, the Indian *ayahs* are singularly kind, injudicious, patient, and thoughtless in their care of children; but to expect anything like *common sense* from them is to lay yourself open to certain disappointment.

Unless you can get a woman from a regular *ayah's* family, the Mahomedan ones are apt to be a nuisance; and the reason which leads many ladies to employ them, viz., the dislike to a sweeper or low-caste woman, is in itself foolish. For no one who has lived long in India can fail to see that the sweeper is very often cleaner in his ways, and certainly in his house, than the Mahomedans. Nor does it follow that because a woman belongs to the sweeper caste she should necessarily do all the dirty work of the establishment. But to whatever class she belongs, the *ayah's* household duties are virtually the same, except that she will not condescend to the broom if she is a Mahomedan. In this connection it may be remarked that the degradation which attaches to the mere act of cleansing anything in India is mainly responsible for the inconceivably filthy ways of its inhabitants. Most of them cannot afford to pay for a cleanser, and so learn to live on contentedly in dirt.

We will begin with the duties of an *ayah* as housemaid and lady's maid. At the time specified by her mistress, she should knock at the door of the bedroom and bring in the early tea, placing the tray on the table, or wherever her mistress directs. She should never forget to *salaam* to her mistress, and ask if anything is wanted, and what time her mistress desires to rise. She should then draw back the curtains and leave the room, remembering to take away the lamp, dirty boots, &c. Having unbolted the bathroom door whilst inside, she should now go round to the outside, and put everything in order, taking special care that the water is fresh, and the jugs, basins, &c., scrupulously clean.

At the appointed time she should bring in the hot water, carefully close the outer door, and after putting towels, soap, &c., in order, go into the bedroom and collect such clothes as her mistress may want. She should never place these in the bathroom till the water has been brought in by the *bheesti*, and the outer door closed. When all is ready, she should take her mistress's dressing-gown and slippers to her. During the bathing time the *ayah* should be arranging and dusting the dressing-table, and carefully putting away everything that is lying about. The bed should also be turned down, and the dress which her mistress is to wear carefully looked over, and hung ready on the back of a chair. Whether the *ayah* does her mistress's hair or not depends upon individual capacity and custom; but most *ayahs* have to do the brushing of the hair, and they generally do it very gently and well.

As soon as her mistress has left the room, the *ayah* should open the windows and put everything in thorough order, making the bed last of all. Not till everything save dusting is finished should the room be swept, especially if she has to call in another servant with a broom. Once a week a more elaborate cleaning should take place, boxes, &c., be moved, lest vermin of any sort should lurk behind them, and both windows and doors receive a polish. Her mistress's room done, the *ayah* will see that the bathroom is set in order, squeeze out the sponge, dry and fold the towels, &c.

If there are no children, she has little else to do during the day, except to lay out walking things, boots, parasols, &c., as may be required. To ensure these being ready, she should come with the other servants after breakfast to take her orders; and if she desires to please, will take her recess between breakfast and twelve o'clock, so as to be on the spot when her mistress is most likely to require her. When the order is given for luncheon, she will take hot water to her mistress's room, and at the same time ask what dress she proposes wearing in the afternoon and evening. At dusk she will go to the bearer for candle and lamp, draw the curtains, if necessary light the fire, and be ready on her mistress's return from her evening drive to take her wraps. While her mistress is dressing for dinner, the *ayah* should arrange everything for the night; turn down the bed, &c., see that fresh water is in the carafe, and lay dressing-gown and slippers ready for use. She must not forget to see that there are matches at hand, and that anything likely to be required is in its place. If a lady guest comes to the house without a servant, the *ayah* of the house should attend to her wants exactly as if she were a mistress, and any neglect in this point should be punished at once.

Where there are no children, an *ayah* should always have time to hem dusters, give out the *khitmutgâr's* cloths, and de many little odd jobs about the house. Indeed, a really good woman will be an immense help, and put her hand to anything, from arranging flowers to sewing on buttons. Being the only woman-servant in the house, the *ayah* should be treated with consideration and respect. Whether she be a sweeper or not, it should be generally understood that you hold her to be the equal of any other servant in the house. If she has charge of children, this point must be still more insisted upon, and you should endeavour to instil into her a sense of her great responsibility, and the confidence you have in her. To treat, however, of the *ayah* as a nurse would involve a chapter on the management of children, and lead us into controversial waters; besides, the employment of English nurses is now becoming so general that ere long such a thing as a child's *ayah* will be unknown.

One thing is certain: Indian children are proverbially captious, disobedient, and easily thrown out of gear. Whether this be the fault of the mother, the *ayah*, or the climate is a moot point; perhaps the safest plan is to attribute it to all three. This more frequent employment of English nurses is no doubt improving the régime of Indian nurseries; but even now it is no unusual thing to see an English child eating his dinner off the floor, with his hands full of toys, while a posse of devoted attendants distract his attention, and the *ayah* feeds him with spoonfuls of *pish-pash*. Appetite is no doubt variable in Anglo-Indian children, but it is possible that a little more pomp and circumstance, and a wholesome conviction that food is not forthcoming except *at* meal-times, would induce Sonny or Missy Baba to treat dinner with graver circumspection. Where, save in India, do we find sturdy little tots of four and five still taking their bottles and refusing to go to sleep without a lullaby? Without going further into the subject, we can only assure every young mother that there is no climatic reason whatever why discipline should be set aside in an Indian nursery, and that it is as possible to insist on cleanliness, decency, and order there as in an Indian pantry or cook-room. The whole secret lies in refusing to listen to the word *dustoor*, or custom.

Few mistresses have been long in India without having had the trouble of scandals between the *ayah* and other servants. In this connection, one word of warning. A steady, well-doing woman may lay herself open to deliberate slanders by her very virtues; and in sifting a story of this kind, it must not be forgotten that the Mahomedan men-servants as a rule have no shame, and will say anything.

The following recipes will be found useful to the *ayah* :—

1. **Brushes, to wash.**—Dissolve one teaspoonful of carbonate of soda or brush powder in a basin of hot water, and whisk the brush on it till clean, taking care not to wet the back lest the ivory or wood should split. Dry in the shade, with handles upwards.

2. **Dentifrice.**—One oz. betel-nuts roasted to charcoal and ground fine, 1 oz. lump sugar, cream of tartar and Peruvian bark, of each ½ oz., powdered cinnamon, 1 drachm. Pulverise. Or equal parts of betel-nut charcoal and common salt. Both these whiten the teeth.

3. **Grease Spots, to remove.**—Use a hot iron and blotting-paper. A piece of cardboard split to a rough edge, and rubbed gently on the spot, will often remove grease from silk. But no house should be without benzine.

4. **Hair, to wash.**—Bruise one dozen soap-nuts (*rēta*), and steep for an hour in a pint of hot water. Pound one tablespoonful of poppy seeds (*kish-kâsh*) on a curry stone, and steep in half a pint of hot water. When wanted for use, strain the water from the soap-nuts into a basin, using pressure to extract all the juice. Into a separate basin strain the liquor from the poppy seeds, which should look like milk. Wash the hair thoroughly with the *rēta* water, rinsing it well out before using the poppy-seed milk. The latter should only be lightly rubbed on to the hair, and just rinsed out. It gives the hair a beautiful softness and gloss, without being greasy. It is also a specific against scurf.

5. **Hair Wash.**—Dissolve in two quarts of boiling water 1 oz. of borax and 2 oz. of camphor; use to wash the hair, rinsing it well.

The Duties of the "Syce" or Groom.

The implements required by the *syce* are :—

2 Dusters.	1 Burnisher.	1 Set blacking and harness brushes.
1 Chamois leather.	1 Body brush.	
1 Sponge.	1 Mane comb.	1 Clippers (?).

The stable may seem outside the domain of the mistress, but as a matter of fact, so many Englishmen in India are over-busy, that, unless the mistress keeps an eye on the horses, the animals are apt to be neglected. Now, if the good house-mother's proudest boast is that not even "the cattle within her gate" fail to feel her kindly care, she will often find it necessary to take an active part in teaching the *syce* his duty, and seeing that the horses receive proper attention. It will, in the authors' opinion, be invariably found a good plan to *limit* the number of servants employed in the stable as much as possible. The old plan of a *syce* and a grass-cutter to each horse is a thing of the past in almost every part of India. Grass is generally bought; but as this costs quite as much as the wages of a man who is available for other stable work, the authors fail to see the advantage. The number of *syces* or grooms should have reference merely to the amount of harnessing and out-work necessary during the day.

If one grass-cutter were given to each horse, one *syce* to every three horses would, as a rule, be found sufficient. The *syce* should be made responsible for the horses under him, and any complaints he may make about the grass-cutters should be attended to at once. He is thus placed in a position of responsibility, and for the extra work involved may be given a small increase of wage. His duties also become those of an English groom. Every morning after breakfast he will come for orders, and again after dinner at night; since, if a horse is to be taken out early in the morning, a good *syce* will wish to know it, in order that he may arrange that the animal gets its food in good time. Without grass-cutters two *syces* should be enough for three horses.

The routine of an ordinary Indian stable should be as follows: At daybreak the horses should receive quarter of their daily allowance of corn, and in hot weather this may be preceded by a limited drink of water. In cold weather this is not necessary; a light grooming should then be given, night clothing removed, the bedding gathered to one corner, and the stall cleaned. After this the grass-cutters should go out for their daily bundle of grass, under orders to return by twelve. It is not by any means necessary for grass-cutters to go out every day for grass, as they can quite well cut a double quantity in the time allowed. In fact, in large stations they invariably do so, and sell one bundle before returning home. Supposing, then, six horses are kept, it will only be necessary for at most four grass-cutters to go out, so that two can remain to help the two *syces*.

The *syce* must be ready at the door to take over the horses which have been ridden, and he should invariably have a light saddle-cloth with him to throw over the horse before leading him away. It is not, of course, necessary, but it will be found a good plan, after district or cross-country work, to put on bandages for the first hour after the horse comes in. The *syce* should have orders first to loosen the girths, then to bandage the legs, then remove the saddle and set to work at once, first with a wisp, then with a pad or cloth, and finally with hand and arm-rubbing. Remarks have been made on the omission of a curry-comb in the list of implements for the *syce*. This is no oversight. A curry-comb is an abomination, and quite unnecessary. Except under unusual circumstances, there will always be two men at leisure to attend to one horse; and as freedom from chill and its many consequent evils depends in a great measure on quickness of grooming after work, it should be a recognised rule in the stable that the grass-cutters are not on *one* particular horse, but on all.

As soon as the horse is groomed, he should be watered and given a small supply of grass. Meanwhile the horses which have not been out will have been exercised, and when all have been looked after and watered, the whole stable should get the mid-day meal of corn. At three the horses may again be watered, at four they get the next feed of corn and should be thoroughly well groomed, so as to be ready for the evening exercise. On their return from this, they should get their last feed and be made up for the night. With regard to the *times* of feeding, people will, of course, consult their own convenience; but it should never be less than three times a day: the gram should be given dry or merely sprinkled with water, and should be mixed with, at least, an equal quantity of chaff or chopped hay, to ensure thorough mastication and digestion. The horses should invariably be given water not less than half-an-hour before, and *never* immediately after, his gram. It is a mistake to feed horses out of their stalls.

In regard to the food, variety is a thing to be looked to, and horses kept from year's end to year's end on nothing but gram are seldom in such good health as those whose food is judiciously changed. Almost every grain may be given, mixed with either bruised barley, gram, or oats. A small corn-crusher will be found both economical and convenient where many horses are kept; you are then certain of getting the food unadulterated, and the horses prefer freshly-crushed grain. Each grass-cutter in turn grinds the corn for the day, and, roughly speaking, it takes five minutes to crush one horse's rations.

The quantity of food must vary immensely with the work given, but it may be remarked that, considering the small amount of work horses do in India, they generally get too much corn. The recognised scale of forage for the largest carriage horses in full work in England is per diem—

Hay	12 lbs.
Corn	12 lbs.
Chaff	2 gallon measures.
Bran	2 quart measures.

For ponies of 14 hands in full work the English allowance is—

Hay	10 lbs.
Oats	8 lbs.
Chaff	2 gallon measures.
Bran	2 quart measures.

In the country in England, a ten miles' drive to the county town and back is supposed to be nothing out of the way; but in India, if any distance over ten miles has to be *ridden*, an extra horse is laid out. Much, of course, depends on the grass, and for this reason it is always advisable to make the grass-cutters bring their bundles into the verandah for inspection at twelve o'clock. If the gram, oats, &c., be kept in lockers in the same verandah, the mistress can then see the grain taken out, and so, at very little trouble, avoid the *buniya's* bill. It is not necessary to weigh out the grain; and if a week's supply is put into the lockers every Monday morning, and the feeds measured with a wooden corn-measure, you will scarcely ever be out more than half a *seer*. Under the ordinary system of a *buniya's* account, you are never certain what kind of stuff the horses are getting, while any change in quantity or kind in the food leads to troublesome complication, and gives cover to cheating. Once, if not twice a week, horses should have a bran mash, a recipe for making which will be found at the end. It also tends to keep horses in health to give them some green food—a *seer* or two of carrots, green wheat, lucerne, grass, or even sugar-cane—and if the mistress takes a pride in her horses, which it is to be hoped she will always do, this little treat will be given during her daily visit to the stable. It will be a distinct pleasure to most women to hear the whinnyings and neighings which will then follow at the first glimpse of the *Mem Sahib.*

Always encourage your *syce* to speak to you at once if anything ails the horses, and never neglect such information. If a horse is reported lame, it does not take much trouble to put on your hat and go out to see. Even if you know little what to do, it impresses the *syces* with your anxiety, and they themselves will look on the matter more seriously.

In cold weather always give out blankets to all the stable-servants, to prevent them from stealing the coverings of their horses. These blankets should be of good quality, marked with your initials, and should be attached to the *service,* and not given to the individual. At the commencement of the hot weather they should be washed and put back into store. The same procedure should be adopted with regard to the horse-clothing, otherwise it will be used to wrap up bundles, &c. &c. Do not grudge warm clothing to your horse; if he is decently groomed, his skin will be very susceptible to the changes of temperature; and with good clothing, he will keep in condition on less food. It is false economy to deny him what is equivalent to an extra feed of corn.

It is not always possible to have *good* stables, but it is in every one's reach to have clean, wholesome ones, by knocking ventilators through the walls near the roof, and converting stalls into loose-boxes by movable bamboos. Heel-ropes should never be seen in a private stable, and the mere sight of them condemns the management. It is said that some Waler horses require heel-ropes, owing to a bad habit of rubbing mane and tail, especially during hot weather; but there can be no doubt that such symptoms point to disease, and these cases may therefore be treated as abnormal. The floor of the stable is nearly always of mud, but it should be quite level; and once a week at least it should be *leped* or plastered with a thin paste of cowdung, sand, and water, as should be the walls to a height of four feet. Stables should always have a verandah in front, and it is wonderful how greatly a cheap bamboo or grass chick to the arches will reduce the temperature in the hot months. The *syces* should not be allowed to sleep *en masse* with wives and families in the spare stalls or verandahs, as they disturb the horses, but *one* man must always do so in case of sudden illness.

If horses are picketed out at night, as they often are during the summer, the safest and most comfortable plan is to have a wooden post about four feet high permanently let into the ground. The horse should have a light iron chain to his headstall, with a ring at the end large enough to slip over the post. If the bedding be arranged round the post in a circle, the horse can always shift his quarters without fear of entanglement or breaking loose. The best bedding in India is rice straw; but where grass is plentiful, many people use *drubh*[1] grass, which a horse will seldom eat.

The best manger for a horse is a square of hemp matting or *tât* on which the gram can be spread on the ground. This enables the horse to eat in a natural position, and prevents bolting; nose-bags are an abomination in a private stable. Watering buckets of galvanised iron are the best; and though it is more reasonable to allow a horse an unlimited supply of water all day long, by means of a suitable receptacle in his stall, yet without constant supervision it is hard, on this plan, to ensure the water being fresh. Therefore, unless unusual care can be given, it is best to keep to the bucket. Hay should never be in a rack. The seeds and spikes are apt to fall into the horse's eyes, and it also conduces to greediness.

In regard to grooming, body brushes, &c., the real secret of a good coat lies in sheer, honest, hard work. As the *khitmutgâr* when pulled up about the dulness of the plate cries loudly for *pureah* (plate powder), so the *syce* will clamour for brushes and curry-combs when brought up for neglect. Elbow-grease is more effectual on a horse's coat than anywhere else—which is saying a good deal—and, while it is quite possible to get on without a brush, it is impossible to dispense with the hand and arm. In fact, a *syce* who does not take off his coat and turn up his sleeves before beginning to groom his horse, knows nothing of his work. There is a great art in making a horse look smart, which is seldom

[1] A kind of coarse rye grass.

thought of in India; but if the *syce* sees that his employers expect it and notice it, he will soon learn, like an English groom, to take a pride in the appearance of his horse. The following rules should be impressed on all the stable helpers:—

1. Give water before and never after food.
2. Do not soak the corn. It may be damped for ten minutes.
3. Report the least injury or symptom of illness.
4. Beat the grass well, and let it dry a day before using it.
5. Always have two men to groom a horse.
6. Never wash a horse's legs except on rare occasions, and then dry carefully at once.
7. If you must steal, steal from men, and not from dumb animals.

The *syce,* however, has other duties besides keeping his horses. He must look after the saddlery and harness, also the dog-cart or carriage, unless a coachman is kept. For saddlery there is nothing like good English soft-soap. If washed with this once a week and carefully dried, scarcely anything else will be required. A recipe for dubbin is, however, given at the end; though we doubt if anything home-made can be cheaper or better than the soaps and *mom roghan* sold by the N. W. Soap Company at Cawnpore.

Bits and stirrup-irons should be cleaned with dry sand or pounded brick and burnished with a regular steel burnisher. If washed in water, they must be dried at once. In hot weather constant care is necessary to prevent insects getting to the saddle stuffing; and it is a good plan to have bags of camphor and *nim* leaves tacked along the top of the saddle-horse or stand. Girths, if white, should be sponged and pipe-clayed, then dusted out; *numdahs* or saddle-cloths dried in the sun and brushed, instead of being utterly neglected.

Carriages, when it is necessary to wash them, require plenty of water, and not half a bucketful, as the *syce* seems to think. But in India the roads are seldom so muddy as to make daily washing necessary. A dry duster is generally sufficient for the most part, and splashes can be removed from the wheels gently with a sponge. A spoke brush or carriage mop is rather a dangerous implement in a native's hands, and we prefer to give him nothing but soft dusters, a sponge, wash-leather, and carriage brush. It is always necessary to have a large dust cloth which will completely cover the carriage almost to the ground. Without this, the most careful *syce* will not be able to send his carriage out as neat as it should be. If the hood is movable, the best plan is to have a hook and pulley to the roof of the coach-house, and so keep the hood out of harm's way when it is not in use.

Harness requires care to keep it strong, and it is usual to put a little lamp-black in the composition used for it. A good recipe for harness paste is given at the end. The mountings should be kept bright with powdered whiting, and the patent leather portions carefully polished with drying oil. Whips should be hung up by the lash, otherwise they will warp.

The following recipes will be found useful to the *syce* :—

1. **Waterproof Harness Dressing.**—Melt 2 oz. mutton suet with 6 oz. beeswax (*kuchcha môm*). Add 6 oz. powdered sugar-candy, 2 oz. soft-soap, 2 oz. lampblack, 1 oz. powdered indigo, and 1 teacupful of turpentine. Use like boot blacking.

2. **Wheel Grease.**—Melt and strain into a tin 2 lbs. fat and 1 bottle common mustard oil.

3. **Waterproof Brown Harness Dressing.**—Melt 1 lb. mutton fat, 5 oz. beeswax; boil and skim. Then add 1 pint turpentine.

4. **Saddlery, to clean.**—Wash with soft-soap. Then apply with a sponge the following recipe: Warm 1 *seer* milk, add ½ *chittâck* dilute sulphuric acid, and when cold 2 *chittâcks* hydrochloric acid. Strain and bottle.

The Duties of the "Dirzie" or Tailor.

These are almost too well known to require description; indeed, they are only referred to here in deference to request. The tailor's duties, briefly, are to give his mistress eight hours *at least* of steady sewing work. If, as is usual, he gets a Sunday holiday, his hours should be longer, but in daily work the tailor should be in his place by eight o'clock A.M., and work till five o'clock, with a break of one hour for food in the middle of the day. In the hot weather it is better to make him work from seven o'clock till eleven, and again from three till seven P.M.

Few *dirzies* can be trusted to cut out without any supervision, and it is far better for the mistress either to do it herself, or to order the tailor to show her the patterns tacked on to the stuff before the fateful scissors are brought into use. In most large towns, however, *dirzies* are to be found who are to all intents and purposes dressmakers, and excellent ones into the bargain. They have not, of course, much taste, and their original draperies are almost always wooden-y; but small dressmakers at home have the same faults. The price charged by such *dirzies* for making a dress varies from five to ten rupees, and as a rule they finish their dresses very neatly indeed. To ladies in out-stations, Butterick's, Schild's, or Weldon's paper patterns will be found invaluable; and by giving the bust and waist measurement when ordering the pattern, there is seldom any radical alteration necessary. If, in addition, the lady is wise enough to have an accurately modelled dress form on which to fit the bodice, the *dirzie* is quite as likely to produce a good fit as the most expensive dressmaker. The difficulty about dress forms is their unwieldiness. Several kinds, however, pack into a fairly small space, while the bazaar dress form, to be had from Butterick's for about fourteen shillings, folds up like an umbrella, and can be altered to any size. All that is necessary to make the bodice part of this form efficient is a wadded bodice made to button over the wire frame. It then answers quite as well as many more expensive kinds, whilst it is nearly as portable as an umbrella. It is an excellent plan to pay five shillings at Redmayne's, or any other good dressmaker, for a scientifically-cut bodice pattern, made to actual measurements.

The *dirzie* should always be supplied with a locking box for his work, a sheet for spreading on the ground, an iron and an ironing board. He is supposed to supply his own scissors and thimble. Where a permanent *dirzie* is not kept, it is an admirable plan to have a man in regularly once a week or fortnight to do general repairs. It must not be forgotten, however, that there is an appreciable chance of infection in giving work out to be done in the bazaars, as the natives are almost criminally lax in all kinds of infectious disease. A permanent tailor almost always saves his own wages, especially if in spare time he is set to do embroidery. Many of them are excellent hands at many kinds of silkwork. Indeed, one of the authors had a complete set of curtains embroidered by her tailor when regular work was slack.

The Duties of the "Dhobi" or Washerman.

The *dhobi's* duties do not bring him much under the eye of the mistress, but there are a few points about his work which require notice. To begin with, it is necessary to fix the place where he is to wash, and insist on his keeping to it. Those who have children, and indeed all who regard their own safety, will arrange for all the washing to be done at their own well. It is both disagreeable and dangerous to have one's wearing apparel steeped in water in which the clothes of smallpox and cholera patients have been cleansed. Yet, if the *dhobi* be allowed to wash at the *ghât*, there can be no certainty that such may not be the case. The *dhobi* should also be carefully watched to see that he does not wash other people's clothes at the same time as those of his ostensible master. It will be found almost impossible, especially in large stations, to prevent the *dhobi* from doing extra washing, but there is no reason why he should wash it in your compound. For this reason it is advisahle, every now and again, to make a raid on your *dhobi's* house, and ruthlessly confiscate any clothes in process of being washed or ironed, which do not belong to you. This generally leads to an *éclaircissement,* in which you, being in possession, have a strong position. As a rule, where there are ladies and children, the *dhobi's* wife comes to count over the dirty clothes, and in many houses this is done twice a week—the clothes given out on Monday coming back on Thursday, and those given on Thursday on Monday. As there is no difficulty—except during the rainy season—in drying the clothes, there is no hardship in giving out the dirty linen even three times a week; in fact, on an emergency, twenty-four hours is sufficient for a small wash.

In regard to the method of cleansing adopted in India, nothing can be more primitive or ineffectual. Cold water, bad soap, and much beating on stones remove the dirt with less certainty than the buttons, and in the effort to bring a presentable *jâogân* (wash) to his mistress, with the least possible labour to himself, the *dhobi* is apt to forget that lace and embroidery is an integral part of underclothing. There is, however, no reason whatever why the recent improvements in cleansing clothes which have revolutionised laundries at home should not be adopted in India. "Sunlight," "Paraffin," "Scotsman," and other soaps make almost all handling needless, the only necessity being warm water and thorough soaping. These, however, owe almost all their efficacy to the paraffin they contain, and this may be used in its pure state with equal advantage. The procedure adopted in most home laundries in England is as follows: A boiler is filled with water, to which one tablespoon of paraffin or kerosene oil has been added to each gallon of water, with a sufficiency of soap to make it blend. The clothes are dipped in this, well rubbed with soap, rolled tight, and set to soak for three hours. The fire is then lit, and the whole boiled for one hour, after which the clothes are removed, well rinsed in two waters, and hung out to dry. No rubbing of any kind being required, the saving in wear and tear is enormous.

Flannels only require steeping for a quarter of an hour, and should *not be boiled;* or if they are simply well rinsed out in warm water in which soap and paraffin have been mixed, they will be found quite clean. They should be at once wrung out and set to dry in the shade. When half dry, pull out carefully and iron. Shrinking is nearly always caused by not having all the waters used of the same temperature, by ineffectual wringing, and slow drying.

Table linen should always be ironed whilst still wet, or it will not glaze. Borax should also be put with the blue.

Coloured clothes are the better of a little alum in the water, and coloured woollen stuffs and embroideries should be washed in water in which bran has been boiled.

It is a good plan to order all flannel things, socks, &c., to be returned the day after they are taken, as this ensures rapidity in washing and drying.

The *dhobi* requires a table, a box for the clothes, an ironing blanket, and a heavy sheet for carrying the dirty clothes.

He will also be the better for a polishing iron—that is to say, one with a convex copper surface. Without some such thing the shirts will never look glazy. It is made moderately hot and rubbed up and down till the polish appears.

It will be found useful to have a supply of "Maypole Soap" of different tints for renovating blouses which fade. The directions are given on each packet.

Scrubb's Ammonia is also useful for woollen tennis dresses.

Capt Geo F. Atkinson

OUR STATION

G.F. Atkinson

Curry and Rice, on forty plates; or the ingredients of social life at "our station" in India. London: W. Thacker, 1911.

"OUR STATION" rejoices in the euphonious appellation of Kabob; it is situated in the plains of Dekchy, in the province of Bobarchy. Far from the busy haunts of a civilized world, and the traffickings of men, and plunged in the wild retirement of a luxuriant jungle, smiles Kabob, "the loveliest village of the plain," basking beneath the rays of the orient sun. Oh! if there be a paradise upon earth,—I suspect it must be this!

The general aspect of Kabob is obtrusively prepossessing; it is bounded on the north and east by a mountainous range of—flaming brick-kilns, whilst on the south and west it is embraced in the tortuous sinuosities of a circumambient ravine populous with pigs. But Kabob—and the truth must be told outright—Kabob is not regarded in the light of being the most attractive station in India. Popular prejudice protests against its secluded locality, and malignant slander whispers, in no faint accents, that a hotter and a duller hole is not to be discovered by the most enterprising and enthusiastic tropical traveller,—

"Remote, unfriended, melancholy, slow."

To be sure, and we must confess it, Kabob is not the capital of the province; the councillors of the kingdom, the great men and the mighty men, do not reside here, nor do the high Church dignitaries, nor any military magnate, not even a general. Then, again, it is not situated on the banks of the holy Gunga; its solitary temple is not reflected in the bosom of that sacred and budgerow-bearing river; nor, again, do its stately dwellings and lofty palm-trees grace the skirts of the Grand Portmanteau Road that intersects the Northern Empire. Steamers do not furrow the waters that flow by its sunburnt banks, dropping as they pass their timely offerings of Allsop and of Bass; nor does the shrill whistle and intermittent puff of the locomotive "molest its ancient solitary reign."—But what of that? Have not the works of the Great Lohar Railroad been commenced upon? Have not the great capitalists of Kabob—the princes, the governors, the captains, the judges, and all the rest of them—taken shares? and does not every one know that in twenty years' time the line will be open, and that Kabob will then be within one hundred and fifty miles only of the nearest point on the line? Ha! ha! What can scandal say then?—Kabob will be isolated no more—benighted no longer. We see it all; the once dim future is now a very meridian blaze of brightness. We see with a distinct vision consignments of bitter beer pouring into our rugged highways. No longer shall the anxious bullock yield his last breath in glorious but unavailing efforts to drag the much-expected load of six dozen chests. The wild tracks shall no longer be made known by the whitened bones which there unburied shine, and tell the startling tale of supplies for British mouths from Briton's isle drawn ruthlessly over many a hundred miles of bleak expanse.

Away with melancholy, then! for Kabob, let me tell you, will be, moreover, a thoroughfare to the lands of the West, when the Great Lohar line is open. Visions haunt me of travellers thronging to our portals—blue-eyed young maidens fresh from dear England; and blear-eyed old Indians, belivered and bedevilled, on their way to England. Visions of claret and Allsop, of choicest delicacies hermetically sealed—all at a reduced tariff. O Kabob! Enviable Kabob, what greatness is in store for thee!

But let us stray through thy sandy meadows and grass-grown streets, fair Kabob! and tell of all thy architectural splendours,—thy accumulated glories of whitewash and of thatch,—thy mud-built edifices and thy mud-built cottages,—thy mud-built enclosure-walls, in all their mud-begotten majesty!

Ah! there is the parade-ground; there, on that bare and barren plain, do our dusky Trojans learn the art of war; there the embryo hero rises from the pristine performance of the goose-step to a full knowledge of brigade manœuvres. In order that Kabob may enjoy the full benefit of the westerly breezes—which in summer, let me tell you, blow with summary and unquenchable fury, but which, nevertheless, are highly appreciated —"Our Station," as usual, faces the west. On the eastern side, then, of the Parade, are the "Lines." First, is a row of apparently magnified sentry-boxes, commonly called Bells of Arms, which appellation denotes their object. In rear of these are the huts for the native troops,—small mud-wall tenements roofed with thatch, amidst rows of sickly plantains.

Immediately behind these are the domiciles for the officers, in two or more lines,—each dwelling, commonly yclept a bungalow, in its own peculiar territory, which varies in dimensions, as orthodoxy had originally designed it, under the fond but fanciful delusion that subalterns had small and field officers great requirements. These bungalows, you observe, look like exaggerated beehives, perched upon mile-stones,—a judicious combination of mud, whitewash, and thatch. Stop; we will go into one presently; let us now see only the outer life of Kabob. There, that square whitewashed edifice, with an excrescence at one end, looking for all the world like an extinguisher on a three-dozen chest!—what is it? You may well ask. It is the church! a regular protestant building! protesting against everything architectural, æsthetic, ornamental, or useful; designed and built according to a Government prescription. Next to it is our assembly-room and theatre; just beyond you see the hospitals; then comes the racket-court, and to the left is the well-stocked burial-ground. This is the course, where the live splendour of Kabob resort when shades of evening close upon us. There is the band-stand, and this is the station bath. On the extreme right are the barracks, for you must know that Europeans man the guns of our battery that is quartered here. That is the artillery-mess, and opposite lives Stickerdoss, who sells Europe goods, and can accommodate you with anything, from a baby's bottle to a bolster.

Now we must turn to the left, and verging from the confines of the military cantonment, we plunge into territory that is under civil sway. These are the civil lines; those flat-roofed edifices in the Brummagen Tuscan order, all pillars, plaster, and pea-green paint, are the courts of law; this shed is the treasury, and those men guarding it are Our Magistrate's own peculiars. This piece of ground, with its five cabbages, three peach-trees, and patch of onions, is the Government Botanical Garden; and, on your right and left, those wide-verandahed habitations are the dwelling-places of the civilians.

And now, as the sun is getting piping hot, let us gallop home; and after breakfast we will make a day of it, and you shall be introduced to all the beauty and fashion of "Our Station."

OUR PADRE.

OUR Spiritual Pastor and Master at Kabob is the Rev. Josiah Ginger, unctuous in appearance, redolent of fat, and with a face beaming like the sun on a gravel-walk!

A worthy divine of the *Ancien Régime* is "Our Padre," as the pastors of our flocks are denominated throughout the East; his views are of the broad and popular kind, he looks upon it that the pastimes and pleasures of this mundane sphere can be participated in by the Clergy without any invested longitude of visage or sanctimoniousness of gait. He cannot discover that holiness must be exhibited by a concomitant exhibition of the whites of one's eyes; that purity of life is necessarily expressed by a white neck-tie, or practical piety by a rigidity of limb. He considers that the duties of the pastor may well be enlivened by the sports of the field; and that creeds and confectionery, doctrines and devilled kidneys, spirituality and sociability, may consistently run hand in hand, while hams and hermetically-sealed delicacies are not entirely irreconcilable with heavenly-mindedness. And we must confess it, that the combinations are effected with striking and satisfactory results, as we find that the salad of the Saturday, as manufactured by "Our Padre" at mess, in no way clashes with the sermon of the Sunday; that the sick in hospital are visited and attended zealously and lovingly, though he does drive a dog-cart, patronize the Sky races, and burn the midnight oil over a pool at billiards or at a rubber of whist.

Mrs. Ginger is in England, looking after a domestic flock of little Gingers, since which time Ginger has become a member of our mess, to the manifest improvement in the cookery; for the concoction of savoury stews, and the ministration of devilled toast on improved principles, have been instituted and established by him with unqualified applause.

To be sure, we do hear it affirmed that "Our Padre" is a little too precipitate in his movements from church, and that his exit from the pulpit, disrobing, and departure from the sacred edifice is accomplished before some of the more devout have recovered from their genuflexions; and that he "polishes off" the service, as it is heathenly expressed, in a manner that suggests hot coffee waiting at the mess.

Then we have allusions, but decidedly of a less objective nature, upon the brevity of the discourses; and certainly Ginger, in his delivery, does not hang fire. He disengages himself of his sentiments with an *aplomb* signally attractive, and which keeps the soldiery awake; for to be borne away from one's couch at the least suffocating hour of the early morning, and then to be deposited under the soporific influence of a punkah, exposed to the drowsy drawlings of a parson who attenuates his words to the fullest limit of his breath, is apt indeed to restore one to the land of Nod!

Now, Ginger, we must confess it, doesn't give his congregation a chance; he tells his tale with telling brevity and unction. And what though scandal does declare that he possesses a series of sermons which are gone through in rotation with as rigid a regularity as the movements of the planetary bodies! What of that? A good thing can't be told too often; and if the matter is pronounced to be of a mild texture, Ginger can, when he likes, preach "tellingly," and touch the hearts of his hearers, I can assure you, as on the occurrence of a recent fatal catastrophe at Kabob, the sermon delivered on the occasion, and which was obviously original, set off some of the "weaker vessels" into explosive sobs, accompanied with hysteria, whilst the main body of the congregation went boo-hooing out of church.

So close to the sacred pile, let us step in and explore its architectural beauties. That sable janitor, who holds the living at the gate, will unfold its pea-green portals. His functions are to protect the sacred edifice from spoliation and wrong. The duties of this other venerable Oriental consist in preparing

"The taper's glimmering light"

for the evening service, and furnishing fire for—"Our Padre's" cheroot.

This, then, is the steeple; but "the soft, sweet chimes of the Sabbath bells, that so peacefully float from afar!" peal only in the lively imagination. The calling to prayers at Kabob is effected by a less elaborate process: a heathen, "simple and unadorned," scales recklessly the lofty walls, through the instrumentality of an infirm ladder, and then and there bangs spasmodically and intermittently on a discordant gong, until "Our Padre" is attired in his vestments, when the lamplighter, with preconcerted views, rushes frantically forth, and shouts "No more, no more." Mark the interior economy of the structure: that timber receptacle, which does double duty—not of "a bed by night, a chest of drawers by day," but of pulpit as well as of reading-desk—those communion-rails, that table now bereft of its cover, that font. Observe the purity of the ecclesiastical style of architecture selected, obviously the early Indian or Carpenteresque, one of the periods of the "Disappointed Gothic."

But there goes Ginger; that is his bungalow into which you see he has just driven, and all that multitude of "the sick, the maimed, the lame, the halt, and the blind," that are thronging in at his gate are the afflicted ones of Kabob, and of the surrounding villages, who come in for the food which is distributed to them weekly from the Compassionate Fund, which Ginger established, and of which he is almoner. Did you ever set eyes on such a mass of infirmity, decrepitude, and human disorganization? There is a genuine leper; and there you may see a real, living picture of those crowds of impotent folk who thronged the highways of Judæa some eighteen centuries ago, and who waited expectantly by Bethesda's pool for an anticipated cure.

Come in and see Ginger; he will give you a hearty welcome and some excellent bitter beer. His sanctum will recall your college days,—gowns, guns, and hunting-whips promiscuously combine: here a MS. sermon lies complacently by a cookery-book and a *Bell's Life;* while there a packet of letters and a prospectus of the Sky races, with the hospital report and a receipt for milk-punch.

But Ginger is engaged. I find a poor gunner died this morning, and he is off to bury him.

Thus, you see, with the sick and afflicted thronging at his gate, and the dead awaiting interment, "Our Padre," amid the flash of light and cheerful pleasures, has many a sterner duty to perform, from which he never flinches; and if he participates in the sports and amusements of the gay and the healthy, he can and does share in the sorrows of the bereaved, sympathize with the afflicted, and cheer the couch of the sick. Ask the soldiers in the barracks, they are the best judges. But you need not go so far, for the fact is well recognized at "Our Station."

OUR BATH.

Nor are we without the charm of a fashionable watering-place, whither the gay resident of Kabob may resort, to enjoy the luxury of bathing, relieved for a while from the oppression of the

"Busy town's tumultuous crowds,"

absolved from the rigid formalities of urban life, and where he can indulge in the glorious liberty of the subject by an unrestricted freedom of attire.

But our watering-place is an exceptive one; it is not situated on the shore of the wide-spreading ocean,

"Where all agree
With one consent to rush into the sea."

Nor are our eyes gladdened by the prospect of lovely woman basking on the glittering shingle, listening to the plash of the receding wave, and watching with attentive eye the sunburnt mariner, or the snowy sail of the bonnie bark as she rides on the waters blue.

We have not our pea-green seats of gridiron build, on which delight to sit those virgin forms of loveliness absorbed in widespreading hats and the latest novel. We have not our groups of rosy-cheeked, laughing children to trundle their intractable hoops against our legs, or to project their incorrigible shuttlecocks into our unoffending eyes. We do not rejoice in chaises with quadrupeds that have acquired the art of compassing the very smallest extent of ground in their hour's trot; nor have we troupes of Jerusalem ponies, garnished with their draperied saddles, wrought into a canter by the impulsive donkey-boys, and bearing on their belaboured backs the merriest of dear England's fair ones.

These things are not in the nature of our watering-place; ours is charmingly situated on the shores of the waterless nullah that bisects Kabob; and the water where the delights of the bath are effected does not come with its rolling waves plashing on a sand-girt shore, but trickles from an adjoining well, from whence it has been forced by the unremitting energies of horned cattle, and where it plashes (when disturbed) against the plastered sides of a brick-built reservoir.

This is our watering-place of Kabob, in which the form of woman—lovely woman—is never seen; where the male species, with all the seclusion of a Parliament House, have its enjoyment entirely to themselves. Let us betake ourselves to the festive scene; the trip, the change of air, the bath, will revive our falling nature.

We find a bungalow of one large room, with its floor scooped out for the reception of the enticing fluid. We find ourselves plunged into a vortex of human society: it is the season, the very height of the season, and all the fashionable world of Kabob, of the masculine gender, have flocked hither—the early risers from their morning ride, the later risers from their sleepless cots; the Coffee-shop has yielded its ample store, and the votaries of Mocha and Bohea, with the subsidiary libations of gossip and of "jaw," have one and all become the votaries of the water and Companions of the Bath.

Here, on the left, is Scrape Doss reaping the beard of some hirsute visitor. See with what dexterity he wields the razor; mark how its polished edge is whetted by its rapid application to his bared and honelike arm; observe the velocity with which the snowy lather is laid on, and then more rapidly removed (the patient's nose acting as a helm, by which the motions of the pliant chin are guided by the skilful excisor). And look how the jovial crew disport themselves in the water,—how they

"Plunge about like porpoises or whales at play."

But what is the prime agent of their fun? A water-carrier's bag!—the inflated hide of some immolated sheep, which is formed into a Neptune's car, and upon which it becomes an object of ambition to learn the art of equitation—an art which combines the difficulties of the saddle with the poising peculiarities of the tight-rope. The simplest thing in the world is to ride upon a "mussock"—just like swimming and skating, when you know how to effect it—but a most incorrigible thing is a "mussock" to an early learner. It is so detestably buoyant, nothing will induce it to let you mount,—no ticklish steed was ever so unmanageable; but you get the better of it, stride across it, and, skilfully balanced, grip its sides, determined to fall neither to the right hand nor to the left; when the remorseless monster slips away backward from beneath you, and you are plunged headlong into the foaming water; or it springs upward at the bows, and in your ignominious fall, while the circling wave closes over your eyes, you witness it shooting up triumphantly into the air. Then, when you regain the surface, and your hair and the water are removed from your eyes, you detect the object of your immersion floating impenitently, and with a sort of sidelong glance of derision, right at the other end of the Bath.

Look at the essayists—those youthful aspirants for "mussock" honours in every stage of acquired skill. Here is one who, to an unimpassioned and unbiassed observer, the "mussock" might certainly be pronounced to be invariably the rider, and not the ridden. There, on that side, are veterans in the art, who have converted their Neptune's cars into men of war, and with energy and vigour contest for the supremacy of the wave. Here are incipient swimmers, endeavouring to overcome that fatal facility for sinking involuntarily to the bottom. There the more experienced, who have acquired the elementary knowledge of the art, and who are in a delectable state of mind at being able to remain on the surface, are floating joyfully about, but occasionally becoming the victims of contending factions, and getting ducked There, on the banks, are those who have disported themselves sufficiently, and are being groomed and rubbed down by their attendant slaves.

But we have joined in the morning's *divertissement*—we have laughed, we have been splashed, we have been shaven, and we have been dressed; and now, as the sun is frightfully hot, we will have the hood of our buggy put up, and rattle home to breakfast, feeling for a time invigorated, and rejoicing to know that we have the opportunity afforded to us of enjoying the luxury of a watering-place at "Our Station."

OUR BAZAR.

AT the eastern side of Kabob are the habitations devoted to the native population,—constructions of mud that frown grimly at each other across the narrow, dirty ways that separate them, and which form the thoroughfares that intersect, bisect, and dissect the Great Bazar of Kabob. The dwellings, in their prevailing feature, combine the attractiveness of the primitive mound of earth with the characteristics of the pigsty. They form blocks of mud, perforated with apertures of very limited dimensions. But there are grand exceptions, for the Great Bazar can boast of at least three mansions, double in their stories, and the amount of brick-coloured paint which adorns their *facades*, in the shape of hideous demons and still more hideous animals, inexplicable in their anatomy, together with portraitures of celebrated Eastern kings, with the very yellowest of complexions and the very widest-opened eyes, would strike admiration into the heart of every beholder. And then the upper stories, with their gorgeous balconies, at least fourteen inches wide, with daintily-carved parapets a good seven inches high, and painted every colour under the sun, shed an air of aristocratic splendour around. These are the palaces of the nobles. There, in that one, more splendid than its fellows, dwells Chouse Lall; and here, in this one opposite, resides Bunya Doss, the great contractor, of the grain caste. There, below, in the open shop, reposing on their hams, and smoking their hubble-bubbles, are his assistants, dispensing grain of every kind to the tempted passer-by; and there, in front, stands a buffalo, sniffing the good things which the uncouth monster has already grabbed at on his way, and for which his dense hide has been punctured accordingly. Opposite is a confectioner's shop; to be sure we miss the ice-creams and tartlets, the jellies, and the buns—Bath and plum, the pastry and the cakes; but do we not see, and do not our mouths water at the contents of those brazen dishes, those savoury-looking mounds of tawny-coloured sweetmeats—combinations of oil, of treacle, and of flour, upon which the eyes of those two urchins have fallen and are feasting; and in which the Oriental damsel, with coin at command, is about to invest, lured by that pungent odour which, penetrating our olfactories, reaches to the very roots of our hair?

But let us pass on, if that gaunt, half-famished hound, all covered with sores—a very Lazarus of dogs—will but gratify our wishes by making way, and adjourning with his bone to some more convenient locality. There goes a native, carrying his bed and walking; and in that you see how such a performance was enacted some eighteen hundred years ago, when those miraculously cured of their diseases took up their beds and walked—not, you perceive, as the imaginative artists of the West love to portray such scenes, by depicting weak men staggering along under huge and highly-carved four-posters; for, you observe that eight short sticks and a few yards of string are all that composes an Oriental's bed. And this act of taking up his bed and walking is the commonest object in an Eastern city that falls upon the eye. There goes a woman with her pitcher of water from the well, bearing it so dexterously on her head,—a performance by which the daughters of the East acquire that uprightness of form which particularly characterises them, and which consequently imparts to them their greatest attraction.

But let us get away from this din. That fellow who is about to feed, and who is blowing so desperately into that confounded horn, is driving the Devil away—quite enough to do it, I should imagine. This is the Hindoo temple, and this violent ringing of bells and banging of gongs would, I suspect, have a similar effect of driving away their gods.

Take care, or that Brahminee bull will have his horns into your ribs. Look at the bloated beast,—he is holy, and the Hindoos reverence him. He is let loose in the streets, and is fed till, as you see, he can scarcely walk, save to reach the grain merchant's open store, and help himself at his will. Capital practice for our Griffs are these bulls: to shoot one openly would be to create an uproar in the city; but great sport they afford, and bullets go plump into their fat sides with a sound delicious to the ear. See, there goes one limping along. I shrewdly suspect a rifle-ball has very accidentally struck that joint, and that rifle the property of some Griff. We sometimes entice them to our gardens, and teach them the art of drawing water from our wells, at which we find they are great adepts, and to which the Hindoos do not object, as it saves their pockets, and their religion is not affected, as the animals are not injured. But if the Hindoos are glad to be absolved from having to feed them, the public at large are only too rejoiced to get rid of what is universally considered to be a nuisance to "Our Station."

OUR WEDDING

OUR WEDDING.

WE all knew it would be so. Mrs. Aunks declares that she distinctly affirmed it would be a match, on the very first night that she saw Captain Cheeny talking to Carry Cinnamon at the Band; and we all know how adhesive he has been to the Chutneys' carriage ever since, and how he is always to be seen sloping away to the Civil Lines at incongruous hours. Then the fact unquestionably must be true, because, when Mrs. McGhee had a vision of Barbara being married to that insane ensign who made proposals to old McGhee, she instantly got the refusal of all the orange blossoms that Pysa Doss possessed, and his are the best in the station; and, as Mrs. Chutney now wanted them, she told Pysa Doss, who announced it to Mrs. McGhee, who told Mrs. Gander, who mentioned it to Bullet (the fat wife of Corporal Bullet, who is in her service, and whom she calls her lady's-maid), who spoke of it to the ayah, who repeated it to Mrs. Gudder, who at once ordered her carriage, and paid fifteen visits that very morning, on purpose to communicate the intelligence to the whole Station.

Our weddings at Kabob have been few and far between: Ginger, our Padre, I must say, has had an easy time of it, so far as the tying of nuptial knots is concerned; and I suspect he will be glad of this event, if it is only to get rid of that detestable and everlastingly-in-the-way license which has been floating about for so many months on his library table, getting most incorrigibly mixed up with recipes for sprained ankles, receipts for resurrection stews; and sharing the cover of his domestic cookery with his own last will and testament.

But the happy day for the lovers has arrived—a "bright sunny" day, and a furious hurricane hurling its burning clouds of dust all over Kabob. The Chutneys are to give the breakfast, or, rather the dinner; for the ceremony of splicing is to be performed at dusk. The sun has betaken itself to its fiery bed. Ginger has arrived, and Cheeney and his best man, Dhalbhat, have rattled up under the portico in a state of excitement and full dress. The guests then begin to invade the church, and, martyrs to stiff-laced collars, the male species wish it was all over; while the ladies, in expectation, and with much fanning, long to see how the bride will look. The night is closing in; Ginger doubts if he will be able to see without lights; but he knows the service by heart, though not from too much practice. Cheeny has been hovering about the door, straining his eyes in the joyful direction of his coming bride, while the best man entertains serious thoughts of rushing off to see what has happened; when the rattle of carriages is heard, the long-expected ones have come, and there is the blushing Carry led up "the long-drawn aisle," supported by Chutney on her left and Cheeny on her right, and backed by her group of bridesmaids, like "clustering constellations." Letitia, and Bella, and Barbara, and Mrs. Byle's Helena—a maiden of full five summers all decorated alike in the whitest of dresses and the bluest of et-ceteras. The bride, in the costliest of silk, with a figured lace veil that "flowed in easy negligence" from her bridal wreath, looking the very essence of a bride. There is Mrs. Chutney, and there are the Capsicums, and there is Mrs. McGhee in the everlasting pea-green, and furnished with her "new dinner set," and there ——. But Ginger has commenced, and very soon are the happy pair irrevocably one. Cheeny, at the altar, is the first to salute his bride;—then Mrs. Chutney showers down her kisses, and the Colonel is the first to call her "Mrs. Cheeny." Congratulations follow—the favours are bestowed—the books are signed—the happy pair drive off in the Chutneys' carriage (the coachman of which, inspired with zeal, has pinned on his favour on the very apex of his turban),—and we all disperse.

Then we take a turn on the Mall to breathe a little fresh air, and display our favours to the bats. We while away an hour, until we gather again at the Chutneys. Then there is a mighty spread and grand display,—

"The polish'd marble and the shining plate;"

the table is crowded, the night more sultry than ever, the punkahs drive about hot wind, and the ices relapse into tepid water. But dinner is over, the health of the happy pair is drunk right cordially, pretty things and jocose things are said, and, in spite of the heat, we are all very merry and all very gay. Then the happy pair bid us adieu, and retire; and as they are to pass their honeymoon some forty miles away, they are to perform the journey in palankeens. The torches are lit; the bride, relieved of her finery, has been packed in her case; the loving swain scrambles into his; they near the portico; we rush forth and give them a lusty cheer, as, in their palankeens "and four," they take their departure.

Then we reassemble in the drawing-room, and though the night is very hot, and "a plentiful moisture encumbers each flower" (of loveliness), we resolve to be jolly.

"Oh, what remains, what lingers yet,
To cheer us in the darkening hour?—
The *hop* remains!"

And so, with some fair ministrant at the piano, we waltz, we galope, and we polk,—we flirt prodigiously with the bridesmaids,—we quaff Moselle so sparkling and so bright,—we feel its convivial effect, and we are so elated at beholding the happiness of the newly-married couple, that a feeling is kindled within us to fling ourselves on the knees of devotion, and resign ourselves to matrimony—and Letitia. The company, however, beginning to depart, rouses us to a sense of our danger;—

"The rattling chariots' clash, the torches' glare,"

dispel our matrimonial illusion; but we fervently hope that the blissful pair just married will enjoy every happiness, and that we may speedily welcome them back to "Our Station."

Maud Diver

The Englishwoman in India.
London: William Blackwood, 1909.

CHAPTER II.

WIFE.

"Jack's own Jill goes up the hill,
To Murree or Chakrata;
Jack remains, and dies in the plains,
And Jill re-marries soon after."

In the above quaint version of the old nursery jingle did Rudyard Kipling record his earliest impressions of married life in India; a life hedged about with dangers, difficulties, and hardships rarely dreamed of in our placid English homes.

If Jill's conduct is not always as exemplary as it might be, it is certain that her life and surroundings are not always of the most elevating description. Nor is she invariably as light-minded as Mr

Kipling here depicts her. His clever little verse presents one side of the picture only. That there is another and brighter side to it he himself would be the last to deny. Jill is not always wafted hillward by the first whiff of hot air from the dread furnace to come. She does, on occasion, stand by her husband, through bitter and sweet, through fire and frost; and what such a standard of wifehood costs the brave women who live up to it, only the wives of India know. For these unrecorded heroines are a nation without a history. At all events, their history—and a noble one it is—rarely supplies effective material for fiction, and in consequence their existence has almost come to be doubted on this side of the ocean.

Mr Kipling's Jill is the type of Anglo-

Indian wife best known to English readers; and yet how much less than little do they know of the subtle temptations which beset her at every turn! So serious are the charges made against India's morals—and the morals of her wives in particular—that it is impossible to present any adequate picture of Anglo-Indian married life without touching upon this difficult question. But, in common justice to our sister-women over seas, it is only fair to say all that can be said in palliation of a state of things which cannot, unhappily, be denied point-blank.

In the first place, the random assertion that the tone of social morality is lower in India than in England, is unjust and untrue. It is a fact that women of the upper middle class—wives of service and professional men—are more strictly encompassed by "the conventions" than Anglo-Indian women of the same standing. Yet it does not follow that the sheltered wives of England are justified in assuming the *rôle* of Pharisee. They will do better to consider, instead, whether the saving grace of circumstances may not be, in part, responsible for their own integrity. Circumstance is, after all, the supreme test of character, and India tests a woman's character to the uttermost. For, with all its surface laughter and lightness, Indian life is real, and you live it desperately from start to finish.

Of the social atmosphere enough has been said. In a Hill station—more especially in Simla—it is irresistibly infectious. But the grass widow in the Hills has pitfalls more definite to contend with; and perhaps the two most insidious are amateur theatricals and the military man on leave. It is hardly too much to say that one or other of these dominant factors in Hill station life is accountable for half the domestic tragedies of India. The proverbial relation between Satan and idle hands is too often confirmed in the Himalayas; and for a woman who is young, comely, and gifted with a taste for acting, Simla is assuredly not the most innocuous place on God's earth. Here frivolity reaches its highest height, and social pleasures are, to all appearance, the end and aim of every one's existence. Yet here, in the midst of this throng of busy idlers, the great task of governing the Empire must go forward, come what may.

A correspondent, writing from the great

Hill capital, makes special mention of this anomaly. "Simla," he writes, "would be a far more favourable seat for Government, and energies and faculties would find fuller development there, if the social current were far less strong; and those leaders of society would be public benefactors who could find some means of stemming it. No doubt the greater part of the pleasure-seeking and holiday-making is done by the ladies, but a very large share in it is visibly taken by the men; and we are disposed to believe that the extreme backwardness of Anglo-Indian society in recognising the modern advance in the intellectual and social position of women is due to the frivolity of the overwhelming majority of Anglo-Indian women, who are not only devotees of fashion themselves, but do their utmost to divert the energies of the men from work (which they cannot share) to pleasure and frivolity likewise."

A grave charge this—the graver since it comes from an Anglo-Indian, not from an English, pen. That the "Simla woman" (by which is meant not all women in Simla, but the typical devotee of Simla society) *is* frivolous, and free and easy both in mind and manners, is a truth which her most ardent admirer could not deny. One plea, at least, may be put forward in her defence—namely, that if former generations of her type helped to make Simla what it is, the tables have now been turned, and it is Simla which makes—or rather mars—the woman of to-day. Moreover, in a country where men and women are constantly thrown together under conditions which tend to minimise formalism and conventional restraint, where leave is plentiful and grass widows—willing and unwilling—abound, it is scarcely surprising that the complications and conflicting duties of married life should prove appreciably greater than they are elsewhere.

One last word remains to be said for Jill before taking leave of her altogether. When society sits in judgment on her and her kind, it is prone to overlook the possible share her husband may have had in making her what she is. If a man be careless of his wife's reputation, if he fail to warn her of dangers to which he alone can open her eyes, if—through indolence, indifference, or a mistaken notion of unselfishness—he leaves her too entirely to her own devices, leaves her to walk blindfold upon difficult ground, he has only himself to thank if his carelessness recoils upon his own head. It is not to be presumed that every case of the kind can be thus accounted for; but it is only just, while condemning the foolishness and frivolity of the wife, to make some allowance for possible indifference or unwisdom on the part of the husband.

And so, enough of Jill—a woman not without charm, whatever her faults and follies; and who are we, after all, that we should cast the first stone at her?

The Anglo-Indian wife who elects to stand fast at her post, come what may, lives in another world altogether. If Fate cast her lot in the North, she is called upon, year after year, to face that pitiless destroyer of youth and beauty—the Punjab hot weather. She learns to know all the horror hidden in that dread word—cholera. She grows intimate with the malicious music of the mosquito, with the habits of crows, squirrels, wasps, and punkah-coolies—a unique revelation this last. She is initiated into the agonies of hot weather house-keeping, and grows skilful, through bitter experience, in grasping the fleeting moment between toughness and putrefaction, when the joint may possibly prove eatable. She learns to sleep in full noonday, and drive abroad at midnight in search of a few whiffs of lukewarm air. At sundown, when her long daily imprisonment is ended, she plays "hot-weather Badminton" in the club garden, or reads the "Home" papers in company with five or six other patient, weary women, under the jerky little outside punkah that so grimly resembles a gallows-tree.

Such is her monotonous round of life from May to October—five red-hot, interminable months; unless, indeed, her husband secures two months' leave, and then . . . What pen can depict the rapture of that hillward journey—that magic transit from the parched, chess-board landscape of the plains to the drenched green glory of the mountains? Only the woman who has dared to brave the merciless furnace of June and July tastes to the full the ecstasy of that wondrous ascent to moisture, coolness—life—a very foretaste of resurrection! And thus she, too, reaps her reward.

But although the wives of India may be roughly divided into the two types already named, these by no means exhaust the list. Nothing has yet been said of the way of life peculiar to those little lonely stations, where five or six English folk—with, perhaps, nothing save their colour in common—are thrown wholly upon one another's society day after day, and month after month; a life wherein social temptations are few, but one that creates temptations peculiar to itself, a fact strikingly illustrated in one of Kipling's cleverest Indian stories. Yet it is possible, even in such unpromising surroundings, for the nest-loving Englishwoman to make herself a home, and an attractive one to boot, provided that she be blessed with a happy marriage, and a cheerful and resourceful mind.

The delights and difficulties of "camping" should by no means be overlooked, since the civilian's wife—more especially in the higher grades—is fated to spend a large portion of the year under canvas. In one marked respect, also, camp life differs from all other modes of existence in India. Here, at least, the woman has no social element to reckon with; here her atmosphere is wholesomely and monotonously domestic, and she is dependent for amusement upon physical exercise, change of scene, and her own mental resources. For a woman who rides well, and possesses an absorbing hobby of any kind, camping is one of the pleasantest and healthiest features of life in the East. But a hobby she must have, or the long lonely hours, during which the door of her husband's office tent is hermetically sealed to her, will hang very heavily on her hands.

And now an end. Be it remembered

only that the foregoing inadequate sketches of Punjab life do not, by any means, represent the ways and worries of India as a whole. Climate and customs differ appreciably in all the four great Presidencies of our vast Empire; yet one dominant feature marks them all. Their men and women are primarily social, secondarily domestic; and the reason of this state of things is not far to seek. English men and women in India are, as it were, members of one great family, aliens under one sky. Their social conditions have been handed down to them from the days when India practically meant life-long banishment; and so long as they hold by these India will be a pleasant and friendly land, even though it be a land of exile.

CHAPTER III.

MOTHER.

"I do perceive here a divided duty."

—SHAKSPERE.

IF marriage complicates a woman's life in India, the advent of children—blessed advent though it be,—scarcely tends to simplify matters. At no time, and in no land, is it an easy thing to keep in perfect balance the conflicting duties of wife and mother. But in India it is hardest of all. If a woman needs loyalty, strength, and fearlessness anywhere, it is there.

From the hour that a nursery is established under her roof, the Anglo-Indian mother must be prepared for a hand-to-hand contest with the two great gods of the East —Dirt and *Dastúr:* a contest in which supervision—constant, personal supervision —is the one weapon that can never fail. But here, as always in India, we find her torn in two between the imperative demands of society and home: and as the small sweet hands cling closer about her heart, the voices of home and conscience will not easily be put to silence, or ignored. She will be a stranger to peace till the problem has been frankly faced—and solved.

Where money permits, the solution will frequently take the form of an English nurse: a step in the right direction. Yet even an English nurse is no less liable than her mistress to suffer from the effects of the climate, from the all-pervading tendency to let things slide: and it is just this insidious atmosphere of slackness, coupled with the absence of nursery discipline, that makes the Anglo-Indian child a byword in England, and too often embitters its first years of life "at Home." Those first years "at Home"—how willingly the young mother thrusts the thought of them out of her heart! Yet, defer them as she may, there is no thrusting them out of her child's life: and every woman worthy of her calling will see to it that the inevitable change shall be as little painful as may be for all concerned. To this end she will be zealous in guarding her children from promiscuous intimacy with the native servants, whose propensity to worship at the shrine of the *Baba-lōg* is unhappily apt to demoralise the small gods and goddesses they serve. There are those who sneer at this form of zeal as a "fad." But facts cannot be sneered away: and the foster-mothers of England could marshal facts enough to silence all such light-hearted scoffers: while, in India itself, the wisdom of entrusting our children to English nurses from the first is far more widely recognised than it was fifteen years ago. Yet is the "base rupee" a factor which even the most devoted mother cannot afford to overlook: wherefore an English nurse still remains a luxury rather than a *sine quâ non* in Anglo-Indian homes.

But the problem of nurse or ayah pales, all too soon, before one of infinitely greater moment—the rival claims of India and England; of husband and child. Sooner or later the lurking shadow of separation takes definite shape; asserts itself as a harsh reality; a grim presence, whispering the inevitable question: "Which shall it be?" A question not lightly to be answered: if indeed, in generalised form, it can be answered at all. Every woman, when her time comes, must face it frankly, from her own individual standpoint; and thresh out her own individual answer according to her lights. An unsatisfactory one it is bound to be, at best; and countless brave hearts have been strained to breaking point during those bitter hours of indecision.

Love him as she may, it costs more for a wife, and still more for a mother, to stand loyally by husband in India, than the sheltered wives of England can conceive: and the rare woman whose heart is balanced equally between the two great loves of her life, finds herself, at the moment of crisis, in a far sorrier case than her more one-sided sisters. Be her decision what it may, it will not be come at without wakeful nights of anxious self-communing and deliberation:

nor may she hope, either way, to escape the poisoned arrows of regret.

But for many—possibly the majority—the struggle is less severe. Strong temperamental bias may even eliminate it altogether; so fatally easy is it to enlist conscience on the side of our urgent desires. The woman who is a born helpmate and companion to the man she loves will inevitably persuade herself that her place is at his side: while she who is primarily a mother will find in the helplessness of her children a conclusive argument against shifting her God-given privileges and responsibilities on to other shoulders, however willing these may be to bear them. In every case the thoughtful woman finds herself hedged about with a host of minor considerations, to all of which due weight must be given: and one of these, at least, is worth emphasising. Wherever there is delicacy, there the keen anxious eye of love is needed to detect and check minor symptoms that may lead to serious illness, or even loss of life. Child or husband, the claim of physical weakness is supreme.

There remains also the man himself, who may greatly help or hinder her in her bitter hour. Mere selfishness apart, some men are unquestionably more dependent on their wives than others: some again will be jealous of their very children, and will stoutly refuse to see why they and their comfort should be sacrificed to a "woman's fad": while, on the other hand, there are always cheerful souls who in no way object to an occasional spell of bachelor life, though the wives of such are not often as grateful as they might be for this amiable idiosyncrasy,—simplify matters how it may. Happily, however, there do exist men and women whom love has so triumphantly incorporated that each is ready as the other to face any sacrifice marriage may demand of them. And verily they have their reward!

But whatever her ultimate decision, there are two resolves that the Anglo-Indian mother will do well to make and keep, so far as in her lies. In the first place, she should at least go home with her children, and see them safely launched upon their new path of life; in the second, she should register a vow, and keep it—Fate permitting—never to desert either husband or children for more than three or four years at a stretch. Think of it, English wives and mothers, and let the thought keep the door of your lips when you are tempted to sit in judgment on the Anglo-Indian woman and all her works!

Nor is the personal problem all. The question of "which" merely gives place to the question of "when." Sooner or later—cruelly soon, it seems to most of us—comes the inevitable moment when the voice of conscience can no longer be silenced; when the very love wherewith she loves her children is become a two-edged sword that shall pierce her heart; and she knows that they must go: knows that there is a limit of age beyond which she dare not keep them without risk of handicapping them, physically and morally, in the race of life. Physically, because the staple foods of childhood have far less nutritive value in India than in England, and the constant moving comes harder every year upon their sensitive nervous systems, to say nothing of the difficulty of obtaining pure and suitable food at Indian rest-houses and railway stations: morally, because routine and discipline are not easily enforced in a land where constant allowance must be made for the climate and the life; and because—let India's champions say what they will—it is still less easy to keep the eager, all-observant little minds fearlessly upright and untainted in an atmosphere of petty thefts and lies, such as natives look upon as mere common-sense and good policy. Children are quick to discover this; and the idea is both inviting and infectious to some temperaments,—far more so than to others. For here, as elsewhere, it is the fine-fibred nature—responsive, impressionable, capable of the highest development—that is most apt to suffer harm in body and mind.

Thus, to the question "when," as to that of "which," no abstract answer is forthcoming. It is a problem every woman must face and solve for herself when her bad moment comes; though most thoughtful mothers agree in fixing the limit of age at seven years; and few will deny that the sooner after the fifth year a child can leave India, the better for its future welfare. This is a hard saying; and it is perhaps needless to add that it is rarely acted upon. For in the depreciated rupee human weakness finds an ally of the strongest; and more young lives have paid dearly for its supremacy than those who cannot or will not face facts are ever likely to believe.

But early or late the cruel wrench must come,—the crueller, the longer deferred. One after one the babies grow into companionable children; one after one England claims them, till the mother's heart and house are left unto her desolate. Empty nurseries, empty verandahs; only the haunting music of small footsteps and clear voices still troubles and glorifies her dreams. Yet in all likelihood she will continue to dance and ride and entertain with undiminished zest. Heartlessness? Frivolity? In a few cases, possibly, but in most the sheer pluck of the race that has a prejudice in favour of making the best of things as they are, and never whimpering over the inevitable. Consider the words of one who may be reckoned among these last: "Indian life is full of fears, which lie always in the background of the bravest minds, and which may at any moment start, fully armed, into the line of vision. Above and over all that tragic shadow of separation, which is the keynote of Anglo-India—unavoidable always, and always a tragedy. And yet one laughs, and is as happy as circumstances will permit. One cannot always be shedding tears of renunciation. If we choose the lesser of two evils and stay with the man, we will not damn his life with sadness and recrimination. He has his anxieties too. We take life as we find it. It is ungracious, ungrateful, always to want what we have not got; and yet . . . well, the ache is there!"

Thus, on a note of courage and endurance, our Anglo-Indian woman closes her first chapter of motherhood in exile, to reopen it afresh, under other conditions, when the great ships bring back her sons and daughters, grown almost out of recognition, yet not always out of sympathy and love. Then, with a heart sobered by experience and self-knowledge, she takes up her interrupted task, and carries it through to the best of her power, till wedding bells "ring out the old, ring in the new"; till the years of her husband's work are accomplished, and it is she herself who must go, leaving a younger generation to tread the same paths, and uphold the same traditions after their kind.

CHAPTER VII.

WOMEN WORKERS: MEDICAL AID AND MISSIONS.

> "Does the road wind up-hill all the way?
> Yes, to the very end.
> Will the day's journey take the whole long day?
> From morn to night, my friend."
>
> —C. Rossetti.

To any woman skilled in the divine art of healing, and courageous enough to push steadily onward in the face of disappointment and soul-sickening apathy, to work her way through a stone wall, and banish from her vocabulary the poor-spirited word "impossible," our Indian Empire offers an inexhaustible field of labour. Its densely-packed cities are hotbeds of disease and physical degeneracy. Dust and the fly sow cholera and typhoid broadcast throughout the land. The sun's arrows smite the unwary by day, and by night the treacherous breath of earth breeds fever in his bones. Conquerors and conquered are bowed down beneath one yoke; for the sickness that walketh in the noonday knows no respect of persons. True, the white man imports doctors for his alleviation, and the brown women are blest by the benefits of the Dufferin Fund: but even so there remains work in plenty for those equipped with the necessary knowledge, plus energy, sympathy, and perseverance. These last are indispensable. The woman who thinks to achieve a successful Indian career without them is foredoomed to failure, overwrought nerves, and a broken heart.

In no climate and under no conditions

is a life-long duel with disease and death a matter to be lightly taken in hand; but in this age of restless nervous energy, a brave woman in search of work worth doing, might do worse than devote her powers to the service of India's stricken millions, black or white. The harvest is plenteous; the labourers none too many; and the field as varied as it is vast.

Four spheres of work, at least, lie open to the qualified aspirant: work that leads neither to fame nor fortune, but which, nevertheless, carries its own exceeding great reward. For wheresoever sickness is, there will assuredly be scope for woman's sympathy, energy, and zeal. Take, as an instance, the chief woman's hospital in Calcutta, the Dufferin Victoria. This institution, over and above its complicated internal work, makes a special feature of out-patients, who are estimated at over 20,000 in the year. It is good to realise that the healing of this multitude of sick is accomplished entirely by English, Eurasian, and native medical women working loyally in concert: a state of affairs that would have seemed little short of miraculous forty years ago.

The Government of India's State-supported service of medical aid maintains over 2000 hospitals of varying scope and size. In most of these the chief appointments are held by men; but capacity and vigour will rarely fail to find employment, irrespective of sex. And though work may be hard, the climate discouraging, holidays rare, and payment disproportionate to the energy expended, yet the woman who sincerely desires to serve her fellow-creatures, will find in the life a satisfaction such as no onlooker would ever conceive to be possible.

Another promising field for medical work exists among the Native States of India, all by now more or less enlightened, and more or less disposed to patronise the lady doctor and all her works. Here, as elsewhere, hospitals have multiplied exceedingly: for whensoever an enlightened maharajah wishes to make a public exhibition of his charity, or, in other words, to "catch the eye" of an appreciative Viceroy, he inaugurates a fine public building,—a hospital for choice.

In addition to this praiseworthy predilection, the wealthier princes more and more tend to engage resident lady doctors exclusively for the benefit of their zenanas. These appointments, though lucrative, are not always so desirable as they may appear to women weary of hospital routine, continuous work, and straitened means. Tact, diplomacy, nerve, and a strong will are indispensable to the Englishwoman who accepts the position of paid dependant to an Indian prince. Whom he pays he rules; and he may even derive a certain satisfaction from keeping the English men and women in his employ fully alive to their anomalous position. There are many to whom such a state of things would be intolerable, and these will do well to keep clear of Native States and their fair-sounding offers.

But generalities are almost as odious as comparisons. For there are princes *and* princes: and given one of the right sort, the work itself must needs be of exceptional interest; rich in opportunities of obtaining first-hand knowledge, and of bestowing practical help and sympathy upon those masses of jealously-guarded women who, having eyes, see not, and having ears hear not, aught of the life that lies beyond their own windowless walls.

To these workers it is given to penetrate into the hidden mysteries of zenana life; to lay up a store of facts that enable them to silence the outcry of the ignorant sentimentalist, who would have England believe that Eastern wives—downtrodden, ill-used, and imprisoned—invariably lead lives of tragic gloom, and water their couches with tears shed for the lack of joys whereof they have never even dreamed. Sorrow and pain they endure, in common with womenkind at large; but, taken as a whole, the abiding feature of zenana life is a very unromantic dulness, enlivened by jealous squabbles and petty triumphs, and glorified by religion, children, and personal sacrifice. Here and there a rare nature will crop up, whose instinct is for freedom, and whose spirit chafes against the bars, as a bird's against it cage; but the majority are very well content with such things as they have—a state of mind which scarce commends itself to Western philanthropists, since content spells stagnation, and discontent progress.

Yes, the Indian wife and mother is happy enough, after her own fashion, so long as she is blessed with health; but in her hours of pain and weakness she is worthy of all pity, all love, all that Western energy, sympathy, and knowledge can achieve for her relief. Neglect of the sick, and callousness to their sufferings, is unquestionably one of the least prepossessing traits of Indian character. "It is scarcely possible," writes one who knows, "to exaggerate the misery of the scenes witnessed by the Zenana medical missionary, as she takes her place by the side of some poor pain-tossed one, and looks round in vain for any sign of comfort or alleviation in the wretched apartment. It may be illness in which the utmost quiet, the most absolute rest, are imperatively demanded; or it may be that the sand of life is running out. Yet the room, roof, or courtyard, as the case may be, is crowded with noisy women, not one attempting to relieve the sufferer; while beneath the bedstead—generally too short for the patient to lie at ease—is assembled the family stock of poultry; and dogs, goats, and children divide between them the little remaining space."

This picture brings us to the third field of healing open to Englishwomen in the East,—medical mission work in all its branches: a field that differs from the rest in that it regards the healing of the body as a means to one great end. In the eyes of the medical missionary, the hospital, over and above its *raison d'être*, affords peculiar opportunities for soul-winning; and it is for this reason that high-caste Hindu and Mahommedan women,—the Purdah aristocracy, so to speak,—are debarred from the benefit of its ministrations. Herein lies the main point of divergence between mission work and that of the Dufferin Fund. The boundary line of the one is the base line of the other. And from that base line rises the stony, uphill road of medical mission work; a work demanding all and giving little in return. Yet are its devotees by no means dismayed, as the following letter (written some years ago from Peshawar) bears striking testimony: "Your heart would be stirred within you to see what the ladies are doing in India. Here and at Amritsar they are working splendidly. Full of energy, bright, natural, and wonderfully brave, . . . they practically give up all the attractions of European society, and spend their lives for the poor women and children. At Amritsar, two or three of them live in the heart of the city, with no European near them; and here they do the same." Whatever be one's opinion of mission work in the abstract, there can be but one in regard to workers of this calibre; women whose record of pluck, devotion, and self-sacrifice may well make England proud of her daughters. Slow uncertain progress, disheartening apathy, bitter disappointment,

—these have they fought single-handed, again and yet again; still, in the face of all, have they persevered, and found some measure of reward.

A letter from a qualified medical missionary may give some idea of the difficulties attendant on doctoring Eastern womanhood: "The Hindus do not want water in their medicine, so we give them powders. The others use shells as measures, and these shells vary very much in size. One woman will drink up medicine sufficient for three days in one night, another will throw away her medicine, and then complain that she is no better. Another will eat the powder with the paper in which it is wrapped! Again, another will come up determined to have an eye powder. You assure her her eyes are not in a fit state for a powder, and give her drops. She refuses them; and if you still refuse her the powder, she demands one for her aged mother at home!" Yet even under such conditions as these patience has had her perfect work; nor has that work been wrought in vain.

The largest mission hospital in India, St Catherine's, in Amritsar, owes its existence to the unquenchable zeal and energy of its founder, and to the liberal help given her by the municipality of the station. Twenty-five years ago St Catherine's consisted of an insignificant building containing six beds, whose occupants were tended by two indefatigable Englishwomen. To-day the hospital stands two hundred and fifty-five feet high; accommodates forty-two in-patients; and provides living-room for a hundred persons. Nor is St Catherine's an isolated instance. India is full of such monuments to the courage, patience, and devotion of the many Englishwomen who have made her peoples' welfare the primary object of their lives.

And last, though very far from least, there are the nurses also,—the women indispensable to doctors as to patients; and happily for both they have multiplied in India within the last two decades. Of all vocations open to the unattached woman, here surely is one of the finest; one that makes the most unsparing demands upon heart and brain and body,—the last more than all in a land of vast distances, interminable journeys, and violent extremes of temperature. Five years of nursing in India will test a woman's nerves and health and zeal to the uttermost; and only the elect in mind and body care to outstay that term. But there is no lack of novices eager to take their places in the ranks;

eager to learn at first hand something of the mystery and beauty and terror of that wonderful India, that "after two hundred years still stands before her captors like some beautiful stranger;—so defenceless, so little understood or known."

E.P. Stebbing

The Diary of a Sportsman Naturalist in India.
London: John Lane and the Bodley Head,
1920.

CHAPTER IV

A HUNTER'S PARADISE

Chota Nagpur once more—The fascination of the study of the natural history of the forest—Malarious jungles—Extraordinary abundance of the large game animals—Big herds of bison—Monsoon and hot weather conditions—An animal census of the forests in the late nineties—Arduous nature of bison tracking—Behaviour of wounded bison—The commissariat question—Start off to fill the larder—A moonlight walk—The decision—A barking deer—Come upon the fresh tracks of a herd of bison—The ·450 express and temptation—Proceed to track the bison—Hot weather conditions—Come up with the herd—I follow the herd—Fire at a bull—Am charged by a young bull—I fire at him—Search for the bison—Am charged again—An ineffective rifle—A third charge—Treed by the bull—A long vigil and a vindictive enemy—A rescue—The dead bull—Carried back to camp.

TWO years later I found myself back in, and now in charge of, the division in which I had enjoyed such fine sport as an Assistant. With a greater knowledge of the jungles and Indian sporting methods I promised myself a good time—hopes that were to be fully realized.

Already, however, my attention had been attracted to the study of the fauna of the great jungles in which my work lay, and I had begun to realize that there was a stage beyond the mere sportsman's pleasure in stalking and shooting and searching for record heads, fascinating as these pursuits proved; that the study of the fauna of the jungles as a whole, and not of the game animals alone, was a most enthralling pursuit before which the mere acquisition of heads would occupy a secondary position.

My work for the next year kept me out in the jungles the year round. This was exceptional and a hardship in its way. For owing to the deadly nature of the malaria prevalent in these forests in the monsoon months, the orders in force enacted that the whole of the forest staff should retire to their head-quarters out in the open country at this period, brief visits only being paid to the jungle.

The reasons which entailed my remaining on the spot proved, as it turned out, a golden opportunity; as unique opportunities arose for studying the fauna of this part of India as I could not otherwise have hoped to do.

They were an extraordinary place those jungles in the monsoon in the late nineties of last century. Teeming with animals they were, in fact, a giant sanctuary in which the shyest members of the jungle folk, such as the elephant and the bison, roamed at will, free and practically unmolested. It is difficult to believe that this state of affairs existed, for the short interval which has elapsed has brought about very different conditions, so far as the numbers of the game animals are concerned.

On one brilliant day during a break in the rains in August of that year three separate herds of bison, two containing over forty animals apiece, were tracked down and put up, whilst two old solitary bulls were seen; one inadvertently run into as he was resting under the shade of a bamboo clump, and the other after two hours' hard tracking. This latter was a fine old bull, his skin jet black and shining like satin, and horns deeply furrowed at the base and blunted and worn at the tips.

The fleeting glance we obtained of the other bull, as he sprang up and crashed away into a bamboo thicket, showed an animal in its prime, with what appeared to be an unusually long and curved pair of horns.

That day, as regards the number of bison actually seen, proved a red-letter one. But we had few blank days—either seeing animals or coming upon absolutely fresh tracks on most occasions.

And the same state of affairs was disclosed with respect to other game. Sambhar were plentiful and many a good head could have been bagged had I not held my fire, being unwilling to disturb the jungles in the hopes of obtaining a good bison.

In the light of the present condition of these forests in this respect I often bitterly regret that I did not keep an accurate daily record of the animals seen. It may be admitted that such a record would not have been absolutely correct, since the same animal may have been put up more than once. But as the tract of jungle visited at different intervals that year extended over some nine hundred square miles, such a record would not have been without its useful side.

It was not only in the rains that the animals were so plentiful. At that season, when food and water were to be had in abundance everywhere, the animals roamed throughout the whole length and breadth of the vast jungles. In the hot weather they were more restricted, as the vegetation died down under the fierce heat of the sun and the streams dried up, leaving only pools. At this season these water-holes and the perennial streams which maintained a much reduced flow of water were the places to visit. In the evening, throughout the night, and early morning such places were the rendezvous of an extraordinary concourse of the jungle folk, and it was quite possible to arrive at some estimate of the numbers of the different classes of animals present in the surrounding tract of country. As the hot weather drew to its close the ground in the neighbourhood of these drinking places became trampled down into a shining, stony consistence, the surface showing a network of fine lines and curves left by the impress of the hoofs of the innumerable animals resorting to the drinking places to quench their thirst.

Here again such figures as might be given, relative to the numbers of the various species probably existing in these jungles at that time, would scarce be credited in the light of the more or less accurately estimated numbers of the various species inhabiting the tracts at the present time. From my own personal observations made in the late nineties it can be said that considerable numbers of wild elephants were present in these forests and large herds of bison, whilst sambhar were very plentiful, big heads, forty inches, being fairly common. Spotted deer, barking deer, and four-horned antelope were numerous, as also pig, hyena, wild dog, and so forth. Tiger and leopard, though difficult to get at, were plentiful. Bear in the more open country, as already mentioned, were easily obtainable.

As has been said, shooting in the Chota Nagpur jungles is done on foot, and if one wishes to track the bison with any chance of success it is absolutely essential to keep in hard and fit condition. One will almost certainly have to spend hours on end tracking, exposed to a hot sun. Camp may be quitted at two or three in the morning, and should a fresh trail be picked up it may be late afternoon before one comes up to the quarry. All will then probably depend on one shot. If the sportsman is so tired out that he cannot hold the heavy rifle straight and steady he will have had his trouble for nothing. And this is by no means a rare ending to many hours' strenuous exertion. For these hours of tramping over rocky hills under a hot sun are terrifically arduous work. One must be abstemious—I do not mean teetotal—and reduce the smoking allowance whilst engaged on this kind of work or success need not be expected.

One of the fascinations of bison shooting on foot resides in the fact that it is not possible to anticipate how an animal will act once he is wounded. The gaur is amongst the shyest and most timid of animals. He is endowed with a most wonderful sense of hearing and smell, and the slightest taint of man's presence in the air or the snap of a small, dry twig breaking the great midday silence of the jungle will send him crashing blindly away on a trek during which he may cover, if seriously alarmed, thirty miles or more before he stops to browse and take matters easy once again. It is a knowledge of these characteristics which necessitates that slow, cautious and absolutely silent approach which is imperative when on a hot trail, if the stalker wishes to obtain a result from his hard work. It is this timidity also added to the natural wildness and constitutional inability to remain anywhere in the neighbourhood of civilization or man, allied to the bulk of the animal and his roaming propensities, which necessitates the maintenance of large tracts of untouched primeval jungle, if the species is to be preserved from extinction.

When wounded this instinct for self-preservation and solitude may prove uppermost in the animal's mind and lead to a blind rush for safety dead away from the direction in which he imagines the danger to be. He may act thus. In many cases he does. On the other hand, in numbers of recorded instances he has exhibited a very different spirit. The wound appears to have roused in him a blind fury, under which all his usual instincts of timidity, fear and cravings for flight to a safe solitude, seem to be overpowered by an overmastering passion for revenge; and to that consuming fury he often adds a cunning which is of the jungle and commonly found in all jungle folk when they turn to bay against their enemies. It is now that the bison becomes one of the most dangerous and vindictive of animals and resembles his cousin the buffalo. With his marvellously developed senses of smell and hearing to guide him he charges down on his antagonist, and if he misses him will wheel, as soon as he can pull up his heavy bulk, and come on again with rigid determination and eye blazing fire and deadly fury. It is on such occasions that a life hangs upon a thread and coolness and a heavy rifle alone stand between the sportsman and eternity.

I had an experience of this kind that hot weather, and although the ludicrous aspects of my position have often appealed to me since that day, there was no possible doubt at the time as to the tight fix I had got myself into.

One night at dinner my Khansamah informed me that the stock of murghis (fowls) had run short, that the commissariat arrangements had gone wrong owing to some unforeseen delay, and would the sahib go out next morning and shoot a sambhar or spotted deer for the larder. We had considerable difficulty over supplies that year and cholera broke out badly in the district, adding to our troubles. It was a bad business for a time, but we managed to weather the storm. . To my Khansamah I replied that his desire could be easily fulfilled without interruption to the work I had on hand. The moon was late that night or I would have gone out there and then. Before I turned in I gave orders to be called at 3 a.m.

Dawn next morning found me several miles from the camp accompanied by a gun-bearer, who also carried a light lunch-basket and a couple of bottles of cold, weak tea, all I ever drank now when out in the jungles by myself. The moon had afforded us plenty of light and the path, a broad elephant track, had been an easy one. We had already seen or heard numerous deer, and a possible easy shot or two might have been obtained had I not wished to reach a certain hill in the cool before the sun rose and whilst walking was pure pleasure. My object was to get the work done, bag if possible a young stag, and be back by ten o'clock in camp, where I had a long day's office work to get through.

As the moon paled before the brightening rays of the rapidly rising sun the surrounding forest became pervaded with a lovely rosy light which gave to the crowns of the great creeper-covered trees a wonderfully soft effect. In front a trappy, rocky hill-side covered with stunted, scattered trees and sparse tufts of sabai grass lay already bathed in a hard golden sunlight, which meant fierce heat later on. It was this hill we were making for, and to my annoyance we had not reached it as soon as I had hoped to do. I was now faced with the problem as to whether to climb the hill and get the work done whilst it was still comparatively cool, or make certain of replenishing the larder and face the greater heat on the hill-side, once the commissariat question was settled. The latter alternative appeared the most prudent, and quitting the track, we entered a narrow deer run to the left, and proceeded slowly, keeping a look out for fresh tracks or animals.

We had not gone far when we saw, away to the right, a small dull reddish shape cropping the grass at the foot of a fine old sál. It was about forty paces away and quite unconscious of our presence. The khakar or muntjac, the so-called barking deer, for such the little animal was, raised its head, listened intently for a second or two and then stamped its forefoot into the turf, emitted a succession of sharp barks, listened again and returned to its feeding. I raised the rifle and then lowered it and signified to my companion to move forward. I had not the heart to fire at the little beast and I had remembered that the camp followers would like to have some meat, and that it would be as well to kill something larger than a khakar.

Within ten minutes we were standing before the absolutely fresh tracks of a herd of bison! The animals could not have passed, by all the evidences, more than an hour before, and were evidently browsing as they went along.

The jungle man's eyes gleamed as he thought of the feast that he would have if the sahib bagged one of them. A corresponding gleam was in my eyes. What would Bishu, the head shikari, say if the sahib bagged a good bison without his being there to show it him. The sahib whom he himself had taught to decipher the tracks and signs of the jungle to some small extent.

My hesitation was but brief, and was perhaps chiefly connected with the rifle I carried. Not wishing to overburden myself, I had only brought with me a light ·450 black powder express. Cordite express rifles had not then come into general use. To those who know its significance their advent alone speaks volumes for the decrease in the game animals of India. Now to face a bison with a black powder ·450 express is madness. Of course, many have done it and wounded their animal and never seen it again or, a far rarer event, killed their beast by a lucky shot; others have done it or tried it and have paid the penalty with their lives. Elephants have been killed with a ·303, but few would care to stand up to a charging rogue elephant with only this weapon in their hands. I had a fair-sized bump of caution about me, but I was young and the temptation was out of all proportion to the size of my caution bump—as it has been to many before and will, in like circumstances, be to the end of time. Nor am I quite certain in my own mind that I should not succumb to the temptation now.

A motion of the head and we set forth to follow the tracks of the herd.

I am not relating this episode with any idea that it redounds to my credit. Far otherwise. It may read amusingly, and I have since been able to perceive the entertaining side of it. At the time, however, as events will show, my attention and interest were held by the serious aspects of the position. Also I have little hope of persuading any other keen youngster to act differently. With the temptation in front of him he will certainly give way to it. But this episode will show him one of the experiences he may have to confront when, inadequately armed, he follows up dangerous game on foot.

The tracks of the herd we now commenced to follow were simple enough to read, and it was evident that there were, at least, a score of animals in it. The difficulty lay in the fact that the forest at this season of the year was all as dry as tinder, and walking without making a considerable rustle and crackle was by no means easy, so thickly did the dead, dry leaves of the sál trees lie in the denser parts of the forest.

Since I could not emulate my companion in his noiseless progression which, in his eagerness, would quickly have left me far behind, I placed him behind and we advanced in this manner for well over an hour and a half. In the period we covered a bare three miles, the tracks leading us dead away from the direction I wished to go in. But this appears to be almost invariably the case in bison tracking, and you must be prepared to follow where the trail leads. Latterly we had been silently walking through a piece of high sál forest, following a narrow path which was more or less clear of dead leaves—swept clear probably by the fierce, hot wind which blows during the day at this season. Gradually the ground began to rise and the forest to open and thin out in front. Evidence had shown that the trail was becoming hotter and hotter, and I was breathless with excitement and anxiety, expecting momentarily to run into the herd or to hear the well-known short, sharp, snorting bellow which is the signal for a stampede.

As soon as we noted the forest thinning again with the rise of the ground, it became evident that the herd must be close. I could not trust my companion sufficiently to send him on to make observations ; nor, at this stage, would I give up the honour I wished to have myself of running down the bison and telling the head shikari about it afterwards. Slower and slower still we advanced. Suddenly I felt a touch on my arm and a hand came stealthily forward, pointing to my right front. I turned my head slightly and at once made out the head and shoulders of a bison. The rest of the body was hidden behind the stems of two sál trees. We stood motionless, not daring to move even an eyelash, as for all we knew there might be bison on our left flank. Gradually I made out three other bison immediately in front of us. They were in the thinner part of the forest and the light fell in large chequered patches on their backs. Look as I might I could see no more. There was nothing for it but to wait till they moved away. The animals were all browsing, and in about a quarter of an hour or so they gradually fed forward and disappeared. We waited another ten minutes and I then motioned to my companion that I would go forward and that he was to follow at some distance behind. He nodded, and may or may not have understood. So far as I was concerned I saw nothing more of him till a much later stage in the proceedings.

I crept forward with infinite precaution, the ·450 at full cock in my hand. The weight of the light rifle had not caused me much trouble or fatigue on this stalk! As I advanced my eye was held by a curious-shaped, forked, almost deformed tree standing at the edge of the forest and directly ahead of me. The tree was thick and stumpy, forked at about twelve feet from the ground with a thick branch growing out horizontally from the trunk about six feet up. This tree was subsequently to play an important part in the day's operations. I arrived at the place where the forest thinned out, keeping so far as possible a tree or two always in front shielding my line of approach. The rise was more gradual here, and as I approached what may be called the edge of the forest the grass, with the lighter overhead cover, at once became thicker and higher intermingled with bushes. Out beyond the hill-side, as is so commonly the case in this part of the country, grew stonier with elevation; being covered with a scattered, rather stunted tree-growth, interspersed with tufts of the sabai grass and bushes growing in clumps. A glance showed me that a number of bison were grazing here. Several were near the top of the slope, whilst others had probably already crossed the ridge out of sight. I was evidently only just in time if I was to get a shot before the herd disappeared—for once on the other side the animals might get into bamboo jungle and give an infinite amount of trouble before I could get up to them again.

I watched the herd with bated breath. In spite of some acquaintance with this fine beast I had not yet learnt to look upon him in his native jungle unmoved, and the sight before me set my pulses tingling and my heart beating a double tattoo on my ribs. My object was, naturally, to pick out the master bull of the herd, and I could form no estimate as to what his size would be. I had not had the practice, and even with it I knew I could never hope to vie with Bishu in his wonderful capacity for picking out the biggest head after a hurried glance over a feeding, or even a bolting, herd. As I surveyed the animals in front of me most fervently did I wish he were beside me. The animals were half and, at times, wholly hidden by the bushes or scattered trees, and as they moved about slowly browsing,

I only got glimpses of their heads. So far as I could perceive there were twenty animals on the slope when I came up, and already three of these had crossed the ridge and disappeared. Again I ran my eye over each animal as his head became visible. The nearest was, I suppose, about seventy yards off, the furthest under two hundred and fifty yards. There were two I had marked down as bulls and their heads appeared pretty level as regards size, and therein lay the difficulty. Surely there must be a larger bull in such a herd !

Patiently I searched the bushes again, starting on the left and working round past the curious forked tree in front of me, until I reached my right front. Ah ! What was that glint ? I waited and watched, and suddenly a black form loomed up above a bush and moved slowly forward. This must be the Lord of the Herd for certain. A fine massive beast in his prime. One long look I gave him and then as he moved diagonally away from me, too diagonally I have since thought, but I had forgotten that I had only the light rifle, I aimed slightly behind the shoulder in the hopes of reaching the heart. The sharp crack of the ·450 was followed by amazed snorts and bellows from the herd and a general stampede ensued. I saw the big bull lunge forward and then my attention was diverted by a crash to the right. I turned sharply to see a bison charging down directly upon me from about fifty yards away. Where he had come from I had not time to consider then. Raising the rifle I aimed hurriedly at the neck just behind the lowered head with the idea of trying to sever the spinal column, and fired my left barrel. He was within about twenty yards when I pulled the trigger. Springing aside I got behind a neighbouring large sál tree, the bison passing within ten yards of me, being carried on by the impetuosity of his rush. The whole thing was a matter of a few seconds only, and I was totally at a loss for the moment to explain the extraordinary action of the animal, for he was nowhere near the large bull at which I had fired. Afterwards I came to the conclusion that the animal, in its first rush, was not charging me at all, but only stampeding away in fright and by chance took my direction. As I silently extracted the spent cartridges and put in a couple of fresh ones I listened intently for any fresh sounds of the bull, but could hear nothing. A deep silence had given place to the turmoil which reigned so shortly before. "Perhaps he is down," I thought, and with the idea I at once started to find out. Leaving my tree I advanced cautiously in the direction in which the bull had disappeared. The dry leaves were a bother, but the tree-trunks, being still fairly numerous, afforded a certain amount of protection

and concealment, and luckily for me I was not encumbered with the heavy boots I used to wear on such expeditions, but was shod in light stalking shoes. I had gone about fifty yards on the line the bull had taken and was beginning to think I must have overshot the mark, when suddenly from behind me a deep bellow sounded, followed by the rush of a heavy body. I sprang round to see the bull viciously charging down on me. There was no mistake about it this time. He had spotted me, and mad with fury meant having me. I was quite close to a big tree and, hurriedly firing my right barrel, got behind it, loosing off the left as he carried on past me. I might have been using a pea-shooter for all the apparent effect on the bull, who only answered to the shots by enraged bellows. He was a young bull, not having yet reached his prime, but brimful of viciousness as I was beginning to discover. I was now becoming seriously alarmed, and as I reloaded the rifle, with fingers that trembled in spite of me, I cast about hurriedly for a refuge. That the bull would return I had no doubt, and I did not like this hide-and-seek business amongst the trees. All round me the trees were large with stout, clean stems and quite unclimbable. Suddenly there flashed across my mind the queer forked tree I had noted on the edge of the forest from my first position. It was an inspiration and I at once set out towards it, my actions hurried by the fact that I heard the bull stop and turn and advance in my direction again. So far as possible I moved backwards in the direction I knew the tree must be, having the edge of the forest on my right hand as a guide and facing in the direction of the bull. I moved very slowly, trying to make as little noise as possible, but I had not gone half the distance before, in stepping round a tree, I walked on to a mass of dry sticks. The sharp crack they produced was immediately followed by an angry roar from the bull. I had by then discovered the position of the tree and so knew the direction to make for. I started running, but realized that I could not get there in time as the grass and bushes were thicker now. Again I sought the protection of a friendly tree and fired a shot at the bull as he passed. But I was now shaking like a leaf and could hardly see out of my eyes for perspiration, and the bullet went in far behind as was subsequently discovered. This charge settled me. I could hear the bull already pulling up and I ran stumbling through the grass and undergrowth for the tree, the instinct of self-preservation uppermost. Panting and swearing and perspiring and in a blue funk, for I heard the bull again advancing, I made a jump for the low horizontal branch, missed my hold and came to earth. Scrambling up I had another try, got on to the branch and climbed up into the fork of the tree. There I clung, shaking with fright, the perspiration pouring down my face and blinding me. Luckily, though I was unaware of it at the time, my topi had not fallen off, as I usually wore it with a stout, leather chin-strap. As I climbed up into the fork I had a dim realization of a great heavy dark mass rushing beneath me. It was the bison, and when I began to recover my senses somewhat I looked about to ascertain the position of affairs. I soon saw the bull. He was out in the open, his impetus having carried him some considerable distance. He was now advancing in my direction at a shambling trot, and, passing quite close to the tree, went on into the forest ; to shortly depart for good, I hoped, when he could not find me. I had read, it is true, of men being " treed " by bison, but I did not imagine then that my position would entail anything but momentary inconvenience now that I was out of his reach. As I recovered from my fright my chief feeling was one of wrath at the young bull whose blundering interference had, I then thought, caused me to lose the old bull. However, I may say at once that no trace of blood was subsequently found on the latter's trail and I do not think he suffered much from the encounter.

As has been said the young bull passed on into the forest, and as I made myself as comfortable as possible in the fork of the tree with my back resting against the thickest stem, I heard him blundering about amongst the undergrowth, though the surrounding foliage prevented me seeing him.

As soon as I was comfortable I concentrated my attention on the bison. He still seemed quite close, and then suddenly the noise advanced in my direction and the brownish-black form appeared about twenty yards away. I could not make out what he was doing. He appeared to be, if I may so express it, routing about in the undergrowth. Routing about was the thought in my mind, and then suddenly I thought of another term, " nosing " about. And with the word my spine ran cold and I remembered what I had read and heard of " treed " men—men in the position I was in, in fact. That when wounded and thoroughly roused a bison, discovering his enemy in a tree, would patiently wait at the foot of it till weakness caused the latter to fall into his power to be gored to death. I confess terror again invaded me at the thought. My whole consciousness was now concentrated on the actions of the bull. He again passed quite close to the tree ; again went out or rather blundered out into the open for fifty yards or so. I thought he might be giving up the quest and following in the tracks of the herd. But he circled round and once more entered the forest.

As I lost sight of him I peered down through the leaves, the foliage was scanty below me, to see if I could perceive the rifle. On jumping up from the ground in my second attempt to get into the tree I had left the rifle where it had fallen after my first desperate effort. So I was unarmed and helpless. From where I sat I could see nothing, but on moving a little I got a wider view, and—yes, there lay the rifle about ten yards from the foot of the tree. Though tantalizing, it gave me some comfort to see it there.

Again the bull approached. This time he came quite close and circled round the tree. His course seemed aimless at first, but I cannot make up my mind that it was. Nor could I say definitely that he ever saw me in my present position. What he actually did was to blunder round the tree at about fifteen to twenty paces away and then sit down. He was in full view when he stopped and sat down, and I was thunderstruck at the proceeding. The only conceivable explanation that I could at the time give to account for this was that he had scented his enemy and was going to wait for him. It really appears the only plausible explanation of this and similar incidents which have been recorded. To say that my heart sank into my boots does not adequately portray my feelings. At first I buoyed myself up with the hope that he was so hard hit that he was dying but I soon had to give up that idea. He was sitting diagonally, head facing me, ears flung forward, the picture of alertness and, so it seemed to my anxious gaze, wickedness. For an hour, or perhaps longer, I did not keep count of time at that juncture, I sat holding on like grim death to my tree, dazed and despairing. The sun got hotter and hotter, and I could feel it beating on to my topi and through it on to the top of my head, in spite of the leafy screen above me. It may have been this intensity of heat that at last woke me to reality again.

Quite suddenly I found myself looking at the bull. He was still apparently in the same position. He surely must be dead I thought. Then I glanced downwards and my eye fell on the rifle. A thought flashed through my brain and I began to let myself down on to the horizontal branch below, keeping my eye on the bison the while. From the lower position I found I could only see a part of him, but still most of the head. Taking my eyes from him I looked down ; there lay the rifle, not immediately beneath me, but still fairly close if I could only reach it without sound. This I proceeded to try and do. I turned over on to my stomach and was commencing to lower myself slowly when the buckle of a leather belt I wore caught in the bark and made a loud scraping crack. I heard a sudden movement to the left, a bellow and crash followed each other instantaneously, and I was sitting palpitating on the fork again. I could not have explained how I got there. The bull, for he it was, passed almost below the tree. What pace he was going I had no idea. But I heard him turn and then sit down again quite close ; but now I could not see him.

I made no further attempts to get the rifle.

The effort had done me good, however, and I now turned seriously to a consideration of the position. I had no watch on me, but calculated it must be between eleven and twelve o'clock. The effect of the sun was what I most feared. Drowsiness would do for me. The noise I made no longer bothered me. I felt the bull knew all there was to know, so I selected a better position, and taking off my leather belt, slit a hole in the end of it, and passing the end of a handkerchief through it, knotted it securely. The added length enabled me to tie myself to a fair-sized branch and thus ensure partial safety if I dozed. The added tightness round my middle also stilled the pangs of hunger that were making themselves felt, for I had not eaten for about nine hours. The thought of food brought to my memory my companion and the tiffin basket. Where, I wondered, were they? And then I began to calculate. Assuming that the man was more or less aware of my position and had returned to camp, how soon could I expect relief? Three hours either way should do it and an hour to collect the men who in my absence might be all over the place. Three o'clock at the earliest, and I wondered if I could stick the heat, always greatest between one and three o'clock, or felt most at that period. I had luckily never taken to the afternoon *siesta* in the hot weather so usual in the East for European and Indian alike, and so the fight against drowsiness was not so awful as it must otherwise have been. But I must have dozed.

Once I thought, or dreamt, that the bull came close up to the tree and I grew cold with fright. But this incident may have been a chimera of the brain. Another time I felt myself falling off the tree. That effectually roused me and I was broad awake. I looked round. The shadows were lengthening. I noted that, and as I did so I heard a faint halloo. I listened, my faculties keenly on the alert. Silence, a dead silence, save for the tiny twittering of a small tree-creeper on a neighbouring tree. Again—surely that was a human voice. With strained faculties I listened intently. There! unmistakable that time, and on the instant I opened my mouth to shout back. But no sound came save a harsh cackle. My tongue was baked dry and hard as a parrot's. Again I tried, with no better result. Despair seized me. Suppose they went away and left me to my fate. I grew frantic and gazed wildly round. My eye fell on the sál leaves. I plucked a couple and crammed parts of them into my mouth and chewed feverishly. Again the hail—nearer this time. I attempted an answer and got out a sound and continued my chewing. I tasted nothing, but I felt a little saliva beginning to form and the blessed hails came nearer. At last I gathered up my whole powers and yelled. A certain amount of voice had come back and my third shout was heard, for a volume of shrieks answered me. I plucked some more leaves and chewed hard, for it was imperative that the men should be warned about the bison. To my wandering senses, after the protracted vigil in the intense heat, he had assumed the form of a devil, armed with the cunning of a serpent, and I did not want my deliverers to suffer at his hands. The voices approached, and I did what I could to warn them. But I doubt whether they understood me at the time. And it was immaterial. They thoroughly understood the wily nature and cunning of the animal they had to deal with. Bishu told me afterwards that the men guessed, from the moment they heard my voice, how it was with me; for my companion of the morning had been apparently convinced that I was "treed" before he left. I did not clearly follow the men's subsequent movements, as in the reaction my senses must have wandered. I was brought back to reality by a great shout and I heard indistinctly voices saying, "He's dead, sahib. The shaitan's dead." They found him lying on his side at the place I had last heard him sit down. And he must have been dead an hour or two before the men arrived !

They took me from the tree and I drank two long whiskies and sodas, and ate a couple of sandwiches whilst they hurriedly made a palanquin of creepers and branches. Into this I got, for I could not have walked a yard, and immediately fell fast asleep, only waking up as we reached the camp.

CHAPTER XIX

A REAL TIGER STORY

Told round the camp fire—The camp in the forest—Feeding the elephants —A tiger shooting party in May—Tigers very numerous in old days —Scarcer now and will require protection—Blank days—A day with tigers—The morning start—Tigers break out—Crusty sportsmen—Advice to youngsters—Plan of campaign changed—Placing the howdah elephants—The beat commences—A tiger's head appears—Fire at tiger—An excited elephant—A second tiger's head appears—Grass—A shot at the tiger—Tiger reappears and charges elephant—Gets on to elephant's head—Exciting moments—Death of the tiger—Elephant takes charge—A hot time—The Collector's luck.

"IT was a blazing hot day in May several years ago, that I had the best fun I have yet had with tigers," said a friend one evening, as we sat round the camp fire in front of the tents. "You have often heard me mention that day, and I have promised to tell you the story. So here goes for the yarn."

The Collector of the District, a fine sportsman, lay back in his deck-chair, took a pull at his cigar, and became reflective for a space.

Night had fallen, the camp was pitched near a small forest bungalow in a clearing in the forest. As the firelight danced and flickered, the trunks of the nearmost trees stood out straight and columnar, and the grass heads gleamed white on their greenish-yellow stalks against the dark depths of the forest behind, whilst overhead the heavens were lit with a brilliant scintillating mass of stars. Now and then a dull rumble, as of thunder, came from the quarter in which the elephants were picketed. The great animals were contentedly chewing their evening forage; a great mass of green boughs of the pipul tree, having been brought in earlier in the day by one of their number for the night's meal; for the elephant sleeps and eats alternately throughout the night. At sundown his mahout gives him his chief meal, a round number of pounds of grain. This has to be fed to him, for if left to himself he will scatter it about and lose half, for the animal is a wasteful and improvident feeder. To prevent this, the mahout binds up a wisp of straw into a mass like a bird's nest, about a foot across, fills this with the grain and places it in the elephant's mouth, the latter advancing a step or two and bringing down its head to receive it from the mahout, who is squatting on the ground the whole time and does not trouble to move. As soon as the mass is placed inside his mouth, the elephant backs a step or two and slowly chews it, straw and grain together. This nightly operation is usually carried out in front of the tents, so that a watch may be kept on the mahouts; otherwise the men consider they are within their rights in feeding the whole of their family and relations out of the grain provided for the elephants, and the latter suffer a shortage in their daily meal. And the elephant is perfectly aware of the shortage and pilfering, and is in his way grateful for the sahib's care. For the elephant is one of the most intelligent of beasts, and rarely forgets a kind act done to him.

At the opposite side of the camp to that where the elephants are situated, is the horses' encampment. Here are to be found the horses' attendants, a man and a boy to each animal, with two or three small single-fly tents, the horses picketed out with heel ropes to prevent them stampeding when a leopard prowls round the camp, or wandering or engaging in playful kicking matches, a game at which some ponies are past-masters. Earlier in the evening I had myself personally inspected this camp, to see that my favourites had been properly fed and groomed: for a perfect understanding should exist between the master and his four-footed friends.

Hard by is the small camp, in which the havildah and the shikari reign supreme over a swarm of lesser camp attendants. The two great men sleep in tents, but the satellites have to be content with the camp fire for their shelter and warmth. To one side, and in the rear of the main tents, are a couple of police tents, for the police guard which always accompanies the Collector on tour. But a short distance from these, and exactly behind the mess tent, the cook and house servants have their headquarters. It is here that the appetising dishes the Indian cook can turn out in the face of difficulties, which none of his European confrères would dream of facing, are prepared. With several holes in the ground, flanked by large stones and filled with burning sticks, and a charcoal brazier or two, the Indian *chef* will prepare culinary marvels which would not disgrace a first-class London hotel.

A hum of conversation arises on the night air from these different encampments, at all of which, with the exception of the cook's, the evening meal of the men is in course of preparation, chaff is being exchanged, and the incidents of the past day—and there are always incidents, amusing and otherwise, in camp life—are discussed.

As I sat and took in the familiar scene, so well known, but one which never lost its fascination, my friend continued :

" You know the —— Jungles ; you were there last year for a day or two, if I remember rightly. Well, it was in that neighbourhood that I had the best and most exciting time of my life. It was in May, one of those real scorching days, that the incidents I am going to relate occurred. We were a party of four rifles, and had already had fair sport. For tigers were far more numerous then than they are now, and there will be precious few left for generations to come, unless some form of protection is extended to them, or to those of the species who are game-killers pure and simple. No one wants to protect a man-eater, of course ; he is a pest to be stamped out as early as possible. Nor should the cattle-lifter, the animal who confines his attention to the cattle of the villagers and makes them his chief food supply, receive any countenance from sportsmen. But the pure game-killer, i.e. wild animal killer, falls within a different category, or so you yourself and I and others who have studied the question think, and he might well receive such protection as would be afforded him by closing some of the blocks of heavy jungle for a few seasons at a time.

But I know you agree with my views on this game protection question, so I'll get on with my story.

"As I have said, we had had fair luck and had bagged some dozen tigers and four or five leopards by the day I am speaking of. We had, however, had several blank days just previously, and though the khubbar was good, we were not over sanguine as the party left camp about nine o'clock in the morning. We had a ride of five miles in front of us, and accomplished this on a couple of pad elephants, the howdah elephants having, of course, been sent on ahead. Part of the ride was up the hard bed of the —— River, and we were pretty well roasted by the time we reached the rendezvous.

"The plan of campaign for the day included four beats, two in the morning and two in the afternoon. You know the big block of sál forest, with open patches of tall grass that runs alongside the —— Forest Road. It is intersected by a rather deep ravine, filled for the most part with tiger grass, and a few scattered copses of the sissu and khair trees. The idea was to beat the two blocks of jungle in two separate beats, each towards the ravine, the first beat to come out in the upper part of the ravine, the second in the lower and towards the road. Jitman knew the country perfectly, as, in fact, did another man and myself, and we had the stops, consisting of elephants and also some men posted in trees, placed at the points where a tiger would be likely to try and quietly leave the beat.

"During the first drive the four howdah elephants were placed in the ravine, and none of us had a very nice stand. The grass was too high and thick. The winter had been a wet one, and rain had fallen in the hot weather, with the consequence that the grass had not died down or opened out to anything like the usual extent. Also we feared we had scarcely enough beating elephants to make success certain, for the area to be driven was a large and difficult one. As it turned out, we were right. Certainly one tiger was afoot in the first beat, but he got past us in the long grass. The same thing occurred in the next, and we were pretty savage, all of us, by the time we reached the lunch rendezvous. Two of the men turned rather crusty, in fact, lost their tempers, and began to swear at the shikaris and mahouts."

There is one piece of advice I would offer to a youngster commencing his career in India, or anywhere else for that

THE LINE OF ELEPHANTS CROSSING A RIVER *EN ROUTE* TO THE TIGER JUNGLES IN THE UNITED PROVINCES TERAI

Sir J. P. Hewett, photo

HOWDAH ELEPHANTS LINED UP FOR INSPECTION BEFORE THE START FOR A DAY'S TIGER SHOOTING

matter. Never lose your temper if you can help it, especially when out with a party. There are bound to be contretemps. Mistakes will be made, and you may be the sufferer. But, save in flagrant cases of disobedience, never swear at your men. Bear in mind the fact that they know infinitely more about the jungle lore of the forest than you do. Very often they will carry out your orders about the direction a beat should be taken, or as to beating a certain jungle, when they know beforehand that the result will be failure, or that there is nothing in the jungle to come out. This being so, you cut a rather sorry figure in their eyes, and also lose their respect, if you swear and browbeat men who could have foretold the result before the beat started; besides displaying your great ignorance of the habits of the animals you are out to shoot, and of perhaps the commonest rudiments of jungle lore as known to the local men. The Collector's story illustrates this point to perfection.

" Lunch," he continued, " was a poor affair that day, made uncomfortable solely by the ignorance of two of the party. And you don't want displays of petty temper when the thermometer is standing in the neighbourhood of 110 degrees in the shade and the hot wind is blowing with a furnace heat.

" The first beat after lunch was about a couple of miles from those of the morning. The plan of campaign necessitated the four rifles on the howdah elephants taking up positions so as to command a small ravine and narrow path right at the foot of the outermost of the foothills, for which a tiger, on being disturbed, would assuredly make. A strip of sál forest, and a considerable patch of grass, with two small areas of sissu copse, through which ran the small stream of water which formed the whole ' river ' at this season—the greater part of the great river-bed being a waste of shingle and grass—formed the country to be beaten. As the beat had been arranged, the ravine and path could just be covered by four rifles. When this disposition was explained, however, the two men who had fallen foul of the shikaris before lunch, asked to be allowed to go in the line of beating elephants, as ' they might then see something of a tiger, if one was afoot,' which was their method of expressing that they did not think much of the way the beat had been arranged. To avoid disagreements, this was assented to, and my friend and myself proceeded to decide how we should station ourselves, in order to command as much as possible of the ravine. Having settled this, we tossed for positions, and to me fell the nearest one, the other man commanding a part of the ravine and the path. My position was an ideal one, provided a tiger broke my way. A narrow offshoot nullah ran down between steep sál-covered hills, which dropped abruptly into the ravine on either side. The offshoot nullah formed the chief, and, in fact, only easy passage into the hills from the ravine. I had only to command it, and this I did. Instead, however, of placing my elephant in the ravine itself, I elected to take up a position a few yards up the offshoot nullah. By this means I not only blocked it, but commanded a wider range of the ravine itself, and had a larger outlook over the tangle of tall grass which here separated the ravine from the wide river-bed.

" So far as I could see, the matter resolved itself into this : If a tiger was in the big sál forest, one or other of the rifles with the beaters might get a chance at and bag him. They were both good shots. If he was lying up for the day in the sissu copses near the water, as was more likely, we stood the best chance of seeing him, as he would probably leave before the beating elephants got up to him.

" The beat began, and indistinct sounds and noises came to us very faintly, too faint to be able to distinguish anything. I was on a fine staunch tusker, not unlike our friend Jung Bahadur over there. He was an old campaigner at his business, and had certainly been in at the death of over one hundred tigers. A magnificent beast he was, with his forehead painted in fantastic white designs, and his great tusks cut down to half their length and tipped with massive, engraved silver knobs. He had been lent to me by a Raja friend of mine, and a rare good sportsman himself. Many a jolly day had we spent together ; for as you know there are no finer gentlemen nor greater sportsmen than some of the old Indian families of Northern India can show.

" Well, the great elephant stood like a rock. He and his mahout below me were two living statues, and only by their eyes could you have known that they were alive. My orderly, just as keen, was sitting in the seat behind me, also motionless.

" What thrilling minutes those are spent in the howdah

during a beat for tiger. The terrific heat is unnoticed. For to the real sportsman there is so much to study during the wait whilst the beating elephants are still distant. I was very interested, I remember, in the movements of some tiny tree creepers in the grass below me. Tiny little birds, as you know, their movements are extremely fascinating to watch. As they climb up the stems of the great grasses, prying their beaks into the sheaths, one wonders whether a tithe of the insects they make their daily meal off are known to science. The little beggars were searching systematically the various parts of the stems and flowers and seeds of the tall elephant grass—the tiger grass, as I like to call it—for to my mind there is no fairer sight than to see a tiger coming open-mouthed and roaring at you through it.

" Meditating on these things, my attention was suddenly attracted by a slight rustle in the grass on the other side of the ravine ; or I thought it was a rustle different from that of the wind in the grass, from which we were somewhat protected here. I concentrated my attention on the spot, and held my breath, my whole body stiff and motionless. Suddenly, without a sound, a tiger looked out of the edge of the grass, just where it dipped somewhat into the ravine. Only his head appeared, the head of a fine, nearly full grown male tiger, framed in the long grass. He must have been on higher ground, or up on a stone, for he was far higher than I had expected to see an animal appear ; in fact, for a moment the thought crossed my mind that he was climbing up the grass stems. This notion was, of course, only momentary, and was replaced at once by my surmise of higher ground. As I recovered from my surprise, the head disappeared and silence reigned. None of us had budged an inch. The elephant very quietly coiled up his

trunk as soon as the tiger disappeared, or may have rolled it up before, as he was probably aware that a tiger was afoot long before it actually appeared. I had time to feel annoyed at being taken by surprise in such a manner, though anyway I should have had no more than a snap shot at the brute. We kept a close watch on the grass, but not a sound or movement betrayed the direction or position of the tiger. Suddenly a rifle snapped out on the right. I muttered something below my breath, in vexation, and at the same moment we heard the grass swishing violently. Something was approaching in our direction. Instinctively I brought my rifle to the shoulder, and at the same moment a tiger appeared bounding towards us. He did not see us at first, and made straight for the off-shoot nullah, which we blocked. As he headed towards it, on the instant he caught sight of the elephant, bared his fangs in a snarl and then charged with a roar. I fired. He came on unharmed with a second savage roar, and leapt for the elephant's head, and dropped backwards with a heavy bullet through the brain. So close was he, that as he fell the tusker lifted one of his forelegs, and the tiger, falling against the knee, shot off it and rolled over and over into the ravine, where he lay still. Silence reigned and I reloaded. The encounter had roused us all, and from the quiet movements of the mahout I understood that the tusker was in a royal rage and wished to go in and have another turn with the tiger. He pacified him by degrees and we waited. The beating elephants were now out in the big river-bed, advancing through the patches of long grass and sissu copses. The shots had driven the mahouts and elephant boys crazy with excitement, and we could hear the voices raised in curses, objurgations and endearments to their respective elephants ; the most frightened, both man and elephant, making most noise, the latter trumpeting shrilly in alarm or indignation or pain, as they felt the goad battered down on their heads, giving off a dull, drum-like sound, or as its sharp point pierced through the skin behind the ear. The infernal pandemonium which always arises near the end of a beat, especially if it is known that one or more tigers are afoot, sets the blood dancing through one's veins, and makes it hard to keep the muscles tensely braced and the nerves quiet. I could see one of the howdah elephants on the wing coming through the tall grass, the man in the howdah bending over now and then and looking downward into the long grass, his rifle half up to his shoulder ready for a snap shot. I began to think that it was all over, as I felt confident that no tiger could have remained out there so long, with that din on top of it.

"Again the grass on the far side of the nullah swayed slightly, and from almost the exact spot at which the tiger had looked out shortly before, another and very large tiger's head appeared. I could not have put my feelings of absolute astonishment into words, had I tried. But it is ever the unexpected that happens in sport. For an instant the big tiger stood at gaze and then came out of the grass and disappeared. There was a drop there, and I now understood the configuration of the ground. He had sprung down this and was in the long grass of the ravine. Whether he had seen the elephant or not I could not say. We were in shadow, so I think not. We traced his stealthy approach by the waving grass heads. Suddenly I saw a patch of him, and fired on the instant. A roar answered my shot, and I saw a bounding streak of yellow, at which I fired again, and it seemed to disappear. Before I had time to make up my mind as to what had happened, however, a second roar sounded on my ears. I hurriedly dropped the empty rifle and seized hold of my second in the rack. As my hand felt and grasped it, an undulating yellow streak came out of the grass and flung itself at the tusker's head with a blood-curdling roar. The elephant never moved, but raised up his head to endeavour to get the tigress, for she it was, on to his tusks. The movement unsteadied me, and I gripped the railing of the howdah with one hand to get my feet again, whilst I lifted up the rifle with the other hand. The tigress was now on the base of the elephant's trunk, endeavouring to make good a purchase, and the tusker was shaking himself in the endeavour to get rid of her. Only those who have been on an elephant in a howdah when the

beast is engaged in this performance can have the faintest notion of what it is like. At the first shake I was as nearly as anything shot out of the howdah like a parched pea. Desperately I clung to the rail and tried to get the muzzle of the rifle on to it. At last I got my feet wedged into either side of the howdah, and pressing my knees against the front, I gripped the rifle with both hands and cocked it. As I did so, I was again nearly flung out by a terrible shake, and at the same instant the tigress was sent flying into the ravine. I recovered myself, and was foolish enough to take a snap shot at her. As it happened, I hit her far back, and this only maddened her still further. Again she came for us, and this time the elephant gave a step or two, preventing me firing until the tigress was about to spring a second time for his head. This time, however, my bullet found its billet behind the neck, severing the spinal cord, and she dropped like a stone, as fine a fighting tigress as I had ever encountered.

"By this time I was bathed in perspiration, could hardly see out of my eyes for it, and was feeling pretty sore from the struggles I had made to retain my footing. But the tusker had now to be reckoned with. He was fairly roused, and to use a vulgar expression, was seeing red. Scarcely had the tigress dropped in a heap on the ground, when he rushed towards her, kicked her some yards with his fore feet, luckily not in the direction of my first tiger, then knelt on her and flattened her out of all recognition. Standing up, he got her between his feet and played pitch-and-toss with her between them, sending her backwards and forwards until she was a jelly. Then he varied his performance by dancing on her, until by degrees his ardour cooled, and the mahout's persuasions finally reduced him to something like sanity, although he remained a very vain, victorious, and exceedingly touchy elephant for a couple of days. The mahout had at first tried to keep him in hand and save the skin, but had then given up, recognizing that it would be as well to let him have his way and feel that he had come out the conqueror over the tigress; for otherwise he might have been spoilt as a tiger elephant. As a matter of fact, he remained as good as ever, if anything more contemptuous of tigers than before.

"By the time the tusker had been brought to a fairly reasonable frame of mind, I was reduced to a state of total exhaustion. To be played battledore and shuttlecock with in a hard-sided howdah, with the thermometer over 100 degrees in the shade, and that immediately after being charged twice by two different tigers, was an experience it is not given to many to go through. With difficulty I retrieved the rifles and put one of them to safety. Why that rifle had not gone off when it had been tossed about at full cock in the howdah is one of the mysteries I shall never be able to solve.

"As soon as I was capable of understanding anything, and that was not until I had had a long and exceedingly nasty hot drink—for it was before the days of the thermos bottle—I heard from my friend, who had come up, that two tigers had been found dead in addition to the mass of pulp which was all that the tusker had left of the tigress. An examination of the second tiger I had fired at, and which I had thought at the time had dropped in the grass to my second shot, showed it to be the fine big male, and this solved the riddle. As he dropped, the tigress, who must have been just behind him in the grass on the far side of the ravine, maddened at his death and at finding her retreat barred, came out bald-headed at us, and very nearly had her revenge for the loss of husband and son. They all came out at the same place, and were evidently using a well-known and familiar line of retreat to the hills.

"But for all that, it was the most wonderful piece of luck man has ever had, to have them all three at once and to get them all charging.

"The congratulations I received were hearty and sincere, as you may guess, and the skins of those two tigers, with the tail of the tigress, are amongst my most treasured sporting trophies."

PART II

GAME PROTECTION AND THE PROVISION OF SANCTUARIES FOR THE PRESERVATION OF THE INDIAN FAUNA

CHAPTER XX

THE INDIAN POACHER AND HIS WAYS

The Indian poacher without firearms—Decrease of animals owing to his methods—Elephant pitfalls—Bison, deer and other animals caught by pitfalls—Sambhar nooses—Light and ring method of trapping chital—Black buck nooses and fish-hook method—Netting pig—Use of poisoned bows and arrows—Light and bell method for hare—Netting hare—Trap-door cage for porcupine—Bow and arrow method for tiger—Trap-door cage and goat for leopard—Gun trap for leopard—Cage for jackal—Call method for jackal—"Flying-fox" netting—The snaring of birds—Liming for insectivorous birds—The peacock tail screen for pea-fowl—Nooses for pea-fowl—And hook and line—Call birds and nooses for partridge—The line of nooses—Netting—Methods of netting for quail—The basket trap for quail—Noosing pigeon—Nooses for duck—Bird-liming—Snaring the kingfisher—Egret killing.

BEFORE treating of the question of Game Sanctuaries and the Protection of the Fauna generally I propose to give a brief description here of a few of the methods employed by the Indian poacher without firearms to capture some of the mammals and birds to which protection is supposed to have been given in the past by the Game Act and Rules.

A great deal of discussion has taken place in India during the past couple of decades on the subject of the decrease of game animals in the country and their future preservation by the formation of Sanctuaries. The decrease has usually been attributed to the inadequacy of the Game Act and Rules made under it; to the increase in the use, effectiveness and cheapness of firearms, and the ease with which the community, including the villager, can secure them, owing to the slackness with which permits for the possession and use of firearms are issued to all and sundry on the easily preferred pretext that they are required for the protection of crops from the depredations of animals; to the former laxity in supervision over the sale of powder and shot; and, finally, to the decrease in the areas of jungle capable of affording asylum to some of the larger animals owing to the extension of agricultural lands, the development of the mineral wealth of the country, the building of railways and roads, and to the conservancy operations of the Forest Department through which the jungles are constantly disturbed.

All of these are, it may be admitted, factors leading to a decrease in the fauna and especially in the game fauna of the country and will be treated of in a subsequent chapter. But as important a factor, perhaps a more important one in its effects on the great decrease which is imperilling some of the species in the country, is to be found in the operations of the Indian poacher. The poacher has remained outside the notice of the Government and has had a free hand to perpetrate his nefarious practices. I propose to deal briefly with some of the methods by which this inhuman class of slayers carry out their operations. They will speak for themselves. Considerable ingenuity is displayed in many of the methods employed by the poaching fraternity. But any admiration one may feel for the cleverness is overwhelmed by horror as one realizes that both animals and birds are often done to death by methods the brutal callousness of which has to be witnessed in order to be credited.

A few of the common practices in force are enumerated below. Some of them I have myself seen and investigated personally. For others I am indebted to Messrs. Douglas Dewar and P. Wyndham, both of the Indian Civil Service; and to Messrs. P. H. Clutterbuck, C.I.E., and W. F. Perrée, C.I.E., of the Forest Service, all well-known authorities who have studied this game- and animal-protection question.

Some Indian Poaching Methods of Trapping and Securing Animals and Birds

I. ANIMALS

Elephants

Pitfalls.—A barbarous method of catching elephants used to be commonly in force, and still is in parts of the country. Pitfalls are dug on the elephant tracks in all sorts of ground and carefully concealed. In spite of this animal's great sagacity and caution it falls into them readily. The pits are dug—

(1) In a confined area such as a narrow pass over a range of hills, the pit being dug at a season when the elephants are absent from the area.

(2) Under certain trees which elephants are known to visit to eat the leaves or fruit.

(3) In groups in areas frequented by elephants.

The arrangement of these pits is very skilful. An open one is often left exposed whilst one or two others, dug close by, are carefully covered up with a light branchwood lattice-work which is overlaid with earth, twigs and leaves, so as to closely resemble the rest of the forest floor in the neighbourhood. In avoiding the open pit the elephant falls into one of the concealed ones. Or, again, a group of pits are dug at varying intervals in a comparatively small area. When an elephant falls into one of these some of the rest of the herd, in scattering panic-stricken, fall into neighbouring ones.

Or, again, the pit may be dug at the end of a large fallen tree. The elephant in going round the tree falls into the pit.

In Mysore the pits dug by the natives are ten and a half feet long by seven and a half feet broad and fifteen feet deep. This space by no means gives too much room to the elephant falling in, especially if it is a large one. The reason for keeping the pits small is to obviate the risk of the tuskers being able to use their tusks to dig themselves out by scraping down the sides of the pits. If left undisturbed for a couple of days after falling into a pit, male tuskers are said to be usually able to perform this operation and so escape. To prevent the animal sustaining injury in the fall either through broken limbs or internal injury due to the great drop to the bottom of the pit or to minimise this danger so far as possible, a strong bar is fixed across the mouth of the pit, about the centre, upon which the neck of the elephant usually strikes. The bar generally breaks under the great weight or at least bends, but its presence causes the animal to fall more or less horizontally on its feet. The shock of the fall could also be reduced by means of a thick cushion of branches placed at the bottom, but the natives digging the pit rarely bother to take this precaution owing to the extra labour involved.

Both in Mysore and in Madras in former times a large

number of elephant pits used to be kept up, in which many of the animals were caught annually. A very high percentage of the elephants so trapped died as a result of this barbarous method of securing them. In fact it may be said that as a general rule only the smaller animals on whom the shock of the fall was not so severe survived. Another cause of the high mortality was due to the inefficient supervision maintained over the pits by the jungle-men who were responsible for watching them and carrying information to the elephant-men. Owing to this carelessness many of the elephants so trapped died of starvation.

Both the Commissariat and Forest Departments in former days used the pit method to trap elephants, with the indifferent success which might be expected from such a practice when the great weight of the animal it was sought to trap is taken into consideration. The method has been given up, but in Mysore and Travancore Native States it was in force till lately, if it is not still in use.

In Mysore, for the sake of catching a few elephants annually to be utilized for State purposes, scores of animals are, or were, killed by this most cruel and barbarous plan.

Bison

Pitfalls.—Many other animals besides elephants fall into the pits which are primarily dug to secure the larger animal. Bison, boars, sambhar and other deer, are often the victims of the pitfall system. These animals, when found in the pits, are killed and eaten by the jungle-men. In fact it is the hope of obtaining the flesh of these animals incarcerated by bad fortune in the pits which forms the strongest inducement to the jungle-men to maintain an efficient watch over their charge. I have heard it said on good authority that in the past considerable numbers of bison were annually killed through falling into elephant pits and that these latter alone have led to a decrease in the numbers of this fine animal. In the interests of the preservation of this species, if we omit the question of cruelty, the pitfall system should be rigidly put down throughout India.

Cattle grazing in the forests also fall into the pits, sustaining broken limbs or backs.

Sambhar

Pitfalls.—Pitfalls are also specially dug in some parts of the country, particularly in the south, to catch sambhar and other deer. The spots chosen for the pits are often on the edge of the cultivated tracts in the neighbourhood of the forest boundary. The pits are usually about four feet deep, narrower at the bottom than the top, with a stout sharp-pointed stake driven firmly into the soil at the bottom, its sharp end projecting upwards.

Sambhar come out at night to feed on the crops in the fields, retiring to the forests at dawn by one of their accustomed "runs." The animals fall into the prepared pits, becoming impaled on the stake where they remain in agony until the arrival of the inhuman beings who have prepared the trap.

The Noose.—In the United Provinces large grass nooses are placed in holes in fences in order to catch sambhar as they go in and out when making their nightly foray on the crops. Mr. P. Wyndham records this method and I have seen it practised in other parts of the country.

The above methods, it will become apparent, have no regard for the sex or age of the animal taken, nor for the season at which it is slaughtered. The Indian poacher counts these points as nothing in spite of the rules in force.

Spotted Deer or Chital

Pitfalls.—The pitfall system as described under sambhar is also used to catch the graceful spotted deer.

The Light and Rings.—The curiosity of the deer tribe is proverbial and advantage of this trait is taken by the native to kill the chital. This beautiful little deer is found in the more open parts of forest lands, as also in the dense jungles in many parts of India. The following methods are in force for trapping it.

Two men go out at night armed with the following apparatus: a lighted bull's-eye lantern and a bamboo some eighteen inches in length on to which two iron rods, bent to form arcs, are fixed. Six or seven iron rings are slipped on to each rod before it is fixed to the bamboo.

The men go out at night into an area frequented by chital, and, taking up their position, display the lighted bull's-eye and swing the bamboo gently, causing the rings to run up and down the rods. A curious grating noise is thus produced.

The curiosity of the deer is excited by the light and the unusual sounds and they come up to investigate the strange phenomenon, when they are promptly clubbed to death or shot without reference to age or sex.

Black Buck

The Noose Snare.—The black buck is a dainty little antelope inhabiting the plains of India, and frequenting the cultivated country. The natives have various methods of trapping this beautiful little beast.

A common method is to tether on the ground a system of nooses. A large number of pegs, to each of which a noose made of gut is attached, are fixed to a line which may be two hundred yards in length. The line of nooses is pegged out some hundred yards from where a herd of buck are feeding. The men then make a detour so as to get the animals between themselves and the nooses. The buck are then driven on to the nooses in which some of them get their feet entangled. The snarers then run up and knock the struggling animals on the head.

The Fish-hook.—A common device employed in the Pilibhit district and elsewhere is infinitely more diabolical and displays a fiendish cruelty. The apparatus is simple and consists of a strong fish-hook baited with the bael fruit. The hook is attached by a small piece of strong string, about eighteen inches in length, to the middle of a small piece of wood similar to that used by boys in England for playing tip-cat. A number of these baited hooks are prepared and scattered about in areas in which black buck are known to feed.

The little antelope is very partial to the bael fruit and takes the bait greedily. The strong hook gets firmly caught in the side of the mouth. To get rid of it the wretched animal makes frantic efforts, pawing at the place with his forefeet. This action sooner or later results in the string attached to the hook slipping into and up the cleft of the hoof, the piece of wood eventually stopping its further progress. The impact of the wood against the hoof drives the hook deeper into the flesh, at the same time causing the tortured animal to fall to the ground where it lies struggling convulsively until the fiends who are practising this devilish form of hunting run up and club it to death.

Pig

Pitfalls.—Pig, the wild boar and his female companions, commit serious depredations in the villagers' crops and our sympathies are with the latter in their efforts to stop the damage. But no countenance should be given to methods which result in torture or a lingering death.

The pitfall system, as practised for sambhar and spotted deer, is also used to trap pig.

Nets.—Pigs are also snared by being driven into a system of nets erected on the line of route they will take on returning to the forest after their foray into the fields. The nets are stout ones with a mesh of four inches by four inches. The nets erected, the men go round and stampede the pigs who bolt blindly for the forest and get enmeshed, when they are speared, knifed or shot. The flesh is eaten or sold in the bazaar.

This trapping of animals into nets with the object of obtaining the flesh, hides and horns, is very commonly practised in India, especially at seasons when the animals are collected together in numbers in a tract of jungle, e.g., during the hot season, near the only available water or in the monsoon when large tracts of country are inundated· Great drives are undertaken in which animals of both sexes and all ages are slaughtered in large numbers.

In Assam at certain seasons such drives are carried out, and great skill is exhibited in driving the animals into the nets placed on the outskirts of some thick patches of jungle. The animals stampede and get entangled in the nets in a frightened, struggling mass, and are then knocked on the head in a barbarous fashion.

Bows and Poisoned Arrows.—In some parts of India, more especially amongst the jungle tribes, trapping is not much resorted to but poisoned arrows are used for killing deer and pig, and even larger animals such as bison.. The poison used is either decocted from some poisonous plant or shrub or rotten meat.

Hare

The native exhibits both ingenuity and his knowledge of the habits and idiosyncrasies of the animals he pursues in his methods of killing hares.

The Light and Bell.—The hare in Pilibhit is trapped in a

manner somewhat similar to the method employed for chital, advantage being taken of its bump of curiosity.

The apparatus employed consists of a bull's-eye lantern, a rug, a bell, and a stout club (lathi).

Two men go out at night. On arriving at a suitable locality they take up a position in Indian file, bend down and throw the rug over them so as to simulate a horse moving slowly along. The first man has the lighted bull's-eye and the bell, the second the club. The light and the bell excite the curiosity of the hare who approaches to investigate and is promptly clubbed to death by the rear man.

A modification of the above is to carry the light and bell, or a jingling apparatus, on what is known in India as a banghi—a long stout stick carried across the shoulder. The light hangs from one end and the bell or other jingling apparatus is suspended from the other. The man carrying the banghi walks ahead and the second, armed with a thick stick or club and a clap net, behind. The hare, attracted by the light and jangling, approaches and sits up to investigate. The second man claps the landing net over him, or clubs him, whichever is easiest of accomplishment.

Nets.—Clap nets are also erected at the corners of fields to catch hares, the net being placed on the run.

Porcupine

Trap-door Cage.—The trap-door cage in common use against panthers is also used to secure porcupines. It is described under panther below.

Tiger

Bow and Arrow.—In Chota Nagpur and the Central Provinces, and perhaps elsewhere, the jungle-men occasionally kill tiger with a large powerful bow. The arrow has an iron tip which is dipped in a deadly poison. The bow is fixed horizontally, at the height of a tiger's shoulder when he is walking, at a few yards to the side of a path the animal is known to use. The arrow is placed in the bow, the latter drawn to its full compass, and the whole fixed in an ingenious manner, so that a slight jar will set free the arrow. This jar is given by the tiger unwarily touching a fine line which is stretched across the path, being attached to the springing apparatus on the bow on the one side and to the base of a tree-stem on the other. The tiger springs the trap and the arrow is shot into its side, with the result that its death is certain provided the poison is virulent enough. The bows used are of tremendous strength and size, and success is achieved on occasions, but the trap is by no means a certainty. The tiger sometimes becomes suspicious and quits the path before reaching the stretched line, or may even have the luck to walk over it without springing the arrow. The plan is more especially employed to endeavour to get rid of a man-eater or a cattle-lifter who has taken a higher percentage of the cattle than even the lazy jungle folk can suffer with equanimity. Ordinarily these men are far too lazy to take the trouble to set traps to kill tiger. This form of snare is very dangerous. Of course all the villagers in the vicinity are aware that it has been set but this does not apply to the casual passer-by. The villagers may forget to warn him or may not know of his presence, a stranger being a rarity perhaps in such remote parts. I believe this form of trap has, in fact, been prohibited, though it was in use when I first went to Chota Nagpur.

Leopard or Panther

The Trap-door Cage.—The panther is amongst the wariest and cutest of the jungle animals—so wary and so cute that the possibility of its being practicable to catch him in a cage would appear to be remote to those acquainted with one side of his character only. But the native of India alongside of whom he lives, and of whose stock in goats and dogs he is inordinately fond, is also possessed of very considerable ingenuity and the feud between the two is now several thousand years old. The leopard's great partiality for the goat is well known to the villager and affords the latter the chance of getting even with the animal. He builds a stout cage with a trap-door provided with stout iron bars and worked by a spring. The cage is set up in a suitable locality in the neighbourhood and a goat tied inside. The trap is in the nature of a sacrifice of old, for the goat is the propitiatory offering to be sacrificed. The apparatus being set the men retire and the goat left alone commences to bleat. The sound attracts the leopard but does not always result in his capture. This latter depends on how hungry he may be and whether hunger or greed will ultimately overcome his excessive bump of cautiousness and cuteness. If the former gets uppermost he enters the cage and seizes the goat. The action releases the trap-door, which clangs down and the animal is a prisoner. His ultimate fate will then depend upon whether he is more valuable dead or alive. If he can be sold to a neighbouring Raja, many of whom keep menageries, his life will be spared; otherwise his death follows on capture. I have seen leopards caught in this manner. It is common. The expression on the trapped animal's face is usually more of baffled rage mingled with shamefacedness that he should have been outdone in cunning by man, than of fear.

A simpler contrivance is a stone or log, so placed that a goat can be tethered under it. The least attempt to pull at the goat results in the stone crashing down and killing the leopard. This method is very commonly practised. Mr. Wyndham tells me that a man in Kumaon recently brought him in three leopards he had killed by this means.

The Loaded Gun Trap.—Sir S. Eardley Wilmot mentions this trap as in use in the United Provinces. The leopard's kill is placed in a zareba of thorns. Across the opening a gun loaded with buckshot is placed in position and sighted. To the trigger a long silken thread is fixed and stretched across the front of the zareba at the height of the animal's chest, the other end being tied to a tree or other convenient purchase. As the leopard comes up to the kill the pressure of his chest against the thread fires the gun and the charge is sent into the animal's side. If the leopard has achieved the reputation of being almost superhumanly cunning, instead of the thread a weight may be arranged to fall at the least touch on to a tight cord attached to the trigger.

Jackals

The Trap-door Cage.—Jackals are trapped by the trap-door cage method already described under the leopard.

The Call Method.—In the United Provinces a practice in vogue amongst the Kanjars and others for killing jackals is by calling them up. A native takes up his position outside a cane field armed with a branch of a tree, a call, and a couple of dogs whom he hides. He then starts calling to the jack, waving the branch in front of his mouth. This latter action breaks the sound of the call and renders it more natural. As soon as the jack comes close enough the dogs are set loose at him.

THE "FLYING-FOX" OR FRUIT-EATING BAT

Mr. Douglas Dewar has given me the following note on the method of trapping that loathsome mammal, the fruit-eating bat, which Europeans in India commonly call the "Flying-fox."

"Certain natives of India consider that Flying-foxes are good to eat; while the fat is said to be a remedy for rheumatism and impotency. As everyone knows, these creatures feed at night on whatever fruit happens to be ripe. Selecting a tree which from observation the men know will be visited after sunset by a colony of flying-foxes, they proceed to rig up a net in front of it, in the direction from which they know the bats will come. In order to put up the net it is necessary that there should be two trees taller than and on either side of the fruit tree the bats will visit; over one of the higher branches of each of these trees a long rope is thrown. Care is taken that neither rope becomes entangled in any twigs. It is essential that both may be readily pulled backwards and forwards. A net is then attached to one of the ropes and the two latter are tied together so that there is now but one length of rope that runs over both trees with a net in the middle. If a man goes to each of the loose ends of what is now one rope, and pulls them, the net is raised and hangs in front of the fruit tree. The net is thus raised just before the bats are timed to appear and is held in position until the first of these arrives. It is caught in the net. The men holding the sides of the rope let them run through their fingers so that the net with the entangled flying-fox falls to the ground. A third man secures the bat and as soon as it is removed the net is again pulled up in readiness for the next victim."

A very similar method was practised by the men who had to protect the crop of lichis and mangoes in the large compound of the house I occupied at Dehra. The bats used to arrive in flocks when the fruit of these trees was ripening, and were a great nuisance.

II. BIRDS

A large number of birds are destroyed annually by the natives without discrimination of species, season or close time, or the fact that the destruction of the parents in the breeding season results in the young ones perishing in the nest. The damage resulting is of varying importance. The common practice of bird-liming by the "chirya walla" might almost be looked upon as an occupation or trade. Hundreds of thousands of useful insectivorous birds of the highest economic importance to the agriculturist must be destroyed yearly by this class of bird poacher. Other birds are snared for their plumage or for sale for food purposes. The methods commonly employed are those of the poacher pure and simple. In England such methods are met by prosecution and punishment. It is high time that many of the practices in force against bird life in India should be dealt with in the same way. The following are but a few of the methods in force.

Pea-fowl

The Peacock-tail Screen.—The man who thought of this was an ingenious dog. It depends, as in so many other instances in India, upon the natural pugnacity and fighting proclivities of the cocks and a knowledge of how to turn this trait to advantage. A screen or shield is made of the head and tail feathers of the peacock. With this screen and a stout heavy stick the man repairs to a spot in the neighbourhood in which he knows pea-fowl abound. As he approaches the locality he holds the shield in front of him with one hand, grasping the stick in the other. The man dances the screen, which completely hides him, up and down, thus making it look like a live cock bird full of fight and ready to take on all comers. The challenge is soon taken up by a wild bird who advances in battle order to fight and when within distance is knocked over by the man.

The Line of Nooses.—To a long line, which may be as much as two hundred yards in length, wooden pegs are attached at intervals. To each peg is tied a noose of twisted horsehair—the sinews of black buck are also used for the nooses—sixteen inches in diameter. The snarer proceeds with a pony to a spot which he knows to be frequented by pea-fowl. As soon as he sees a cluster of the birds feeding he crouches down behind his pony which continues to walk forward, and pays out his line of nooses, which is carried on the wrist. Each peg is stuck into the ground, the stiff noose projecting vertically upwards. When all the line has been paid out it stretches more or less tautly in a straight line along the ground, the nooses at the end of their pegs projecting vertically from the ground surface. The man then continues on with the pony until sufficiently far away from the fowl to be able to make a detour, when he reappears on the far side and drives the birds on to the nooses. With luck he makes a good haul in this fashion.

Hook and Line.—Another method employed is to "fish" for the birds with a hook, baited with fruit, fixed to a long length of line.

Partridge

Call Bird and Nooses.—A tame partridge is placed in a wicker cage to which three or four double horsehair nooses are attached. The cage is set down in a locality known to be frequented by the birds and a network of similar nooses is pegged out all round the cage. The man then hides himself close by. The partridge is a pugnacious bird, always ready for a scrap. The bird in the cage commences calling and soon attracts a bird who considers the ground belongs to him. He commences attacking the caged bird unless previously snared, and soon gets caught in a noose. Others come up to join in the fray and the snarer is often rewarded by a good catch. As previously mentioned, and the point bears insisting upon, no respect is paid to season or sex by the men who ply this business.

The Line of Nooses.—This has already been described under pea-fowl. Crows are also trapped in this way.

Netting.—Clap nets are also set up at the corners and edges of fields with the object of taking partridges.

Quail

Netting.—Quail are probably more poached by netting than almost any other bird in India. Call birds are commonly used, the part of the field in the neighbourhood being netted. Another method is to draw a rope, held at each end by a man, through the standing crop (dál), the birds running before it being netted at the other end.

In a kodo field the net is drawn over the crop till the end of the field has been nearly reached. The net is then stopped suddenly and held down and the birds beneath it caught.

In the Central Provinces, according to Mr. Clutterbuck, the following method is employed, and I think in parts of Bengal also.

The Cul-de-sac Net.—The term best describes this

ingenious method of snaring quail. Two lengths of net, each about thirty feet in length and four and a half inches in height, are pegged out on the ground at an angle of about 130 degrees, a small opening being left between the two interior edges of the nets. A covered net about six feet in length is then pegged out, the opening ends joined on to the interior edges of the long nets, the rest of the net being stretched backwards from the latter so as to form an elongate conical channel, joined at the top and upper end, forming a *cul-de-sac*. The man commences operations by imitating the quail call and as soon as he gets a number of answers and hears the birds coming up, he pegs out his nets and then makes a detour so as to get the quail between himself and the nets. He then walks forward slowly in a zigzag manner towards the nets and when near enough drives the quail on to the nets. On reaching the two long nets the birds run along, seeking an opening instead of hopping over. Those that turn inwards, and they preferably run along the outward slope, eventually reach the opening into the *cul-de-sac*, into which they run and are thus trapped.

The Basket Trap.—The basket trap is another method made use of. An elongate basket with a hole at the top through which the hand can be inserted is used. The man ascertains, by careful observation and search, the bushes under which quail roost on the ground at night. This is determined by their droppings. He proceeds in the evening towards the spot marked down and as soon as the quail are asleep, a little after sunset, he approaches and drops the basket over the bush. He then inserts his hand and with luck will have the lot.

Pigeon

Noose.—A common method is to catch the pigeon round the leg whilst sitting on a tree, by means of a fine horsehair noose affixed to the end of a long thin rod like a fishing-rod.

Duck

Noose.—Strong bamboo uprights are pushed firmly into the bottom of a jhil (lake). These bamboos project some six feet above the water. They are connected together by a strong line tied to them about four or five feet above the surface of the water. From this horizontal line a row of nooses is suspended, about two feet apart, the noose being about ten by seven inches. When the duck are flighting in the evening or early morning those passing just above the water in the direction of the snare are, unless they spot it in time and rise over it, caught by the neck and hang in this position until the snarer comes to fetch them. The method is successful, since it is not easy to see the line in the gloaming until the birds are up to it and almost impossible to perceive the much finer nooses.

Another method is to peg down a line, or lines, of horsehair nooses on the edge of a jhil and place a little rice in each snare, the snares being of course on the ground. The lines of nooses are all attached to a strong main line. This method does not appear to be quite as successful in its results as the former since it is common to find many more coots in the snares than duck.

KINGFISHER

Liming.—I have already mentioned the bird-man (chirya walla) whose occupation is catching birds by liming. He is a common sight. He uses a long pole which can be extended to a considerable length by jointed pieces. It would be of very considerable interest, as it is of importance, to know the number of useful birds which this professional bird-catcher secures in the year.

He catches the large kingfisher by staking out a captured bird near the water and placing sticks of bird-lime close by. The free bird comes down to fight the staked one and is bird-limed and taken.

EGRET

Net.—Some species of egret are of value for their plumage. A merciless war has been waged upon them and there is every danger that the species will become extinct. Since the plumage is borne in the breeding season the indiscriminate destruction of the birds by netting, shooting and so forth results in the young nestlings who have lost their parents inevitably dying. No species, however abundant and prolific, can stand this sort of merciless warfare waged on it without disappearing. If the plumage sellers are really concerned in maintaining the supply of articles of this nature for their commercial operations, it is time they asked the various Governments in the countries from which they draw them, to institute such methods of collection as shall ensure the proper preservation of the species.

Edward John Buck

Simla Past and Present.

Bombay: Times Press, 1925.

CHAPTER III.

Viceregal Hospitality and the A.-D.-C.

IN this Chapter I propose to make some remarks on the subject of Viceregal hospitality in India, but before I do so I would recommend all who are interested in this delicate subject to peruse Lord Curzon's most interesting final chapter in his last book, which deals with 'Forms, Ceremonies and Entertainments' and gives a vivid description of Viceregal pomp and entertaining in early days. Very few people I fancy have any idea of the enormous amount of entertaining which the King Emperor's representative is expected to do to-day. Usually the first action of any distinguished visitor to Delhi, or Simla or wherever the Viceroy is residing, is to inscribe his name in the visitors' book which is always placed in charge of a scarlet liveried servant at the entrance gate of Viceregal Lodge. All officials of Government of a certain standing are expected to call as a matter of course, just as they are expected to attend levees, drawing rooms, and certain state functions. The majority of people who perform this act of duty, or courtesy as the case may be, then sooner or later receive an invitation to some Viceregal function or other, be it lunch, dinner, garden party, or dance. It is the special duty of one of the Aides-de-camp to attend under their Excellencies' orders to the issue of invitations, and needless to say, there are some heart-burnings in the course of the year when, as must happen, certain people feel themselves aggrieved at being omitted. At a big ball like that held in honour of the King Emperor's birthday when the guests may be over a thousand in number, the Viceroy naturally cannot know all of those present, and on one occasion a certain Governor-General remarked to a Secretary to Government at a birthday ball, "Do you know who all these people are"? The Secretary made one of those unhappy replies which might have been expressed differently, and said, "Good Heavens, no Sir ; you always see people at this ball you never see anywhere else"! "Really," replied His Excellency in a peculiar tone which for the time being quite collapsed his faithful Secretary. In Calcutta in the olden days it was more or less understood that if a man wrote his name in the Viceregal book, and attended the Viceroy's annual levee that he had an actual right to be asked to the State Ball and State Garden Party. To attend these functions was to receive the prized hall mark of society by being recognised as on the Government House list, and Lord Curzon was the first Viceroy to intimate diplomatically to the Indian public that when a Viceroy practically paid for entertainments out of his own purse he was at liberty to select his guests. This was done in consequence of a certain Calcutta resident actually demanding an invitation to a State function. The mention of Lord Curzon's name reminds me that it was an open secret that he and Lady Curzon personally spent nearly £15,000 in entertaining their guests at the famous Delhi Durbar of 1904. The actual salary drawn to-day by the King's representative in India is Rs. 2,40,000 a year and his official allowance to-day for entertaining is only Rs. 40,000 or under £3,000 a year. This salary has been the same for many years past, and when the rupee stood at two shillings or more in the days when the obligations of a Viceroy were comparatively light, it was what might be called an attractive salary. Lord Curzon I note has recorded that the salary given has commonly sufficed for the performance of the obligation of entertaining on quite an adequate scale, and he has also stated that he has known of a Viceroy who in the last half century managed to save £30,000 during his tenure of office. But no one seems to know who this Viceroy was. To-day however prices are very different and the cost of living since the war has risen enormously, while the calls on the Viceregal purse in many directions are heavy and continuous. I have heard it said more than once on good authority that no Viceroy in recent years has saved a rupee out of his official salary, and that several have had to dip heavily into their private purses in order to preserve that dignity of position which means so much to the ordinary Indian world. To the vast uneducated mass of the population the "burra lat sahib" (Great Lord Sahib) is still the embodiment of all that is powerful in the country. However in these days of retrenchment and reform the splendour of the Viceregal court has suffered in common with other institutions, and within the last few months His Excellency's brilliant Bodyguard has undergone a reduction. Indeed in a recent Legislative Assembly debate on the financial budget the grants for the Viceregal establishment were severely criticised, and the cost of an extra short-hand writer for the Viceroy's personal use was actually objected to by certain Indian critics of expenditure. But there are many men who think the more state a Viceroy can preserve, without undue extravagance, the better it is for the Indian Empire. In this connection however those are not wanting who wonder how the next Viceroy will appreciate being called upon to upkeep the huge palace which is being prepared for him in New Delhi. I might add that Lord and Lady Reading have been a charming host and hostess, and have nobly preserved all the best traditions of princely Indian hospitality, for their official residence has scarcely ever been free of visitors from abroad. More than one European and American travellers will, I know, bear me out in these remarks.

At Viceregal official functions it is always the custom for an aide-de-camp to inform guests courteously that the Viceroy, or his wife, who is sometimes incorrectly called the Vicereine, would like to converse with them, and the aide then conducts the guest to the spot where one of their Excellencies is sitting. A sensation was caused in social circles in Calcutta when a well-known American lady at a dance at Government House on being informed that Lord Lansdowne, then Viceroy, wished to talk to her, declined to accompany the aide-de-camp to the other end of the ball room. In answer to the latter's explanation that it was the custom in India, and the Viceroy's privilege to send for ladies he wished to speak to, she retorted that gentlemen in America and other parts of the world who wished to converse with her always sought her side, and she had no intention of obeying any man's summons be he Viceroy or not. Nothing would persuade the fair visitor to alter her mind, and eventually she and her husband returned to their yacht on the Hooghly, and were not again invited to the Viceroy's residence during their brief visit to India.

It goes without saying that Viceregal invitations are much prized, and there is a story of a lady, who resided some years ago at a Simla hotel, making her appearance at a Viceregal party at which she was not expected. On being politely interrogated she informed the aide-de-camp who addressed her that she had received an invitation card. Then the Military Secretary took the matter up, and having previously obtained an assurance that her card would at once be sent back to her, madame despatched it to Viceregal Lodge for inspection. It was duly returned to her with a very ample apology for the inconvenience she had been put to. Subsequent enquiries however proved that her body servant had indulged in a little financial transaction with a subordinate official of the Viceregal invitation bureau, and shortly afterwards both lady and official disappeared from Simla. But the fair dame took with her to the plains the invitation card as well as the apology !

When a Governor of the Punjab, a Commander-in-Chief, or a member of His Excellency's council vacates his office, the Viceroy of the day usually gives a banquet and makes a speech in honour of the departing guest. Sometimes these speeches are given to the press, but now and then no reports are permitted. On one occasion, when a colleague was giving up his office, the Viceroy, whose personal antipathy to this high official was no secret, very briefly alluded to his services, and then in so many words said, "That is quite enough about Sir—we will now allude to Lady—and proceeded to pay her several compliments." The latter, however, was so aggrieved at what she considered a slight to her husband that after dinner she deposited a decoration which had been awarded to her for public service in a flower pot in the corridor, whence it was sent back to her the next morning.

When Lord Minto arrived in India he introduced a custom which at first struck terror into the hearts of ladies who were bidden to dinners at Viceregal Lodge. I refer to the fact that they are now required, when they leave the dining room, to curtsey to His Excellency as they make their exit. I believe that one or two big wigs were much struck with the idea, and proposed to introduce the custom into their own houses with somewhat disastrous results so far as their domestic happiness was concerned. Be this as it may all the official ladies began to practise curtseying with much vigour. On one occasion a charming lady at Viceregal Lodge in attempting to rise after her curtsey, unfortunately fell over her dress, was assisted to her feet by an A.-D.-C. and retired in some confusion. As she disappeared through the doorway where stood as usual the imposing figure of Mr. Jordan, the Viceregal butler, a witty Secretary to Government gently murmured, "Sorrow ended, labour vanquished, Jordan past." And the curtseying was afterwards not inappropriately called 'passing Jordan.'

The Aide-de-Camp in Simla is such an important person that I make no apology for alluding to him. It has been said that he can make or mar a Viceroy's reputation ; certainly he has much to do with His Excellency's social success.

The Viceroy, the Commander-in-Chief, and the Governor of the Punjab all possess these necessary adjuncts in numbers suited to their high degree, and without them it is no exaggeration to say that the dignity and prestige of these important personages would be sadly deficient. "Ali Baba in his "Twenty-one days in India" has so aptly described the A.-D.-C. that I dare not endeavour to improve upon his effort to give a proper idea of this very superior young man in scarlet and gold. Not to know the Viceregal aides-de-camp, as a married lady said, is to admit that "you are not in it" ! She was of course alluding to Simla society. To show how the A.-D.-C. is admired by the maidens in the Himalayas may perhaps be best understood if I tell a little story. One Sunday morning a fair damsel who had only recently arrived from England, accompanied by her mother, attended a morning service at Christ Church. On emerging from the sacred edifice the young lady remarked, "Oh mother was'nt it a lovely service this morning?" "Why was it so lovely Molly?" replied her parent, "I did not see anything very unusual about it." "Oh mother," came the quick response, "how could you say so, did'nt you see that there were five aides-de-camp in Church?" There may be advantages in having an aide always at your back and call, for the Viceroy and his consort are really never allowed to go anywhere without one accompanying them, in either undress uniform or mufti, but on the other hand some men heartily dislike being constantly escorted. I once asked a well known high official why he had declined to officiate as a Lieutenant-Governor of a Province for six months. There are two main reasons he replied, "The first is I want to finish some important work I have initiated, and the second is that if an A.-D.-C. followed me about I know I should shoot him."

On one occasion an aide-de-camp was rather startled to find the Viceroy of the day standing by his bedside in the middle of the night. The great man had been disturbed by some of the household retainers who were making a noise in the lower regions of the lodge and he was very angry. In a few words he told the A.-D.-C. to go down and quiet the offenders. As the A.-D.-C. quickly descended the stairs a hoarse whisper from above arrested his progress, and the Governor-General who had had to deal with more than one case in which an Indian had been assaulted, cautiously instructed him, "Kick them on the shins, and be careful of their spleens."

The A.-D.-C. of to-day may be interested to read the remarks of the anonymous author of "Observations on India" which was written about 1844. He says "Lord Auckland arrived at Simla in company with two elderly maiden ladies, his sisters. Handsome aides-de-camp were here and there and everywhere, and if plain people did not know what the duties of aides-de-camp were, and why so many of them were paid by the State, they might here learn that their employment was to follow the ladies and make themselves generally useful as upper footmen. What swarms of idlers in mountebank finery does the shadow of Monarchy collect around it! Pious youths were not particularly in request in Lord Auckland's house, but good looking ones held the same premium as with his predecessor."

The mention of aides-de-camp naturally recalls the memory of Lord William Beresford, who was on Lord Lytton's staff in the seventies, and Military Secretary to Lord Dufferin and Lord Lansdowne from 1885 to 1893. Lord William's language to aides-de-camp on the steps of Viceregal Lodge when they failed in what he considered their duty was extremely refreshing, for he spared the use of few adjectives suitable or unsuitable. He was a great character possessed enormous influence in all circles, was an enthusiastic racing man, and he often did things which astonished the public. On one occasion he challenged the proprietor of Messrs. Symes and Co., chemists in Simla to a pony-trotting race round Jakko. The race started at Bank buildings, and after a close contest to the convent along the ladies' mile, Lord William came down the steep hill to Chota Simla at such a break neck pace that he won easily. The race took place in the middle of the day and all the work in Government offices ceased while it was being run.

Lord William's name carried terror to the ordinary Indian and there is a story of a servant of his who, being unable to obtain a ticket at the railway station at Amballa complained to his master. Lord William went to the third class window and asked for it, but the babu took very little notice of the request and continued working on some paper or other.

Then the Military Secretary thundered, "Babu, I want a third class to—, I do not think you know who I am, I am Lord William Beresford." The babu gazed at him for a moment in speechless horror, ejaculated "Oh my Lord God," and fell backwards with such violence off his high stool that he was forced to relinquish his duties, for the day. Lord William Beresford was really a most kind hearted man, and 'Bills Babies Ball,' a fancy dress affair which he gave to the children of Simla when he finally departed, was a party which was talked about for years. But I fear I have digressed from my subject of the A.-D.-C. and I will only tell one or two more stories about him. It was one of Lord Elgin's aides-de-camp who began the practice of riding about Simla without a hat. When asked why he did so he said it was too much of a nuisance taking it off to such a lot of people and besides it ruined its brim! When the Viceroy read of this incident in a newspaper he cut out the paragraph, attached it to a sheet of foolscap and wrote—"Captain P. If the cap fits wear it," and his A.-D.-C. took the hint.

A couple of ladies were once discussing as to which was the better aide-de-camp of two young officers whom we will call 'Captain A' and 'Captain B.' After each had briskly defended her own favourite, one of the matrons brought the discussion to a close by remarking, "Well my dear I am sure you'll agree that 'Captain A.' tucks you into your rickshaw most perfectly."

Finally there is the delightful story of the A.-D.-C. (the Viceroyalty shall be nameless) who, at dinner *en famille* one night, was listening intently to the general conversation which had turned on the somewhat extraordinary titles given to modern dance tunes. As the subject was one of which he had a considerable experience in his capacity as an exponent of the "Brighter Simla" theory, he quoted to Her Excellency the tune entitled, "I shall remember your kisses when you have forgotten my name." Her Excellency however was listening to conversation across the table, and did not properly hear what had been said, so turning to the A.-D.-C. she invited him to repeat his remark. With the premonition that something out of the ordinary was about to occur, the general talk ceased and all eyes were turned upon the aide-de-camp who, somewhat confused by this marked attention stammered out, "You will remember my kisses, Your Excellency, when I have forgotten your name." Tableau!

So far I have dealt with the lighter aspect of the A,-D.-C. and his duties, but let us turn to his more serious side—for people are not wanting who think an aide-de-camp's life is one long day of ease and enjoyment. There are others however who know that if the A.-D.-C. has his ornamental side, he also has his useful one, for more than one A.-D.-C. has risen to high office in after life. I find that Captain R. Pole-Carew and Lieutenant G. C. Kitson were on the Earl of Lytton's staff in the eighties. The former died recently full of honours, the latter became Quartermaster-General in India. Captain Lord William Beresford on the same staff afterwards held the post of Military Secretary to three Viceroys.

Was not Lord Rawlinson, the late gallant Commander-in-Chief in India, once A.-D.-C. to Lord Roberts with Colonel Neville Chamberlain and Colonel Ian

Hamilton, as companions on the same staff? Lieutenant W. F. Furse, at one time aide-de-camp to Lord Roberts, retired in 1920, after being Master-General of Ordnance, and a member of the Army Council. Is it not a fact that Lord Ronaldshay, aide-de-camp to Lord Curzon, utilised his great opportunities to such an extent that he became one of the most popular and successful Governors Bengal has ever possessed, and has more than once been mentioned for an ever higher office in India? Field Marshal Sir William Birdwood's name will be found amongst those who were on Lord Kitchener's staff, and he is now Commander-in-Chief in India. Other names that occur to one are those of General Sir George Barrow, once A.-D.-C. to Sir William Lockhart and Sir Power Palmer, and now an Army Commander in India, also General Sir Reginald Barnes, who was with Lord Kitchener and who won his laurels in the Great War, while Brigadier-General F. Maxwell, V.C., who had been his fellow aide-de-camp fell in battle in France. Sir Fritz Ponsonby and Colonel Clive Wigram, who are now holding high postitions in His Majesty's household, were both youthful Aides-de-Camp to Lord Elgin. General E. A. Fagan, now Military Adviser-in-Chief of the Indian States, was once upon on Lord Curzon's staff, the late Sir Rollo Grimston, A.-D.-C. to Lord Lansdowne and Lord Elgin having previously held the appointment, and Viscount Errington, once aide-de-camp to Lord Chelmsford, is now the Earl of Cromer and Lord Chamberlain to His Majesty.

Delhi Sketch Book, 1854.

THE ONLY PLAUSIBLE REASON FOR THE C-IN-C LIVING IN CALCUTTA.

G. G. in Council (Lord Dalhousie) Hoot awa mon what the deevil do you think I know aboot the cut of a drummer's 'breeches'. Dinna ye ken we don't wear breeks in the Heelands, where's that Commander-in-Chief skulkin and idlin in the 'mountains' We'll hae him doon immeediately to settle this deeficult question.

CHAPTER XIV.

Simla Society.

IT is not without somewhat serious misgivings that I venture to write on the delicate subject of this chapter. For it must be admitted that, to a large majority of people both in England and in India, Simla, although the initiated well know that all its women are beautiful and all its men are clever, possesses a social reputation which cannot be described as altogether enviable. How this has arisen, and how far it is to-day capable of being refuted, I will endeavour to show. But before attempting the latter task let us examine the opinions of those who have written of Simla in bygone years.

Let us read what Mr. C. J. French, who was in Lord Auckland's camp in 1838-9, and who dedicated his journals to Sir Frederick Currie, Baronet, then wrote :—

"Mount Jakko seems to be the pivot around which the Simla community revolve in their morning and evening perambulations. The circuit round this hill is about two or three miles, and consists of a broad pathway rendered as level as the nature of hill roads will admit, and in the evening it forms the nucleus around which groups of ladies and gentlemen are observed to congregate. Sometimes the road is entirely taken up with conveyances, when to avoid accident or inconvenience they are obliged to proceed in slow order, but when no such interruption exists a lady or two escorted by a gay cavalier may be seen on their steeds dashing by thicket and grove. While the evening is so often a scene of animation at this spot, in the morning it is generally one of perfect solitude. At a time when the atmosphere is supposed or proved to be the purest—the more so at this elevation—the people neglect the most favourable opportunity of enjoying the exhilarating effects of an early ramble."

In his 'Travels in India,' 1844 to 1866, Colonel S. Dewe White, of the Bengal Staff Corps, wrote as follows :—

"A little farther to the north there was another hill station, more resorted to than any other, which was quite an accessible sanatorium to Bareilly : this was Simla. To this spot would flock all seekers of appointments. An officer aspiring to get a civil or military appointment, who desired to get to some place where, by currying favour with the great, he might create an influence for himself sufficient to secure that object, would select Simla, which was, and is, pre-eminently the most fashionable sanatorium in India. Here the place-hunter would stick during the whole period of his leave, taking every opportunity to ingratiate himself with all who could do him a good turn, as it is to Simla that the Governor-General, Commander-in-Chief, and other magnates annually take their flight to escape the scorching heat of the plains. These great personages draw after them a host of minor swells, too numerous to particularize. Simla, then, for six months, becomes the head-quarters of the civil and military government of India, and for that time endless festivities and gaieties and frivolities are the order of the day."

Referring to a *bal masque* given in 1845 in honour of Prince Waldemar of Prus-

Delhi Sketch Book

SIMLA, IN SEASON, 1851.

sia, then a visitor to Simla, Dr. Hoffmeister, his physician, wrote :—" It was a bright and merry party, for there are here a great many sprightly old ladies who, loaded with perfect gardens of flowers, rush about in the polkas with incredible zeal. They did not appear, as I had heard they were to do, as Dianas or the Graces, but on the contrary in remarkably pretty antiquated costumes, hooped petticoats and stiff brocades : the elderly gentlemen being equipped to correspond. The fancy dresses were all very successful, and selected with much taste. The oriental masked travesties were also very numerous and natural to a degree which doubtless could never have been attained in any other part of the world ; for you may easily imagine, considering the generosity with which all eastern Princes delight in lavishing presents to the right and left, that the British officers, many of them newly arrived from the remotest parts of the East Indies, having been ordered now to the Punjab, now to Scinde or Afghanistan, are richly supplied with costly stuffs which they can turn to account only on occasions such as this. There was however by no means a lack of young ladies, for the kind and thoughtful relatives at Simla never fail to bring up from the plains everything in the shape of young and marriageable nieces or cousins ; and here where so many agreeable officers are stationed for pleasure's sake alone, many a youthful pair are thrown together, and many a match is made."

Dr. Hoffmeister also wrote :—" Every evening after five o'clock, according to Oriental custom, the most stirring and animated scene begins ; especially in the broad street in which our hotel is situated the so-called ' course.'

No one ventures to make his appearance there who is not mounted on a handsome horse ; or who cannot sport the whitest linen, the most stylish cut of coat or showy uniform, and white kid gloves ; for one must need make special toilet here, in order to enjoy the open air. Every creature is on horseback ; even the fair sex dash along on fine, spirited, Arab coursers ; and many an English lady may be seen galloping down the street, followed by a train of three or four elegantly equipped officers, while others of sedater age, are carried about in Jampans. The *Jampan* is a sort of machine, in form resembling an arm-chair, suspended at either side, by means of straps, to a short pole, and borne on the shoulders of bearers in gay and varied liveries ; twelve of these harlequin-like follows running behind. You may thus form some estimate of the immense number of domestics constituting the train of a single lady ; for these bearers never move hand or foot in any other employment than the carrying of the *Jampan*."

In the life of General Sir Hope Grant we find the following passage written in 1846 :—" I returned to Simla (from Kotegarh), and my association with bright ladies and gay gentlemen, all dressed in the height of fashion, for a time caused my love of the quietude and simplicity of a rural life to ooze out of me, and I too thought of nothing but dressing gaily, and wearing polished boots and well turned hat, and attending balls and parties. Music too there had become a great craze."

The ' Delhi Sketch Book,' or Indian Punch, of 1851 contained an amusing skit on a season at Simla showing ' Why they all went up,' and much that was true seventy years ago holds good in the present day. The skit runs :—

" The Governor-General wished to make himself acquainted with the Punjab, so by the advice of Sir Henry * he went up to Simla to take a bird's-eye view of it. On

* Sir Henry Lawrence.

being informed of His Lordship's intention of passing the hot weather in the hills, both His Excellency the Commander-in-Chief of India and His Honour the Lieutenant-Governor of Agra felt it their duty to follow him. The Commander-in-Chief went up at a great deal of personal sacrifice, the hot winds always agreed with him, and he had formed a number of very pleasant acquaintances in the barracks. But the head-quarters were at Simla, and so was the Governor-General, and where these two were, he felt it his duty to be also. 'It's a—nuisance,' as he observed to one of his Aides-de-Camp, 'having to go, but still duty is duty, and the Commander-in-Chief, who would avoid going to the hills to shirk it, is a—,' something we leave the reader to imagine.

"Mr. Thomason* was also very unwilling to leave the plains; he liked his 'tatty'; he liked his bath, and for taking exercise he much preferred his carriage and four to a 'ghoont' (hill pony). Besides there were other reasons that would render a trip to Simla productive of much annoyance. His Honour had always set his face against the hills; and he had left no stone unturned to prevent his subordinates, even the sick, from having access to it, and if there was any truth in common report, he had even gone so far as to remove several persons from their appointments merely to place them out of the way of temptation. His Honour could not help feeling that after preaching so much one way, to practise just the reverse would be giving a great handle to his enemies. How Mr.—would sneer, and say he knew all along what it would come to, and be more than ever confirmed in his opinion of human nature. How Mr.—would chuckle and rub his hands. What hollow interest Sir Henry would begin to take in his health? All this was very disagreeable, but when Mr. Thomason feels a thing to be his duty, it is not a few disagreeables that will deter him from doing it. He had a good deal to say to His Lordship in favour of vernacular education that could not be well put in a letter. The Ganges Canal required a friend at court, and last, though not least, in case Sir Henry Lawrence broke down, it was very desirable that there should be some one at hand who could carry out the Punjab settlement.

"The correspondence of the Governor-General, the Commander-in-Chief and the Lieutenant-Governor, taken collectively, is beyond all question the most important in Upper India. On ascertaining therefore that these illustrious personages intended making Simla their place of residence during the ensuing season, the Post Master-General felt it his duty to ascertain by personal inspection and observation that the post office at that station was in a state of efficiency.

"If, as Pope says, it is only high life that produces high characters, by parity of reason, great official virtue can only be expected to be found in those individuals holding great official situations. Although, as I have shown, the heads of the Government and the head of the Post Office went up to Simla from nothing but the purest regard for the good of the State, I fear the mass of their subordinates were drawn up by much more mixed motives. Some went up for health, some for pleasure, and some few who had an eye to appointments, or a taste for cards, went up on business. Some because they were ill, some because they feared they would be, and some because they were in excellent health and had a mind to enjoy it. Some took sick leave, some took private leave, and some few, I am sorry to say, took no leave at all, but this was only for short periods and from contiguous stations. Old Mr. Slowcoach of the Sudder had only one year more to serve and wished to serve it in the hills, so by great luck his liver broke

* Lieutenant-Governor of N.-W. Provinces.

Delhi Sketch Book

SIMLA OUT OF, SEASON, 1851.

down and enabled him to do so. Young Mr. Mivins, a very rising man, had rather overworked himself and required change of air. Mr. Pringle was getting middle aged and began to want a wife, so he took four months' leave to inspect the new arrivals. Captain Flint, the great shot, wished to try his luck among the 'gurral' (chamois), and Lieutenant Snorley, that celebrated waltzer, his among the ladies. Captain Lounge of the Dragoons had been up every year since his arrival in India, so he went up this rom mere force of habit. Major Drill wished to see the snowy range to tell his friends at home what it was like (he was thinking of selling out), but this being the first leave he had applied for in seven and twenty years, he had some difficulty in obtaining it. Captain Rook and Mr. Sharp went up because they were clever at cards and billiards, and Mr. Spoon and Ensign Jones because they thought they were. In sending in their applications these gentlemen did not think it necessary to state their reasons in too much detail, but hinted in general terms at the existence of urgent private affairs requiring their absence from regimental duties, which indeed was all that was necessary, it being received at that time (I need hardly inform the reader the story is laid under the old *regime*) as an undeniable axiom at head-quarters that every man must be better acquainted with his own private affairs than any third party. If, therefore, an officer thought that they required his absence from his regiment, or his presence in the hills, it was not for those who possessed less information on the subject to contradict.

"Excepting that neither play nor sport were among the inducements, the ladies went up from pretty much the same motives as the gentlemen. Good motherly Mrs. A., because her children's health required it, and little flirting Mrs. B., who had no children, because her own did. Mrs. Clare certainly lived at the dullest of out-stations, and everybody knew the weather half killed her, but I do not believe anything would have induced her to leave her husband, if he, dear old man,—he was a *leettle* her senior—had not absolutely insisted upon it, and then, of course, it was her duty to obey. Miss O. went up because she was Miss O, and did not wish to be so any longer. But what made old match-making Mrs. F. take her (unless, as the gossips said, it was to keep her hand in till Sophia came out) is a mystery. Captain F. wanted staff employ, but had no interest, so he very wisely sent his wife, that very agreeable woman, to make some. Mrs. Lennox was determined her daughters should not be in the plains more than she could help, so she took them up the very first season."

An observant visitor in 1858, whose opinions are tersely recorded, was Dr. W. T. H. Russell, the famous *Times* correspondent, whose graphic description of the United Service Club I have already quoted. Discussing society nearly fifty years ago Dr. Russell said :—" The social distinctions are by no means lost sight of in India ;—on the contrary, they are perhaps more rigidly observed here than at home, and the smaller the society the broader are the lines of demarcation. Each man depends on his position in the public service, which is the aristocracy : and those who do not belong to it are out of the pale, no matter how wealthy they may be, or what claims they may advance to the consideration of the world around them. The women depend on the rank of their husbands. Mrs. A., the wife of a barrister making £4,000 or £5,000 a year, is nobody as compared with Mrs. B., who is a deputy commissioner, or with Mrs. C., who is the better half of the station surgeon. Wealth can do nothing for man or woman in securing them honour or precedence in their march to dinner, or on their way to the supper table, or in the dance. A successful speculator, or a 'merchant prince,' may force his way into good society in England; he may be presented at court and flourish at court balls, but in India he must remain for ever outside the sacred barrier which keeps the non-official world from the high society of the services. This is, to some extent, a necessity of position, and at a place like Simla, where there is an annual gathering of all sorts of people, it is desirable to take care whom you know."

Dr. Russell also wrote :—" Soon after our return the reports from the bazaar which reached us—in other words, the stories of the natives respecting the proceedings of the young gentlemen who are up here on leave and sick-certificate—show that Simla must be entitled to a high position as a sanatorium; for its health-restoring properties, to judge from the wildness of these gentlemen's spirits, are well-nigh miraculous.

" There can be no more convincing proof of the very lax notions of discipline and decency of these young men than the excesses of their conduct, which would not be endured in any place where a sound public opinion existed, or indeed any public opinion at all. In former days, when Cashmere was visited by the British, their wild exuberance of spirits was so great that the Indian Government was forced to appoint a diplomatic officer of rank to look after these young gentlemen; and I am decidedly of the opinion that a senior officer should be sent to all our hill-stations to exercise a proper, but not a too rigid, control over the fast invalids and riotous sick who recover themselves so boisterously. . . . . I think that every Englishman in India ought to look upon himself as a sort of unrecognized unpaid servant of the State, on whose conduct and demeanour towards the natives may depend some of the political prestige of our rule in the whole empire. He is bound to keep the peace, to obey the law, to maintain order and good government. In the hill-stations he certainly does not exhibit any strong inclination to adopt those views of his position. Our manners are said to be much improved recently, but even now gambling is carried to an excessive and dangerous extent, and there is not a season passes without damage to reputations, loss of fortune, and disgrace to some of the visitors; which are serious social evils affecting the British community directly, but which also bear a very grave aspect in relation to the influence we exercise over the natives."

The same writer continued :—" Somewhat better and able to crawl on my crutches to the verandah " (Dr. Russell was then living in 'The Priory'), " whence I turned from my monkeys and birds to the young ladies and gentlemen who were flirting and philandering, a horse and a foot, on the road below us, and from the lovers to the monkeys till I was tired. Jacquemont says English society in India is less frivolous than society in general in France; but I do not think he would apply that remark to Simla, if what my gossips tell me be true. Probably Jacquemont's notion of an agreeable evening was realised when he had a party of nice women sitting round him,—in silence if possible,—whilst he held forth in broken English *de omne scribili*. Here we have ball after ball, followed by a little backbiting; the great event of every day being the promenade which is almost of a sacred and devotional character in honour of the god of the mountain who is called Jacko, and who is 'gone round' as if he were a holy well. If he be propitious—' *Veneres cupidinesque*,' he leads to the altar of Hymen."

Mr. John Lang in 'Wanderings in India' published in 1859, said :—" Simla differs from Mussoorie. It is so much more sedate; more than one-half of those who prefer Simla do so in the hope of prepossessing one or other of the great authorities by being brought into contact with them, and thus obtain staff employ or promotion, and very

Stout Gent.—"WELL, SPINKS, MY BOY, YOU'RE A RIDING MAN; AIN'T YOU ASHAMED OF YOURSELF, FOR ALLOWING THOSE LADIES TO RIDE ALONE?"

Equestrian.—"WHY, IT *does* LOOK ODD; BUT YOU SEE, I'VE BEEN TO SIMLA BEFORE, AND KNOW THE CONSEQUENCES OF TACKING ONESELF ON TO A WOMAN, SO EARLY IN THE SEASON!"

Delhi Sketch Book.

A COMPETENT JUDGE.

SCENE, SIMLA—*the day breaking—two Gentlemen returning home from a Dance.*

1st Gent.—'RATHER A NICE PARTY, JEM!"

2nd Gent.—"OH! PRETTY WELL; BUT I NEVER IN MY LIFE SAW SUCH A LOT OF UGLY WOMEN CONGREGATED TOGETHER BEFORE!"

amusing is it to look on at a public entertainment and witness the feelings of jealousy and envy that swell the hearts of the various candidates for notice and favour. . . . The season I spent at Simla was a very pleasant one, and notwithstanding that it was enlivened by several exciting incidents, to wit a duel, a police affair, a court-martial and an elopement, I was very glad when it was over, and we could return to the plains.'

In 'A Mingled Yarn,' published in 1898, by Edward Spencer Mott, (formerly Lieutenant of the 19th Regiment and later 'Nathaniel Gubbins' of the *Sporting Times*), the author, in referring to gambling, said :—" Everybody played some game of cards or other at Simla, and here, again, but little actual cash was ever paid out. In 1862 loo, the 'unlimited' brand, flourished like a green bay tree in the highest circles. A select coterie used to assemble in a private house most evenings for the worship of the goddess . . . . . On one occasion the play had become so thoroughly exciting that there were 'chits' (pieces of paper) representing over £4,000 on the table. And for this amount was the senior player 'looed.' I think he parted with some cash, but his payments were mostly in kind, and consisted of a furnished house, a mail phæton, and other chattels. When the scandal reached the ears of 'the Chief,' all the gamblers were ordered to return to their regiments with the utmost promptitude. Of that party of 'exiles' Colonel——is, to the best of my belief, the only survivor. Two, at least, of it were in straitened circumstances—one was driving a hansom in London—the last time I met them."

It was in the early sixties that the feminine chignon attained such a size that it sorely troubled the masculine mind, and a few subalterns in 1863 decided to signify their disapproval of the fashion. They accordingly appeared one evening at the band stand with their ponies' tails tied up in chignon form. Great was the sensation they caused, but history relates that their punishment was greater. Not only were they sent to 'Coventry' by the fair sex, but they received a plain hint from a high military authority that the plains were more suitable for such jokes than the hills. And down they went.

" If the Indian hills only possessed the gifts of speech and the ability to compose, as well as the powers of enduring for ever what a book they would write! A story of wealth unlimited and extreme poverty cheek by jowl ; of pure atmosphere and foul rumours, ruined prospects, guilty passions, frivolity, intrigue, disappointed hopes, jealousy, madness, triumph, gallantry, meanness, nobility of character, crime, infamy, universal health, remorse unmitigated, of the canker of corruption in the midst of the bud of youth, hope, and freedom—even as the native bazaar exists, stuffy and malodrous, in the midst of palaces and sanitary improvements." So wrote a visitor in 1862.

I have already alluded to Mr. W. H. Carey, a Simla architect, whom it may be mentioned was once the owner of 'Melville Lodge,' 'Comely Bank,' 'Argyll House,' 'Balmoral,' 'Eglantine' and 'Boxmore,' the latter now the site of a mosquein the Simla bazaar, but which once had a pleasant orchard in its grounds. Mr. Carey formerly owned a press at Allahabad, and is reported to have assisted in the launching of the well known paper 'the Pioneer.' He collected many old books and prints while in Simla and eventually retired to England and lived at Teddington until his death. Mr. Carey wrote in 1870 :—" There are two classes of visitors here—once seeking health, the other amusement,combined no doubt it may be with a renewal of bloom and strength. Many a man pinches himself, or, worse, runs into debt, to enable the drooping wife or the ailing child to take a new lease of life at Simla. Many make a point during their sixty days' leave at least to shake themselves loose from the dreary months vegetated through at some quiet station in the plains. This is their all to look forward to till they can get home. Amusement is to them the *sine qua non,* and *coute qui coute* they will have it. Then you have the headquarters of the army, their gallant chief at their head. Amalgamate these, and when you have done this, pack them in the small compass they must occupy, comparatively speaking, in Simla, meeting on the mall at least once a day, thronging to Annandale, to balls, picnics, everybody knowing every one,—this alone begets a manner so familiar that it in itself strikes a stranger as something very unusual. It is difficult to understand this world of Simla without seeing it. You go up for a few months, you make acquaintances for the season, many of whom you are not likely to meet again, so what matters it you think what they say or do? . . . . The utter absence of occupation on the one hand, and on the other the keen search after amusement, let it be what it may, makes life go at a reckless hand gallop that many come out of in a sore plight."

It was about this time that 'A True Reformer,' by General Francis Rawdon Chesney, R.A., the explorer of the Euphrates, and the founder of the overland route to India, was published by Blackwood & Sons, and the book, which was really written of Simla, contains several vivid descriptions of the life of the day. Writing of a wedding in the hills the author said :—" It has always struck me that the bridegroom looks rather out of place at a wedding, being, so to speak, an awkward, although perhaps a necessary, ingredient in this affair ; but nowhere does he appear more so than at a wedding in the Himalaya. The bride must of course return in her sedan, for, to say nothing of the sun, the dust would utterly spoil her dress were she to walk : sot he bride-groom must perforce either walk or ride by her side, and most men would prefer the latter alternative, since it is not every one who can keep up gracefully with the pace of four shuffling sedan-bearers in the prime of condition. But even then, ride he never so well, the general effect is a good deal marred by the need which arises every minute either to push on in front or drop behind, at the numerous points where the narrow road affords room for only the sedan to pass, and on such occasions he hardly looks as if he belonged to the bride, or the bride to him."

In " London Society " in April 1872 an article runs :—

" The Rotten Row of Simla is called the Mall, whereon fair equestrians weep round the sharp curves at full gallop knowing well that there is no Hyde Park peeler at hand to prosecute them for riding furiously. The most fearless of these gay cavaliers —the flying brigade—as they are called there, hearken not to the cries of man, neither make way for the approaching jampan, but regardless of life and limb surge furiously round the Jakko mall. These would be leaders of men possess neither the power of Lais, nor the charms of Aspacia ; and some of them would scarce find admission within the portals of Juno. The refined and more youthful of Simla are not found in their ranks.

" The club overlooks the Mall, buried in the trees up there, and from that sacred fane, tearing themselves from whist and billiards, the flower of the bachelors descend, slowly sauntering along, or listlessly leaning over the treacherous rails, or peradventure, gazing into the abyss beneath. Mingled with all this, are numberless jampans and jaunty dandies—hammocks slung on poles—borne along by six or eight bearers arrayed

NEVER GO FAST ROUND THE CORNERS OF JAKKO.
Simla Season 1854.

Delhi Sketch Book,

A LITTLE SCANDAL ON THE MALL.
Simla Season 1854.

in flaunting apparel. His Excellency's jampan bearers are habited in royal red, Judge Snout's lady is carried by darkies in green tunics and crimson knicker-bockers, while Col. Qui Hi has a taste for black with gold facings ; all colours may be seen, but perhaps the adipose Bengalee Baboo trotting past with ten coolies grunting aloud as they go, and resplendent in their orange and green vestments and garish turbans, commend the greatest attention."

Mr. Andrew Wilson, the author of the 'Abode of Snow,' appears to have been one of the few of earlier writers who formed a favourable impression of Simla society. His book written in 1873 contains the following passages :—"According to some people, and especially according to the house-proprietors of Calcutta, who view its attractions with natural disfavour, Simla is a very sinful place indeed ; and the residence there, during summer, of the Viceroy and his Members of Council ought to be discouraged by a paternal Secretary of State for India. The 'Capua of India' is one of the terms which are applied to it ; we hear sometimes of 'The Revels upon Olympus' ; and one of the papers seemed to imagine that to describe any official as 'a malingerer at Simla' was sufficient to blast his future life. Even the roses and the rhododendrons, the strawberries and the peaches, of that 'Circean retreat,' come in for their share of moral condemnation as contributing to the undeserved happiness of a thoughtless and voluptuous community. For this view there is some show of justification. Simla has no open law courts to speak of, or shipping, or mercantile business, or any of the thousand incidents which furnish so much matter to the newspaper of a great city. The large amount of important governmental business which is transacted there is seldom immediately made known, and is usually first communicated to the public in other places. Hence there is little for the newspaper correspondents to write about except the gaieties of the place ; and so the balls and picnics, the croquet and badminton parties, the flirtations and rumoured engagements, are given an importance which they do not actually possess, and assume an appearance as if the residents of Simla had nothing to do but to enjoy themselves and 'to chase the glowing hours with flying feet.'

"But, in reality, the dissipation of Simla is not to be compared with the dissipation of a London season ; and if the doings of any English provincial town or large watering-place in the season were as elaborately chronicled and looked up to and magnified, maliciously or otherwise, as those of the Indian Capua are, the record would be of a much more scandalous and more imposing kind. Indeed, unless society is to be put down altogether, or conducted on Quaker principles, it is difficult to see how the Anglo-Indians, when they go to the hills, could conduct themselves much otherwise than as they do ; and probably more in Simla, than anywhere else, there exists the feeling that life would be intolerable were it not for its amusements.

"But no one who knows European society will accuse Simla, of the present and preceding Viceroyships at least, of being an abode of dissipation or of light morality. Wherever youth and beauty meet, there will, no doubt, be a certain amount of flirtation, even though the youth may be rather shaky from long years of hard work in the hot plains of India, or from that intangible malady which a friend styles as 'too much East,' and though the beauty be often pallid and passe ; but anything beyond that hardly exists at Simla at all, and has the scantiest opportunity for developing itself. Overworked secretaries to Government and elderly members of Council, are not given either to indulge in levity of conduct or to wink at it in others ; the same may be said of their ladies ; and the young officers and civilians who go up to Simla for their leave are usually far-seeing young men who have an eye to good appointments, and, whatever their real character may be, are not likely to spoil their chances of success by attracting attention to themselves as very gay Lotharios. Moreover, at Simla, as almost everywhere in India, people live under glass cases ; everything they do is known to their native servants and to the native community, who readily communicate their knowledge of such matters to Europeans."

In July 1877, Mr. Val. C. Prinsep, the artist who had travelled out to India in the previous winter to paint a picture of the Delhi assemblage, came up to Simla for a few weeks, and devotes a chapter of 'Imperial India' to life in the station. His impressions of Simla during Lord Lytton's residence are of special interest, as, if Dame Rumour can be believed, life in Simla was never faster than in those days, and even now allusions are sometimes made to the society scandals of that time. Mr. Prinsep's remarks, if not altogether complimentary, are brightly recorded.

"The day after my arrival," he writes, "I went to a ball at 'Peterhoff' to see the beauty and fashion. I came to the conclusion that there are a great many captains. I forget what jealous husband it was who said he was glad of the Crimean war. 'For now,' he said, 'there will be fewer captains.' By 'captains' he and I mean people on leave with nothing to do. This place is full of such people, who have a difficulty in passing the day. Of course the devil is busy and provides mischief. Sad tales are told of the place no doubt ; but like all such tales there is a great element of exaggeration therein. Of course people gamble, and what they ought not. They do that everywhere. The play is very high, the whist execrable, and I hope the money lost is paid. I suppose this is the blood-letting necessary after the heat of the plain, and the monotomy of regimental duty—excitement provided for by kind nature to restore the equilibrium of the system. . . . . The gaieties of Simla go on wet or dry. Rinking is greatly on the increase, being the only exercise many men and all women can take. . . . . The world of Simla jogs on, or rather pushes along, at its usual pace. All are bent on enjoying themselves, and champagne flows on every side. Every evening at eight the roads are full of 'jampons' conveying the fair sex to their festivities. . . . . Simla society is a curious study. Simla itself is like an English watering place gone mad. Real sociability does not exist. People pair off directly they arrive at a party, as a matter of course, and the pairs happy in their own conversation do not trouble themselves about the general hilarity.

"Indeed the 'muffin' system, like that in Canada, is the order of the day. If you have not a pair, as in my case, you are likely to die of inanition. When such a state of society exists, there must arise most frequent and terrible squabbles, especially among the fair sex, and it is difficult to find two of the dear creatures who are on friendly terms. . . . . . Everything is so English and unpicturesque here that except that the people one meets are those who rule and make our history—a fact one can hardly realise—one would fancy oneself at Margate. . . Officialism is also rampant. The new order of precedence has just been published, and in this new order everything is settled as to India ; but the visitor, however high his rank, has no precedence except by courtesy. I do not find any mention of artists in this document, either with or without Government commissions, and I am in consequence frequently left out in the cold."

Delhi Sketch Book

THE KHYBER PASS, (SIMLA,) 6. P. M. 1851.

On leaving Simla about 15th October Mr. Prinsep wrote, evidently with some relief :—" At length I have left Simla and its civilized gaieties and scandals, and can resume my journal with some chance of recording something more than the flirtation of Captain A. with Mrs. B., or the quarrels and jealousies of C. and his wife, which form the staple conversation of the modern Capua swelled by tittle-tattle of the Viceroy, and his eccentricity, and idle speculation as to the doings of the far-off Turk."

So much for the opinions of those in earlier days of the station. Let us now come down to more recent years. No record of Simla in later times, however, would be complete which omitted mention of Rudyard Kipling, who in the eighties spent several months in the station, and whose 'Plain Tales from the Hills' first appeared in the columns of the *Civil and Military Gazette*. Wonderfully clever as these short stories were, I fear, they led many to regard Simla as a town populated by 'Mrs. Hawksbees,' by frivolous grass-widows, idle hill captains and the genus known as 'bow-wows,' and no writer has perhaps done more than the brilliant genius I have mentioned to give the outside world the idea that Simla is a centre of frivolity, jealousy, and intrigue. Possibly, were he asked, no one would be more ready to admit that several of his characters were exaggerations of an author whom Simla will always be proud to have possessed among her most famous residents.

In an able and interesting article published some years ago on 'The Hills' by A. H., in the *Pioneer*, the writer has said :—" Nowhere possibly in the world are the passions of human nature laid so open for dissection as they are in remote hill stations on the slopes of the eternal abodes of snow. In the very small communities the round of gossip is incessant, probably inevitable. Resources there are none, save such as are afforded by amusement committees. The men are mostly deprived of sport, the women are overladen with calls and dressing and admiration. . . . . The groove into which Anglo-India is forced by circumstances in the plains becomes narrower still in the hills. There, where every advantage of climate is combined with every imaginable beauty of nature, with few house-keeping cares, with many luxuries, with a constant flow of amusements which few save in the richest society at home can attempt to enjoy incessantly ; there, where even the rainy season has its compensations, and the miraculous beauty of a troubled sunset after a storm is a joy to be treasured in the memory always, and where all being more or less equal, none has cause to complain—there discontent breeds, and jealousy and scandal dominate. The smallness of society, eddying round in such a tiny backwater, makes for stagnation."

In several of his statements I am obliged to agree with A. H., though I venture to think that, to those men and women who desire them, Simla offers more resources than the casual visitor to the hills imagines. Botany, gardening, the United Service Institute, mission and charitable societies, the Fine Arts Exhibition and other matters —all have a certain following in Simla.

Women, too, are constantly found in Simla who spare neither time, trouble nor personal expense in the interests of local hospitals and orphanages ; and the station as a matter of fact has reason to be proud of many English ladies who, I venture to maintain, have set examples not only as wives and mothers, but also as hostesses and leaders in a society which is often overexacting, critical, and captious.

In 1909 Mrs. Walter Tibbits wrote a little book called 'The Voice of the Orient' having previously paid a visit to Simla when few suspected she would record her impressions. One of her chapters was devoted to Simla under the heading of 'The Hill of Doomed Hopes.' I fear Mrs. Tibbits did not altogether enjoy her sojourn in the so-called Queen of Hill Stations, for she had very little that is kind to record of Simla society, though she admitted that "more beautiful than any drop-scene by the greatest stage artist is Simla in the spring, and like a drop scene almost unreal in its exquisite daintiness." But of the people she wrote :—"There are many worlds in Simla. The noisiest is that circle of men and women who have no higher ideal in life than to win a prize in a "bumble puppy," to be seen speaking to a Vicereine, or to have an A. D. C. as an attache. When they die these people go to a Valhalla, not above the snows in Heaven, but down the khud to Annandale." Mrs. Tibbits admitted too that the Anglo-Indian man is the finest type of the Anglo-Saxon race, but she vied with Kipling in her denunciation of the 'Mrs. Hawksbees' who are met with in every society. The tongue, she writes, "is the most potent weapon known in Simla. It is indeed mightier than the sword, and the fear of society grips the firmest foundation of morals. Men who would step unflinchingly up to the cannon's mouth walk warily before the eagle eyes of the Simla dowagers."

The fact is that there have always been two distinct sides to Simla life, *viz.*, the official, and the social. There are two communities—the bees, and the butterflies. The former are the working classes, the men who conduct the work of the Empire, and of whose laborious days I have already written under 'The Government of India;' the latter are those who come up for a holiday, with the express intention of getting as much enjoyment out of that holiday as time and funds will allow. Among these last are the grass widows, the hill captains, already alluded to by other writers, who are encouraged to more or less extent by the wives and daughters of Government officials whose duties are not so heavy as those of their husbands and fathers. In somewhat recent years doings, their picnics, theatricals, dances, and luncheon parties are continually, as Mr. Andrew Wilson remarked in 1873, given an importance they do not actually possess. In a word, it was in great measure the fault of the Anglo-Indian journals themselves that Simla attained a reputation for frivolity for not long ago, each week a column or two was invariably devoted by the leading papers to social gatherings which in any other capital would pass unnoticed or unheard of. It is, moreover, an undeniable fact that the work and play of society in Europe are not brought together as they are in India, where the workers themselves are obliged to provide or patronize the amusement which society demands, and which at home is catered for in much larger profusion by professional contractors.

So, as Mr. Andrew Wilson explained, there was often little for newspaper correspondents to write about except the gaieties of the place, and it was largely due to this reason that the tittle-tattle of the hills, the bulletin of the daily doings of the Viceregal court assumed monstrously exaggerated proportions, and induced jaundiced critics at home to believe that the air of the Himalayas had no other effect but to lighten the heels of the dwellers on the mountain tops.

The principal Simla summer festivities may be said to consist of balls at Viceregal Lodge, and at the residences of the Governor of the Punjab and Commander-in-Chief, some eight or nine plays by the Amateur Dramatic Club, tennis and polo tournaments, weekly gymkhanas on Thursdays at Annandale, and constant tennis, dinner, and evening parties. Dances given at the Cecil Hotel, at the Masonic Hall, at Messrs. Davico's

Delhi Sketch Book.

THE FASHIONABLE USE FOR A CHILUMCHEE AS PRACTISED AT CERTAIN PICNICS NOT 100 MILES FROM SIMLA IN 1855.

new ballroom, and the meetings of the Rifle, Polo, Cricket, and Football Clubs are naturally of frequent occurrence.

Add to these an official garden party or two, a few concerts, picnics for which the surroundings are peculiarly well adapted, rides in and around the station, a few days racing in May and October, an occasional bazaar for charitable purposes, and there is little else to mention. In the autumn a limited amount of partridge and pheasant shooting is obtainable by energetic sportsmen on the neighbouring hills, and last, not least, most delightful excursions of eight or ten days can be enjoyed by those who are able to afford the time, to the woods and forests of Huttoo, on the Tibet high road, which ought to be included in the 'Wonders of the World.'

Not many years ago B. C. V. in revisiting Simla wrote to the "Civil and Military Gazette" saying disillusionment was ever the fate of those who return to a favourite station after many years, and there added,—"Harrassed men bolt an insufficient breakfast in silence and in haste, and flying down the hill side vanish until evening. They are concerned in running the Government upon commercial lines. Economy and efficiency are their watch words." He continued.—"Were another Kipling to arise among us, his Plain Tales would take the form of memoranda, notes and tabulated statements. Life is real, life is earnest—painfully so—and because some giants may be seen to wipe great drops of sweat from their brows it behoves all "to play the sedulous ape." All are given over to demoniacal possession. A demon in the brain cries "Work! work! work!" and the evil-eye of petulant authority drives men to a furious scratching of the quill or a frenzied tapping of the type-writer. It avails not to cross the fingers after the manner of superstitious Italy : no charm nor amulet can break the spell ; no exorcism can drive out the evil spirit, nor any incantation revive the past. Romance is dead. Panting youth no longer walks by Beauty's rickshaw : the Hill Captain, gay and *debonnaire*, has followed the Dodo into extinction ; and there are no grass-widows ; or if there are, they are utterly given over to good works. The days of love in idleness are past : Mrs. Hawksbee is no more ; and no one now "takes ices at Peliti's with another *bunder's* wife."

Conditions regulating Society in Simla have certainly changed greatly in the last twenty years. It is larger, less 'cliquey', and more tolerant. Moreover the fact that Indian ladies and gentlemen are now joining freely with their European friends in social entertainments has made a sensible difference. This fact has perhaps been inevitable with the appointment of Indian gentlemen to hold high official positions, but there are certain Indian ladies and gentlemen whose social qualities and generous hospitality have had a marked effect in this direction. This movement may be said to have begun in Simla when Mr. (now Lord) Sinha was appointed to the Viceroy's Executive Council. He and his family quickly became favourites in social circles, one of his daughters, Mrs. Gupta, being a brilliant tennis player. Sir Ali Imam who succeeded him was another notable Indian gentleman who left his mark in this direction. I hope I may also particularly allude to Sir Mohammed and Lady Shafi, and Sir Maneckji and Lady Dadabhoy as outstanding examples of Indian social leaders who played a prominent part in bringing about for this happy state of affairs. Sir Guy Fleetwood Wilson and Sir Harcourt Butler were English officials who by constantly entertaining their Indian friends at 'Peterhof' did much to promote good feeling between East and West. The Chelmsford Club, to which reference has already been made, has also not been without a useful influence in bringing many European and Indian gentlemen into more intimate relations. Pardah parties in recent years have been more than once held at Viceregal Lodge, and Viceroys' wives have also attended them at private houses. Not the least successful of these latter gatherings have been given by Lady Harnam Singh at 'Summer hill'; and Lady Hailey has likewise actively interested herself in this direction.

There are differences of opinion as to whether Simla is musical or not. If the attendance at a musical play by Gilbert and Sullivan at the Gaiety is any criterion it certainly is. Many maintain that the absence of a Townhall with a public concert room has had a deteriorating effect upon music in Simla. Certainly largely attended and excellent public concerts for all kinds of purposes used to be given in the main room of the defunct Townhall. Mrs. H. Hawkins, Mrs. Yeates Hunter, Mrs. Iggulden, Miss A. Watson, Miss Ribbentrop, Miss Macquoid, Mrs. Twining, Mrs. Elsmie, Mr. C. Halle, M. Nabakoff and Major J. Turner (singers), Mrs. Mallaby (violin), Major Sanford, Lady Franklin and Miss Toussaint (piano), Herr Buchner (conductor) are among the names of popular performers that occur when I allude to this subject. There have from time to time been successful concerts at Viceregal Lodge, sometimes for philanthropic purposes and at these the Viceroy's band has always been the main attraction. When Lady Reading gave a concert in 1921 Madame Melba was a guest at Viceregal Lodge, and a Simla audience was privileged to hear her wonderful voice. A lady whose singing has been much appreciated on her occasional visits to Simla is Mrs. H. S. Crosthwaite well known in the United Provinces. Lady Rawlinson conferred great a boon on Simla society by permitting the meetings of the Simla music club to be held in the 'Snowdon' ballroom during her residence in Simla. This Club was started on a suggestion by Mrs. Kisch in 1921, and thanks to the hard work of Mrs. B. Bevan Petman its Honorary Secretary, for a time it flourished exceedingly. But since she recently gave up this post there has been no musical society in the station.

And now for a few words on the 'calling' question which came prominently to the fore, and caused much discussion some years ago. As all Anglo-Indians are aware, the custom of paying the first call is one which, in Simla, as elsewhere in India, is performed by the newcomer. And one of the things which first strikes the visitor fresh from Europe, is the way in which each residence displays, on a neighbouring tree, its 'not-at-home' box for the reception of cards, when the lady of the house happens to be 'darwaza band' (door closed) to her friends. Gradually, as Simla grew in extent and population, calling, from becoming a pleasurable duty developed into a serious social nuisance, and at length many ladies found it a practical impossibility to return all the calls made upon them. Especially was the performance of this duty made difficult by the absurd rule which demanded that visits must be made between the hours of twelve and two o'clock, the hottest hours of the day. So a number of leading ladies held a formal meeting, and passed a resolution that those already acquainted, should in future be privileged to call by posting their cards to each other, only strangers being required to make the first call in person. Then a further concession was allowed, and all ladies in Simla, whether newcomers or not, are permitted, if they choose to join the 'calling league' and to despatch their cards through the medium of the post. It would not be right to say that the new system is devoid of drawbacks, or that it is universally approved. But, that it has come to many as a much-needed relief from an intolerable

H. H. THE MAHARAJA OF BHARATPUR IN HIS RICKSHAW.

burden cannot be denied. For calling was fast developing into a farce. Servants were often sent out with 'tickets' which were to be quietly placed in Mrs. So-and-So's box, intimate friends perpetually dropped each other's cards on a third person; 'box-hunting,' instead of visiting, became the rule; every one openly spoke of calling as a bore, yet no one condoned social laxity or remissness in others. Innumerable complications, heart burnings, and squabbles resulted, and the time had clearly arrived for some drastic reform. But the new scheme was not introduced without a certain amount of difficulty. Anonymous skits were circulated; strong protests emanated from the male sex, especially from those tied to their office desks, to whom no relief was suggested, and numberless letters were written to the press decrying the innovation. While the permanent residents welcomed the new custom, the casual visitors and strangers condemned it as unsociable and discourteous. But I think the development is one which arose from a difficulty which had made itself acutely felt, and that time will prove its wisdom. Simla has for some time been growing into too large a town for everyone to know his neighbours as was customary in earlier years.

Stories of 'calling' are of course numerous, and many little squabbles have arisen through fair ladies sending out chaprasies with sheaves of cards to drop in boxes, or arranging with friends to call for them. For instance on one occasion when Mrs. A. a newcomer called in person on Mrs. B. who lived on Jakko the latter welcomed her profusely, and sweetly said—" Do you know this is the third time you have called on me in four days "? And all that Mrs. A. could say was " My dear are not these hills too puzzling for words " ? Mrs. A. and Mrs. B. however became quite good friends until the following season, when they met on the Mall. Then Mrs. A. said—" Why my dear I have not seen you for weeks ". Where have you been ? Oh how stupid I am, of course I saw you last Monday walking with Captain D. Do dear tell me what sort of a man is Captain D. ? " Captain D " replied Mrs. B. " Oh he is really most amusing, but why do you ask "? " Well you see " said Mrs. A. he has asked me to go for a walk with him on Friday next. " Oh has he ?" replied the other in a different tone of voice, " Well let me give you one piece of advice my dear. You keep on walking " ! And for the rest of the season the phrase caught on, and people were advised to keep on walking, dancing, riding, flirting, or whatever they happened to be engaged in doing at the moment.

Another lady once set forth on horseback to call upon a member of Council's wife, and not finding her at home, told her syce to give her cards to a chuprassie. The syce afterwards informed her that he had handed them to the sweeper, so when she met the Councillor's wife later on she apologised, and told her what had happened. The latter simply replied that she was delighted to hear of cordiality being extended to the depressed classes. And that is the end of the story !

Among calling incidents there is, one of a popular but absent-minded bachelor secretary who in the olden days put into his pocket the cards of all the men who had called upon him, and then proceeded to drop them in boxes until he luckily found a lady at home who pointed out his error. There was also a very short sighted man who carefully distributed a sheaf of cards round the station only to find out at the end of a long morning that his bearer had given him blank ones.

It has also been handed down that not so very long ago a judicial officer, now sitting in a High Court, used to entrust the bailiff—a well known character—with the duty of dropping cards for him, and that a lady of high degree caught the latter placing cards in her box, and was not pleased with his explanation.

To return however to the serious subject of 'Calling.' To-day by paying the sum of one rupee ladies can register their names at the Simla library, and despatch their cards by post to all others whose names are on the list. But names must be written in the books of the Viceroy, Commander-in-Chief and Governor of the Punjab, and it is an unwritten law that the wives of members of Council should be called on in person.

So long as Simla lasts so long will stories be told of its Society.

A charming young widow who dressed in a fashion which roused the envy of all the women, and who sang naughty little French songs with a delightful ease which captured most of the men, once arrived in the summer capital. After a few days spent in a study of her surroundings she remarked to a friend, "My dear there are only three things to do for people in this place; you must either feed them, amuse them, or shock them. Now I am not rich enough to feed them, nor clever enough to amuse them, but I think I can shock them." And she eventually did so most successfully!

Simla has always been a great place for nicknames especially among the fair sex, and some old residents will probably recollect three famous sisters being known as 'the world, the flesh, and the devil.' Three other sisters were named "wriggles, giggles, and goggles," and all were charming, and have been long since married. Then there were "Perrier and Jouet" the pretty twin daughters of a cheery and popular civilian who was also nicknamed after a brand of champagne. Other ladies in turn were given names which more or less explain themselves such as 'the painted snipe,' 'the great unwashed,' 'la vie Parisienne,' 'the Boojum,' 'Piche jawab' (literally 'I will give you an answer later,' and she still writes 'miss' before her name) 'the boosa queen,' 'undulating Ursula,' 'the happy hippo,' 'the destroying angel,' 'the bosom friends' (two rather massive ladies) 'the subalterns joy,' 'the amorous goldfish,' 'rosy rapture,' 'the cannibals dream' (a very buxom lady), 'the cannibal's nightmare' (a lady who was not buxon), 'the passionate carrot,' 'the smouldering Vesuvius,' and 'simply awful and awfully simple' (mother and daughter). Nor have men escaped for 'the rogue elephant,' 'old Nick', 'Naughty Arthur,' 'the ace of spades,' 'For ever with the Lord,' (an A.D.C. who remained with at least three Governors), 'K.C.M.G.', 'the laughing cavaliers,' 'the pilgrim of love' and 'the hardy annual' (an officer who arrived in Simla a good many years running to propose to a certain young lady) were well known characters in past days. Many too have been the alphabets and rhymes which from time to time have tickled the society of the day. An amusing little guide book called 'Simla in Ragtime' was published by the station press in 1913 in which some of Simla's peculiarities were not unkindly criticised.

Prominent among Simla institutions, and I use the word institution advisedly, is the "Most Hospitable order of the Black Hearts". This order which was founded in 1891 consists of a Grand Master, Prelate and Knights associated for the purpose of entertaining their friends at Simla. The first Grand Master, the late Colonel Newnham Davis (The Dwarf of Blood) so wisely fixed the statutes, that there has been little apparent change in traditions, through a long series of Grand Masters, down to the

Major J. A. Douglas. Major W. J. Bythell, R. E. Mr. J. Lang, C. S. Mr. O. V. Bosanquet, C. S. Captain M. H. P. Barlow.

Mr. H. Hensman. Mr. E. Maconochie, C. S. Colonel H. Goad. Captain G. Lubbock, R. E.

Mr. C. F. Bennett. Mr. G. R. Irwin, C. S. Sir William Cuningham. Surgeon-General R. Harvey. Mr. R. Egerton.

Colonel G. Money. Major Colin Campbell.

THE BLACK HEARTS, SIMLA, 1897.

present day. The motto of the order is "He is not so—as he is black" and the hiatus in the knights motto has been the cause of much innocent mystery for thirty years. It was reported years ago that the correct solution was 'devil,' and that a fair dame was given a prize for guessing it. It was also said that the motto was really a quaint rendering of a well known saying given to his pupils by an Italian teacher of English idioms. But the knights of to-day emphatically deny the correctness of the word 'devil'. So apparently the secret has yet to be guessed. The rules of the order, which are kept very secret, are as far as is known very simple. One is believed to be "worthiness" which seems to imply that no knight must commit the offence of living in open matrimony in Simla, and "bachelordom," or at the least "grass widowdom," is a vital qualification for brethren who are elected to this hospitable but select order. Their social entertainments are invariably run in perfect taste and contribute in no small degree to the success of a Simla season. When in evening dress, the knights don their picturesque uniform, consisting of black knee breeches, evening dress, with the black heart of their order suspended by a red ribbon round the neck, and a red cape ornamented with a black heart suspended from the shoulder. The Grand Master wears an imposing golden chain of office.

It has always been the custom that in the State Lancers at a Black Hearts ball the maidens of Simla should take precedence of the dames, and the Viceroy of the day, who generally attends these functions, always selects one of the youngest damsels for his partner. The absence of all formality is indeed one of the reasons why these dinners and dances are such a success.

A particularly successful and memorable fancy dress dance was given by the knights in Delhi on the 10th February 1922 at the Imperial Gymkhana Club when H. R. H. the Prince of Wales joined the order for the evening, and after dinner danced into the small hours of the morning. Shields with the family crests of the various knights, both past and present always decorate the walls of the ballroom at their entertainments, and the ostrich feathers of the Heir to the British throne is now not the least prized possession of the Black Hearts. Since they came into existence there have been fifteen Grand Masters commencing with Colonel Newnham Davis who was largely responsible for the creation of the order.

The others have been Sir William Cunningham, Surgeon-General Sir William Taylor, Mr. Albert Williams, I.C.S., Col. H. S. P. Davis, Sir F. R. Upcott, Sir R. A. Gamble, I.C.S., Col. G. A. Robertson, General Sir J. S. Cowans, Col. F. A. Beatson, Col. J. A. Tanner, R.E., Major-General R. C. Broome, Sir Ludovic Porter, Mr. M. H. Harrsion, I.C.S., and last though not least Mr. A. H. Ley, I.C.S., a popular civilian, who as a temporary member of the Viceroy's Executive Council, has been the first Honourable Member to hold this distinguished post.

To return, however, to my defence, if such indeed be needed to-day, of Simla society. Were Simla social letters brought within the scope of the Official Secrets Act, and gossiping epistles from Poona or Ootacamund condemned as treasonable documents, the bees would be less often accused of making no honey, while the flitting and flirting butterflies would continue to fulfil the natural object of their existence. More than one critic on Simla life has declared that its society lives in a glass house. This I think is undeniable, and it is equally true that Simla in considerable measure takes its tone from the example set to it by the wife of the Viceroy who presides over Viceregal Lodge. For the last forty years at any rate, no one has found it possible to advert, save in terms of admiration, to the example set by the wives of the Rulers of India. Lady Dufferin's 'Viceregal Life in India' is full of allusions to a delightful and happy home life ; and has not Kipling, in 'The Song of the Women,' described with consummate feeling the great work which she inaugurated for the relief of the women of India, which still bears her honoured name, and which has since been so greatly developed by her successors ?

There are some in Simla to-day who still warmly cherish the memory of Lady Lansdowne, whose winning grace and charm of manner endeared her to all classes of society, and whose visit to a hospital I well remember being likened to 'a ray of sunshine passing through the wards.' I shall always remember too seeing her Indian bodyservant in Calcutta bursting into a flood of tears at the mere mention of her departure from India some days before the event took place.

Did not Lady Elgin leave behind her a reputation for many kind acts performed in secret, for the keenest interest in all charitable institutions, for her example as a pattern mother ? And though state and Viceregal functions at times proved for her gentle frame a somewhat heavy task, were not her duties performed with a kindliness which all her guests appreciated ? Of Lady Curzon, who for five years filled a difficult post with not less success than her distinguished predecessors I have already written. The youngest wife of a Viceroy who had ever come to India, a charming hostess, the possessor of natural and well cultivated talents, and of beauty and strength of character, she earned the respect and admiration of all who came into contact with her. Of her qualities as a sympathetic friend to those in distress there are many in India who can testify, and to those who would read a further appreciation of Lady Curzon let me recommend Mrs. Craigie's (John Oliver Hobbes) 'The Impressions of an Englishwoman,' written from India during the Delhi Durbar, 1901.

And have not Lady Minto, Lady Hardinge of Penshurst, Lady Chelmsford, and Lady Reading in their turn added still further lustre to this splendid record ?

Surely it is women such as these who have done, and who continue to do, more to raise the tone of Simla society, its morals, and its general influence than a dozen carping detractors of ordinary innocent amusements. As Hope Huntly wrote in 'Our Code of Honour,' a novel dedicated to Lord Roberts, and which dealt in some degree with Simla life :—" The Anglo-Indian lives 'en evidence' from morning till night and night till morning, and many a peccadillo is enlarged into a scandal in consequence, in which a Londoner might indulge and go scot-free. Society at home is not, as many suppose, more irreproachable than it is at Calcutta and Simla ; and perhaps were the recording angels to compare records, London could not show quite so clean a bill of moral health as would our Eastern City of Palaces."

Finally no one has left a more valuable testimonial regarding Simla than Lord Hardinge of Penshurst for in reply to an Indian deputation he told it, after the dastardly attempt on his life in Delhi, that though offered a holiday at home he preferred to recuperate in the superb climate of Simla.

And in his farewell speech at the U. S. Club dinner on the 8th October 1915, he said :—

" When as I read, as I have sometimes read in the English Press, that Englishwomen in India are frivolous and think only of amusement, I grow fairly indignant,

Standing. Mr. H. G. W. Meikle, Air Vice Marshal Sir E. Ellington, Major-General Sir E. Atkinson, Mr. E. Burdon, C. S., Mr. J. E. C. Jukes, C. S., Mr. C. C. Garbett, C.S., Major D. Pott, Mr. C. Latimer, C. S., Major-General Sir G. Cory.

Sitting. Colonel B.A. Needham, Lieut.-Col. G.N. Molesworth, Hon'ble Sir A.P. Muddiman, C.S., Hon'ble Mr. A.H. Ley, C.S., Lieut.-Col. W.W. Muir, Hon'ble Mr. H.D. Craik, C.S. *(Grand Master).*

THE BLACK HEARTS, 1924.

for although it may have been the fashion in the past for certain journals to write of Simla as an abode of frivolity and the home of scandal, I can honestly say that during the five summers that I have spent here I have never seen or heard of any but the most harmless and healthy amusement, nor has the breath of scandal ever reached my ears. And what is Simla now? You have only to go to the workrooms to see the true spirit of the women of England in India devoting their whole time and energy to making, receiving, and despatching necessaries and comforts for our brave troops at the various fronts, and I have good reason to believe that the same is to be found in almost every big and small town in India. And it should not be forgotten that without the unselfish efforts of these ladies our troops would not be provided with many of the comforts they now enjoy and which it is not the business of the military authorities to provide. At the same time I should like to draw attention to the splendid work and co-operation of the Indian ladies in the despatch of comforts to our troops."

CHAPTER XXI.

Simla's Future.

THE question of Simla's future is a serious matter in which very many people are keenly interested. It has been said that there is no instance in the world's history where a railway running to a centre has not caused that centre to increase in wealth, prosperity, and population. Certainly since the Simla Kalka Railway, on which I may incidentally remark 171 lakhs were spent, came into existence, Simla has developed vastly. But what of its future with new Delhi rising apace, and the constant outcry in various quarters against the practice of Government recessing in the hills in the summer months ? Will the majority of the members of the Legislature prevail on the Government to hold their meetings in the rains in the enervating and steamy atmosphere of Delhi, or will they vote for the cooler climes of Simla where excellent Council Chambers have been specially erected for them ? Will Simla gradually fall away from her high estate, and lose her prestige by becoming only a temporary abode for two or three months for the Viceroy and his Executive Council, or will she continue, as she certainly ought, to be the summer capital in fact as well as in name ?

Whether Government was wise in the first instance in coming to Simla scarcely matters to-day. A previous chapter in this book shows how she came into existence. Some people think that Mussoorie, coupled with Dehra Dun, would have proved a far better permanent arrangement than the present one. Perhaps so, but let us examine the question as it now exists from the financial point of view, What is the annual cost of the Supreme Government's exodus from Delhi to Simla ? Only £24,000 or so, according to a reply recently given in the Assembly. If Government are now expending twelve to fourteen crores in manufacturing a new city at Delhi what amount of money has been sunk in Simla ? From enquiries I have made, it appears that the amount spent on the Viceregal estate to date has been nearly 35 lakhs, excluding the cost of the Council of State Chamber, the Commander-in-Chief's residence has cost 4½ lakhs, the Civil Offices of the Supreme Government 56 lakhs, the Military Offices 22 lakhs, the Legislative Chambers 13 lakhs, the Post and Telegraph Offices 13 lakhs, and residences for officials and departmental establishments, 97 lakhs or a total of 240 lakhs. 'Barnes Court,' the residence of the Governor of the Punjab, is valued at 6 lakhs, and the Punjab Government offices and residential quarters at about 22 lakhs. Government property may therefore be approximately valued at about two and a half crores of rupees.

The Simla bazaar is valued at something like 106 lakhs, and other houses in the station at 175 lakhs, while 54 and 24 lakhs have been respectively spent on water and electric light schemes, and more is being spent.

All these figures amount to nearly six and a half crores of rupees. Then there is the question of roads and sanitation schemes. In the last three years nearly two lakhs has been spent on communications, and an equal amount on improving the sanitation of the station. The total sum which has been expended in these directions in past years must be very heavy. Is the major portion of this expenditure to be virtually thrown away ? If this should happen there will be many who will curse an administration which has been the direct means of causing heavy loss to hundreds of private individuals. That there is little faith in Simla's future is possibly shown by the fact that the only properties which are being bought to-day are being purchased by wealthy Indian noblemen and gentleman, and by Indians doing business in the bazaar.

'The days are long past when European officials usually bought their houses when taking up a five years billet, and always sold them at a profit when they left. Very few Europeans save one or two who have been settled here for years own a house to-day. Everyone may, in a word, be said to be waiting to see what the next two or three years will bring forth. New Delhi may in years to come prove a popular place to reside in, but I fear that even in ordinary Government circles it has at present few admirers. As a conception it is magnificent, but more people, so far as my experience goes, curse Raisena than bless it. I except of course from this remark the clever architects and engineers who have laboured so industriously in making the new city, as well as some of the highest officials whose residence have been constructed with unusual care, and who are practically forced to defend the new capital. If after thirty years experience of Simla I were asked what I thought of it to-day as compared with the station of say twenty-five years ago I should say that much of Simla's attraction from the European point of view is disappearing. True the town itself is far bigger, and possesses finer buildings, better shops and more amenties of life in the shape of a more satisfactory water supply, electric light installation, and communications. But life in Simla has much changed, it is far more expensive than it used to be, servants' wages and the cost of both necessities and luxuries have risen enormously, and there is no longer one big family circle, and altogether existence is more strenuous. Moreover increasing numbers of officials, both civil and military, are taking advantage of the improved facilities for making trips to Europe, and the business houses in Simla generally complain of poor trade compared with that of some years ago. There is no doubt too that the European population in Northern India, both resident and migratory, is gradually decreasing ; the steady reduction of the British army—over two thousand young officers have been demobilised in the last two or three years—and the introduction of the Reforms scheme whereby Indians are gradually and very properly, obtaining a larger share in the administration of their country, are all causes which are having their inevitable effect on the conditions of European life in the summer capital of India.

The opposition to Simla as the summer seat of the Supreme Government on the score of its remoteness from the plains is scarcely one which can hold much water. A couple of years ago in December the station suffered from a severe snowstorm which caused serious interruption to both the telephone and telegraph communications. But directly this happened an aeroplane service from Amballa, some 90 miles distant, carried all the accumulated mails and telegrams to Simla and dropped them there on the main Ridge in an hour's time. Some people are convinced that the attack on hill stations which has been made in recent years by the Indian community has been deliberately made in more than one quarter for the purpose of forcing Europeans to live in the plains all the year round. For many English women and children this would be a distinct hardship, and were it not for the fact that sojourns in the hills are possible for their families in the scorching summer months probably more Europeans than have already done so would give up Indian careers. While there is a powerful moderate Indian opinion which recognises the need of the British element in India for the country's welfare, and knows full well that the country is not yet ripe for self-government, there is a big Swaraj party for self-government gradually gaining power in the Legislative Assembly which is apparently keen to get rid of the present Government of India at all costs. Hence in the opinion of some competent judges this continued agitation and objection to the long established custom of the exodus to the hills. I much doubt if any Viceroy would ever agree to the condition that he could never retreat to the hills in the scorching summer months, and it would be worse than cruel to condemn European clerks to endure the heat of Delhi while they can so easily reside in Simla. Moreover, there is not the slightest doubt that if the subordinate clerical Anglo-Indian and Indian staffs were consulted in the matter they would vote solidly for Simla.

Now all this constitutional advance has naturally had a marked influence on the history of Simla, for the sittings of the legislature have brought numbers of notable and distinguished men on visits to the station, and Simla has shared with Delhi, the honour of being the legislative seat of Government for several weeks in the year. It is only natural therefore that she should to-day resent any suggestion or attempt to deprive her in future of the prestige and dignity to which she has attained. However while this book is being written the question of further reforms has been engaging the earnest attention of the Governor-General and Secretary of State, in London, and now that Lord Birkenhead has spoken in the House of Lords, India is anxiously awaiting to hear if Lord Reading has anything further to say when he returns to India from his visit to England. Within the next two years it will probably be definitely settled whether the legislative bodies will meet in Simla in the hot weather or not.

On 12th March, 1917, there was an interesting debate in the Legislative Assembly at Delhi, when Mr. Sastri moving that three lakhs estimated as the cost of the exodus be omitted from the Budget, made a strong attack on the move to the hills, and Mr. Dinshaw Wacha as vigorously opposed Mr. Sastri. A powerful speech was made on the occasion by Sir Reginald Craddock (Chief Commissioner of the Central Provinces, and Lieutenant-Governor of Burma) who described himself as a 'sun dried bureaucrat,' and who after 27 years of service, of which 18 had been spent in the plains, said—" I am bound to give my testimony that the work which one could do on the heights of Simla is far more efficient than what one could do in the plains." Authorities whom he quoted in support of his view were Sir Henry Maine, Lord Northbrook, and Lord Dalhousie. " The workshop of the Indian Empire," he continued, " was really at Simla, and if Government decided to stop down in the plains very long and protracted noonday siestas would occupy many more hours than any amusements in Simla." Mr. Sastri then withdrew his motion.

In connection with this important subject, I may also refer to the interesting debate which took place in the Legislative Assembly in March, 1921, when Mr. Seshagiri Aiyar moved for the exclusion from the Budget for the provision of five and a half lakhs for an Assembly Chamber in Simla. The real object of this motion was to bring forward the question of the Simla exodus. The mover based his objections on three primary grounds, namely expense, inconvenience, and undesirability. The only constructive suggestion put forward was that the Assembly should sit in Delhi practically for six months from October to March, and then there would be no necessity for proceeding to Simla. Mr. R. A. Spence, a prominent non-official from Bombay, immediately put his finger on the weak spot in this proposal in that it would exclude from the Assembly merchants, lawyers, and professional men who could not afford to be absent from their business for the entire winter. Sir William Vincent speaking on behalf of Government said, as a possible permanent stay in Delhi was not likely to affect him personally he was in a position to take a fair and disinterested view of the position, and as he had spent three-fourths of his service as a district officer in the plains of Bengal and Bihar he thought he could testify to the advantages of a stay in Delhi if any could be shown to exist. Considerable significance therefore attaches to the following remarks he made in the debate :—" My own information and experience of Delhi in the summer months," he remarked, " is that it is amazingly unhealthy and hot in certain seasons of the year. There is no question about that, and I defy the late Chief Commissioner of Delhi (Sir Malcolm Hailey) to deny this." He went on to say that Delhi was notorious for extremes of climate, and pointed out that owing to the construction of the railway, the accessibility of Simla and the accommodation there available, all the objections advanced by Mr. Seshagiri Aiyar had been removed. He was strongly supported by Sir B. N. Sarma and Dr. Sir T. B. Sapru, members of the Executive Council who had spent their lives in the plains. The former contradicted the myth that equally good work could be done in the plains as in the hills, for he declared that he could do better work in Ootacamund and Simla than in Madras or Delhi. The mover of the motion did not receive much support from his Indian colleagues for the proposal was condemned in more or less unmeasured terms by Dr. Nand Lal, Baba Vjagar Singh Bedi, Mr. S. C. Shahani, Mr. S. Singh and Sardar Bahadur Gajjan Singh. Curiously Mr. Seshagiri Aiyar's chief supporters were Mr. Rangachariar and Mr. Jamnadas Dwarkadas both of whom hailed from distant provinces and who could not therefore have been expected to know the conditions in Simla and Delhi as intimately as the up-country members. In the end the proposal was somewhat summarily rejected, as the supporters of the Delhi scheme were unable to secure the votes of more than 21 members. Mr. Eardley Norton and Mr. Price were the solitary European members to vote with the mover, while 67, of whom 51 were Indian members, voted against the proposal.

ABOUT THE EDITOR

Pramod K. Nayar teaches at the Department of English, University of Hyderabad. His works on British India include, *English Writing and India, 1600-1920* (2008), *The Great Uprising* (2007), *Colonial Voices* (2012), *The British Raj: Keywords* (2017) and *Indian Travel Writing in the Age of Empire* (Bloomsbury 2020). He has edited *The Trial of Bahadur Shah Zafar* (2007), *The Penguin 1857 Reader* (2007), *Days of the Raj* (2009), *Women in Colonial India* (5 volumes, 2013), *English Siege and Prison Writings* (2016), *Indian Travel Writing, 1830-1947* (5 volumes, 2016) and *Colonial Education in India* (5 volumes, 2019). Besides these, he has also published extensively on Human Rights and Literature, the graphic novel and celebrity culture.